Managing Relationships in Transition Economies

"Napier and Thomas offer significant and timely insights into how transitional economies work and how foreign managers can survive doing business there. This is a 'must read' for those managers entering the transitioning economies, providing powerful background knowledge based on years of practical experience."

—Marjorie A. Lyles, Professor of International Strategic Management, Indiana University Kelley School of Business

"Doing business in countries outside US borders requires flexibility, education and, as Napier and Thomas point out, relationships with those familiar with the country and its particular approach to 'Kapitalism.' *Managing Relationships in Transition Economies* provides insight into the minds of foreign managers and points out the importance of understanding the economic culture and management style of a country's administrators."

—Patrick J. Mills, International Project Manager, Washington Group International, Integrated Services Division

"Napier and Thomas have clearly extended the limited previous literature on how to effectively manage in transition economies. They have driven home the point that the key to success is not grand strategic calculation but on-the-ground relationships between domestic and foreign managers who participate in these transitions day in and day out. In the strategy jargon, it is strategy implementation—not merely formulation—that counts, a message with which I totally agree. I am confident that this book will be well read, cited, and debated by students, scholars, and practitioners interested in transition economies in the years to come."

—Mike W. Peng, Professor, Fisher College of Business, The Ohio State University; Editor, *Asia Pacific Journal of Management*; Author, *Business Strategies in Transition Economies*

MANAGING RELATIONSHIPS
IN TRANSITION ECONOMIES

Nancy K. Napier and David C. Thomas

PRAEGER

Westport, Connecticut
London

Library of Congress Cataloging-in-Publication Data

Napier, Nancy K., 1952–
  Managing relationships in transition economies / Nancy K. Napier and
David C. Thomas.
      p. cm.
  Includes bibliographical references and index.
  ISBN 1-56720-565-8 (alk. paper)
    1. Organizational change. 2. Economic policy. 3. International economic relations. I.
Thomas, David C. II. Title.
HD58.8.N365 2004
658.4′062–dc22   2003060014

British Library Cataloguing in Publication Data is available.

Library of Congress Catalog Card Number: 2003060014
ISBN: 1-56720-565-8

First published in 2004

Praeger Publishers, 88 Post Road West, Westport, CT 06881
An imprint of Greenwood Publishing Group, Inc.
www.praeger.com

Printed in the United States of America

The paper used in this book complies with the
Permanent Paper Standard issued by the National
Information Standards Organization (Z39.48-1984).

10   9   8   7   6   5   4   3   2   1

To HSN, who has the wisdom to know the difference
To AWO, who has the heart to make a difference
From NKN

To SAT, who knows it's OK to be different
From DCT

CONTENTS

ILLUSTRATIONS

FIGURE

TABLES

ACKNOWLEDGMENTS

Like building a house or raising a child, writing a book is a team effort. I'd like to thank several groups of people who made this project not only possible, but also enjoyable. First, thanks to Hilary Claggett of Quorum (now Praeger) who helped an "idea" seed grow into a book. She encouraged Dave Thomas and me to pursue a project bigger than we intended, and we learned and gained much from it. As a coauthor, Dave was an outstanding and understanding partner, as we met in airports and conferences, talked by phone and emailed chapters to each other in France, Vietnam, Canada, and Idaho. Of course, the managers who offered their stories and experiences to us are the reason we have a book— their experiences, insights, and questions showed us the complexities and challenges they deal with daily in their global business lives.

Many wonderful students and colleagues supported my effort by being detectives in the library and beyond, reading parts of chapters and offering comments and feedback, and generally being willing to listen to meandering thoughts when I needed to think them aloud. They include Gerhard Fink, Lynn Gabriel, Nigel Holden, Suzanne Hosley, Miki Ishibashi, Murli Nagasundaram, Georg Rothwangel, Sameeta Sahni, Zorina Sendler, and Sully Taylor. Colleagues at the National Economics University in Hanoi, Vietnam, deserve special thanks for their willingness to let me learn from them as we worked together for nearly nine years on a project funded by the Swedish International Development Cooperation Agency and the U.S. Agency for International Development. I hope there will be more years of learning together in the future. Finally, I appreciate the support of Boise State University for granting me the sabbatical time needed to carry out this project.

My husband, Tony Olbrich, and sons, Chase and Quinn, continue to be baffled yet supportive as I've commuted to Asia to work, disappeared to our mountain cabin to write, and lived through countless adventures as we experimented with new sights, sounds, and tastes. Thank you for letting me be your eccentric wife and mother.

Nancy K. Napier

I'd like to add my thanks to those individuals who have contributed, both directly and indirectly, to our efforts. Additionally I wish to thank Nancy for involving me in this project. I have learned a lot, not only though our research into management in transition economies, but also through our collaboration. I am also grateful to the Social Sciences and Humanities Research Council of Canada for their support of my research over the past three years. My research assistant, Alexandra Lebedeva, contributed to this project by conducting interviews in Russian and translating them into English as well as by assisting with myriad other details. Thank you, Sasha! And, as always, there is Tilley, who must think obsessive-compulsive behavior is somehow attractive, and who provided the encouragement and support that I needed to complete this task.

David C. Thomas

Chapter 1

CHANGE: THE NEW ORDER

There is a certain relief in change, even though it be from bad to worse! As I have often found in travelling in a stagecoach, it is often a comfort to shift one's position, and be bruised in a new place.
—Washington Irving, writer (1783–1859)

FROM PLASTIC SANDALS TO LEATHER SHOES

Hanoi, Vietnam, 1994

During an afternoon's break in their work together, one of the authors and several Vietnamese university colleagues talked about the economic changes evolving in the country. Vietnam's central government had introduced its policy of *doi moi,* or "market renovation under socialist guidance," in 1986, and policy implications slowly made their ways into the economy. By the early 1990s, the changes gained steam. Urban Vietnamese were beginning to see (or hear about) changes like greater availability of and access to goods and services, performance versus seniority as a promotion criterion, opportunities for high(er) paying jobs, and more open movement of labor. In fact, Vietnam was touted as a "new little tiger," with dreams of becoming a favored investment destination for Asian and European multinational corporations. In February 1994, the United States lifted its embargo, and the Vietnamese aimed toward opening diplomatic relations and, eventually, securing a trade agreement with the United States, to boost investment and trade.

Our conversation on that hazy May afternoon moved on to the wish lists that the Vietnamese held. What sorts of things they would like in the new Vietnam economy? What did they lack that they wanted, assuming the market economy developed as hoped in Vietnam? A Vietnamese man in his late 20s, wearing the white, short-sleeved shirt and black trousers he wore nearly every day said, "Leather shoes. I want to have real shoes, not plastic shoes. And food. I want to eat more food. I am too thin." Indeed, this man was one of the many who wore a belt that looped around his waspish waist, with the end flapping against his back as he bicycled home. His plastic sandals looked like the jellies, popular among small girls in the United States at the time, closed toes and heels, easy to wear in the floods, but sweaty and uncomfortable in the heat. His male colleagues chimed in with their own wishes—a motorbike, a watch, books. "We would like more than two shirts, more than two pants. And glasses, I can't see, so I would like glasses."

The women had different wish lists. One woman, thick hair in a braid down her back, reflected a moment and then said, "I want another child. Before we can do that, we need money. And I want money to give to my parents. They are old and sick." Other women nodded and added to the list. "We want to have our own place to live, a house or an apartment—more than one room in the house of our parents."

Doi moi promised to be hard work.

Hanoi, Vietnam, 2003

The Vietnamese man who in 1994 wanted leather shoes completed his doctoral education at a top American university and returned to his university, one of Hanoi's most prestigious and advanced in educating students in international business practices. He and his wife, also a faculty member, have a five-year-old child, have traveled to the United States at least three times each, and have built a house (and paid cash for it). The man is able to send money to his village in the countryside, and he wears only leather shoes. Although he is still slender, his belts no longer wrap his waist; they fit his body.

The Vietnamese woman still has her long braid but also has a second child. She provided financial support to her father during his illness and to her family since his death. She also has received a doctorate from a prestigious university in Asia, has her own motorbike, and with her husband, built a house in 1998, for which they paid cash.

Most faculty carry mobile phones, many have home computers in addition to the one in the office, many talk of sending their children abroad for education, of traveling to conferences, and of having leisure time.

Hanoi has changed in other ways. In the early 1990s, traffic moved at the pace of bicycles, because 85 percent of the vehicles on the roads were Chinese- and Vietnamese-made, single gear bikes. Motorbikes, ranging from the guttural, Russian-made Minsks to sputtering 80-cubic-centimeter Honda Cubs, represented about 5 to 8 percent of all vehicles. The remaining percentage was split among aid-development-project vehicles (the ubiquitous Toyota Landcruisers), lumbering Russian-made trucks and busses unable to move faster than the bike pace even if their drivers had wanted to, and the odd sedan or taxi.

By 2003, motorbikes dominated the vehicle mix (about 80 percent), followed by private sedans and taxis (about 15 percent), and trucks. In Hanoi, the bicycle had become the urban middle-class family's second, or even third, vehicle. Increasingly, urban Vietnamese wear leather shoes and snazzy jeans, baseball caps and gold rings. Men and women have several changes of clothing and carry mobile phones, instead of waiting for an expensive in-house line. New U.S.$30,000 houses go up in two months; their owners pay cash, and then hire a housekeeper to clean and cook for their families. Young people play video games, go to nightclubs, and increasingly, study abroad.

Yet in this world of rapid change, life outside the cities of Hanoi, Ho Chi Minh City (Saigon), Da Nang, or Hue remains as it has been for decades, or perhaps, centuries. Tea farmers still plant and harvest by hand. They fire up charcoal stoves to dry tea leaves, their children turn the tea dryers by hand, and families pack leaves in bulk plastic bags, recycled from other uses. Rice farmers follow the back-breaking practices they always have in planting and harvesting rice, using water buffalo for pulling plows and wooden buckets for transferring water from one area to another. Electricity is still a luxury, and families of four or six may still share a bed. The pattern is not unlike other transition economies, where people in urban settings increasingly move toward regional or international standards in products, buildings, infrastructure, and education, while people in rural areas continue to live lives very similar to those of their grandparents.

BACKGROUND FOR THE BOOK

Although the dramatic (and televised) fall of the Berlin Wall on November 9, 1989, is often cited as the trigger or symbol of the end of the planned economy legacy, rumblings—and suppression—began long before. Hungary's 1956 reform program, Czechoslovakia's "Prague Spring" of 1968, the Solidarity Trade Union's (rise and) fall in Poland in 1981, and the liberty movement in China's Tiananmen Square in June 1989 foreshadowed economic and, often, political changes to come. Major shifts emerged in 1989, when 12 countries began the tumultuous route to change. Those 12 have since become 30, and range from the merger of West and East Germany, to the dissolution of Czechoslovakia, to the division of the Soviet Union into 15 new states (Peng 2000).

Other than India's transition from a colonial to a democratic state, no other transition in recent history has affected as many people. The impact of the transition process, gauged in rough measures of people and economic value, is astonishing. In the 1990s, transition economies included some 1.63 billion people—more than 360 million East Europeans and Russians and over 1 billion Chinese, Vietnamese, and Mongolians. This group of states represented about 30 percent of the world's total population and about 7 percent of the global gross domestic product (GDP) in 1990, not an insignificant cluster of countries.

The enormity of such a transition has fascinated many observers, ranging from scholars and journalists to artists and novelists, over the last decade. A simple Internet search on transition economies generates several hundred thousand references to articles in research and journalistic publications. Most are in English, but many have appeared in other languages, especially German, Polish, and Hungarian.

The Challenge of the Literature: Unraveling the Information

The literature on transition economies relating to implications for business is wide-ranging, diverse, and overwhelming in its volume. As is to be expected, publications typically reflect the interests and expertise of the authors—many of whom are academic economists. As a result, research about transition economies in the last decade began with a decidedly macroeconomic orientation, focusing on institutional, governmental, and economic policy changes. The books or articles that resulted from the research (e.g., Edwards and Lawrence 2000; Kornai 1992; Litvack and Rondinelli 1999) frequently describe broad policies and changes, but they do not often suggest how such policies will affect the business managers, local or foreign.

Other publications (e.g., Boisot and Child 1999; Robinson and Tomczak-Stepien 2000; Soulsby and Clark 1996; Vamosi 2001) concentrate on a particular country or region. While this geographic approach makes sense from a research standpoint, it is cumbersome for the manager who may work in China, Russia, Hungary, *and* Vietnam. Even worse, the variances within countries themselves, among managers, and across industries can be daunting. For instance, while observers talk of the significant changes brought by transition in cities such as Shanghai and Moscow, the impact can be negligible in Polish agricultural communities or in Vietnamese fishing villages. Rather than having a set of common themes or issues to consider when they shift countries and conditions, foreign managers must assimilate the information contained in an armload of books or articles that provide (some) depth in specific geographic areas.

Thus, the immense amount of information and its diversity make it nearly impossible for a single manager—or even an enthusiastic academic!—to sift through the available data to find critical gems of knowledge and implications for business. It is an even greater challenge to sort through how the information can help business managers understand and manage better their daily interactions with counterparts in transition economies.

Transformation of Firms

While many articles examine the transition process from a macroeconomic perspective, only in recent years has the literature begun to examine microeconomic implications for organizations (e.g., Bjorkman and Ehrnrooth 1999; Mathur, Gleason, and Mathur 1999; Robinson and Tomczak-Stepien 2000; Stanojevic 2001) We have drawn upon the insights of two scholars in particular who have provided such a perspective (i.e., Newman 2000; Peng 2000). Newman (2000) examined organizations undergoing transition in the Czech Republic to understand how an environment of radical change influenced their abilities to cope and thrive. She discovered an inverted, U-shaped curve relationship between extent of extreme change and ability to cope over time with a quick, positive change in organizations at the beginning of the transition process, followed by a comparably dramatic downward reaction later. In other words, radical change (i.e., both political and economic simultaneously) proved too much for many organizations over the initial decade of transition (Stiglitz 1999). The implications for such dramatic change, likewise, may affect the ways that foreign and local managers react and interact during the course of change in transition economies.

Peng (2000) describes the reactions to change of four types of transition economy organizations—state-owned enterprises, start-ups, privatized firms, and foreign firms. He suggests that each type of firm reacts to influences differently, forming different strategies resulting in different outcomes. Again, we drew upon Peng's (2000) work as we examined the nature of interaction among foreign managers and those from transition economy firms.

How Managers React

While authors like Newman and Peng focus on changes at the firm level, others (e.g., Clark, Lang, and Balaton 2001; Feichtinger and Fink

1998; Illes and Rees 2001) examine the psychological or behavioral impact of transition on local and foreign managers. With this book, we seek to add to this research and offer an overview of the situation in transition economies, the influences that affect organizations and the managers who work in transition economies, ways that foreign managers can better understand the psychology and behaviors of their transition economy counterparts, and suggestions on how to comprehend the interaction between the two groups.

Thus, we emphasize the managerial and practical aspects of doing business with transition economy managers and, in particular, their interactions with foreigners. Rather than concentrating on macro-organizational or firm-level strategies or actions, our focus is at the manager-to-manager level, which we feel is crucial, from our own experience and that of the business people and managers who have worked in transition economies, to understanding the nature of interactions between managers. We hope this book will help those people, primarily from North America, understand the nature of the interactions that foreign and local managers experience during different stages of the transition period and during their business dealings.

A word about words: we recognize fully that the words *manager* or *business person* are distinctly North American in flavor. In many transition economies, the terms did not exist prior to transition—instead, terms like *boss, leader, or director*, were more common. Although we recognize the range of names that business people may use, for simplicity, we chose to use primarily *manager* to refer to the groups of people—both within transition economies and those who work there but come from other countries. While we also realize that not all of the persons we talk about are managers of other people or units, most are or were, and thus we use manager to denote a broad category; for variety and accuracy, where possible, we use the term *businessperson* as well.

Information Sources

Beyond an extensive literature review of publications available over the last decade, our insights and understanding of what is happening in transition economies also comes from our experiences and those of others we have talked with over the years.

Each of us has done research or project work in several transition economy countries, ranging from Vietnam and Poland, to China, Hungary, and Russia. Like other scholars, we have experienced and written about the challenges of doing research in locations outside North America, as well as working with colleagues on training and educational programs in transition economies (e.g., Michailova and Liuhto 2000; Napier, Hosley, and Nguyen Forthcoming; Napier, Ngo, Nguyen, Nguyen, and Vu 2002; Napier and Thomas 2001; Thomas 1998; Thomas and Ravlin 1995). Our research, consulting, and project assignments have been as short as a week and as long as nine years. In addition to our own work and travel, we have conducted training courses for managers from transition economies, either in the countries themselves or in our home universities. We have worked with all four types of firms that Peng (2000) describes as key in transition economies—foreign, state-owned enterprises, start-ups, and privatized firms, again in a variety of countries.

Also, since the mid 1990s, we have talked with more than 100 local managers and educators from transition economies. Their experiences and reactions to the changes they have undergone have helped us build a base of knowledge and insight that lead us to write this book. In our work relating to transition economies, we also have interviewed, formally and informally, over 75 foreign managers and educators who have worked in several transition economies in Eastern European countries ranging from Albania to the Czech Republic and Slovakia, from Hungary to Poland and Romania, from western Russia to the central Russian plains, from Vietnam and China to Mongolia and the Russian Far East.

When the idea for this book became a reality, we sought an update of conditions in transition economies from the perspective of local and foreign managers. We talked to 25 managers in semi-structured interviews, lasting from one to two hours, that followed a common protocol focusing on understanding the ways that managers from western and local settings had (or had not) changed their respective behaviors over time, how they adjusted to each other, and what recommendations they each had for foreign managers working in transition economies. In the interviews, we also asked about the changes in mind-sets that local managers experienced over the years, from the perspective of both local and foreign managers. Some of the foreign managers with whom we spoke had worked in transition economies over many years, some for more than 20 years, and thus had seen changes and had long-standing interactions with certain transition economy managers. Other interviewees had spent only short-term assignments in transition economies and so had snapshot views (in time, place, and activity) and interactions. Likewise, some of the transition economy managers we interviewed had longer-term or shorter-term interactions with westerners.

This book, then, was in the making for several years before we formally decided to write it. During those years, we developed our own informal hunches about what was happening in transition economies, how managers were reacting, and what that might mean for foreign managers who worked there. Part of the work on this book involved testing our hunches on the managers we interviewed. We looked more systematically for examples of how the mind-sets and behaviors of transition economy managers had changed so that we could understand their current roles, how they approached their jobs, and how their approaches might be different from those of foreign managers. Our goal was that this book would give foreign managers insights on what they needed to know now, in the decade-old environment of transition, to operate successfully with those local managers and employees.

Given the widely reported range and depth of change in transition economies since 1989 (e.g., the inflow of foreign firms, of training and education in western business practices, of governmental focus on policies to encourage market-oriented practices), we assumed local managers were increasingly using western practices to run their companies: to hire, evaluate, and motivate employees and to conduct relationships with their partners (foreign and local), customers, and other key stakeholders. We hoped that understanding how their thinking and behavior had changed over time and how they viewed their own roles in the new environment would be helpful for foreign managers going for their first visit or their fiftieth.

We expected to hear that much had changed in the past decade, that doing business in Beijing or Moscow or Prague was increasingly like working in Germany or Japan or the United States in terms of the level and understanding of global business practices. We expected that a decade of training, dealing with foreign firms, studying abroad by younger people, accessing television and the Internet, mobile phones and McDonald's would have changed the ways local transition economy managers ran their firms, people, products, and budgets.

Initially, we were surprised when we didn't find far-reaching evidence of significant changes in local managerial behavior and mind-set. Instead, it increasingly appeared that change had occurred more on a surface level, in terms of increases in material and tangible items, like leather shoes and mobile phones, than in the mind-sets and behaviors of managers. Many local managers admitted themselves that they had been disappointed or frustrated at how difficult the shift in thinking and behavior had been. Likewise, foreign managers had been baffled at the reluctance of some local managers to absorb the (to foreign managers) proper approaches to business. In essence, the pace seems to have followed what Feichtinger and Fink (1998) predicted about collective culture shock: that adaptation by transition managers to the new culture of a market economy will take much longer than initially expected, perhaps 20 to 30 years, rather than a decade.

Nevertheless, as we talked to more managers, we found common patterns emerging in the ways local and foreign managers were interacting in the new environment of transition. The changes then have involved how local and foreign managers interacted with each other, rather than how they have behaved with their own employees and colleagues. The process appeared to have been one that each side could recognize and adjust to, and both sides seemed to realize that they could learn from each other. Thus, while mind-sets and behaviors may not have changed as much as people had anticipated, the interactions between foreign and local managers have altered in subtle ways that are possible to understand and track.

Book Structure

The book is divided into three parts, with a final chapter that offers suggestions, particularly for foreign managers, on ways to interact with their transition economy counterparts as well as ideas about how to build successful relationships. Part I covers two sets of contextual factors that influence the interactions between local and foreign managers (Figure 1.1). The factors include the external environment that managers work in and the organizations, or firm types, that have emerged in transition

Figure 1.1
Overview of *Managing Relationships*

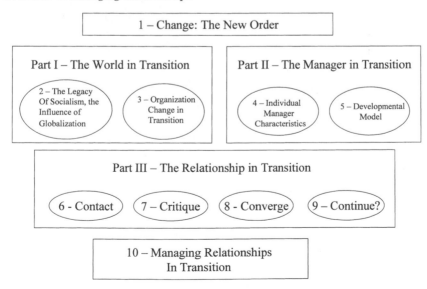

economies. Each chapter presents the current conditions and situations and then argues that, at each level, the change encountered is dramatic, strategic, and radical.

Part II provides a conceptual basis for understanding the managers—both foreign and local—who work in transition economies. Chapter 4 examines the attributes and characteristics of the individual manager, both local and foreign, that can affect interactions. Chapter 5 provides a conceptual framework for understanding the interactions between the two groups of managers. This framework forms the basis for Part III, which describes the stages through which the interactions between local and foreign managers progress as the relationship develops.

As outlined in Figure 1.1, contextual factors (discussed in Chapters 2 and 3) provide the background for understanding the managers and their interactions (Chapters 4 and 5). Illustrations of the interaction stages appear in Chapters 6–9. In the next section, we describe briefly each chapter.

Chapter Synopses

Part I, "The World in Transition," comprises two chapters. Chapter 2, "The Legacy of Socialism, The Influence of Globalization," examines key environmental issues that provide the context in which foreign and local managers interact in transition economies. Chapter 2 begins with a presentation of the legacy of socialism, a description of the fundamental concepts and beliefs that grounded managers in transition economies for, in some cases, more than 50 years. Then the discussion moves to a brief description of the types of approaches to economic (and sometimes political) change pursued in transition economies—some have undergone a "shock treatment" approach, others a more gradual one. The types of issues that have emerged from those approaches are also examined. Finally, while the transition economies have been undergoing unprecedented change within the borders of individual countries, so too has the world economy experienced dramatic change through globalization. Thus, both foreign and local managers face significant environmental turmoil—change within change—at several levels.

Chapter 3, "Organizational Change in Transition," turns to the enterprise level, providing an overview of the types of organizations that have emerged within transition economies (Peng 2000). The four types, state-owned enterprises, entrepreneurial start-ups, newly privatized firms, and foreign firms, are themselves in various stages of development, so the chapter suggests ways these types of organizations may react to change at a firm level, which of course, eventually affects interactions at the managerial level.

Part II, "The Manager in Transition," contains two chapters that set the framework for understanding interactions between local and foreign managers working in transition economies. Chapter 4, "Individual Manager Characteristics," presents insights from our interviews and experience that confirm and add to the research and practitioner literature about individual level influences on management in transition economy settings. The chapter discusses three key attributes of managers that may affect the ways they interact with one another: the nature and extent of business knowledge that each holds; the motivation, or psychological makeup, of each group; and demographics.

Chapter 5 of Part II provides the theoretical underpinnings for a developmental model used to identify and explain how manager interactions may evolve over time. One of the unique areas explored in this book is the reaction of the foreign manager. Much has already been written about the local manager's situation, challenges, and frustrations as he or she experiences transition. This chapter discusses both the process and outcomes of the necessary interaction in international businesses between local managers and their foreign counterparts, which are indicated by the levels of trust among the parties, the nature and type of information flow or communication, and the expectations that each group has about the other. Our interviews revealed that, in these relationships, the quality and nature of interaction starts out positively, typically dips into friction, and eventually works back to some state of equilibrium or acceptance. Since the curve of the stages can range from quite dramatically positive to negative, one of the goals of our research was to find ways to smooth out the dips in the interactions.

Part III, "The Relationship in Transition," includes Chapters 6 through 9. Each chapter explores one of the stages in the development of the relationship between local and foreign managers, based on the findings of our own experiences and on our interviews with both types of managers. The titles of the chapters were chosen to highlight each stage; however, titles alone—in a word or phrase—cannot fully capture some of the subtleties and nuances considered within the chapter itself.

These chapters, which form the core of the book, examine how a relationship starts (or does not), how it grows, how it changes, and how it ends (or continues). Chapter 6, "Contact: Getting to Know You," focuses on the early stages of a relationship and on the nature of the interaction in that early "getting to know you" stage. Both local and foreign managers have strong reactions toward building a business relationship, and the chapter considers each perspective. A typical (if not inevitable) subsequent stage of a relationship is critical evaluation of the relationship, including perhaps some disharmony or discord. Such evaluation may happen early on (e.g., during negotiations), or several years into the relationship. Chapter 7, "Critique: Surprises and Frustrations," addresses issues—in trust, communications, expectations—that emerge when counterparts move beyond the initial stage and begin to discover the realities of the relationship. Sometimes, they confront tension and, possibly, conflict. Both local and foreign managers may face dissatisfaction, frustration, and sometimes, anger in their relationships, and their interactions will reflect such feelings. The chapter provides several examples of what can happen and how each side may view the discord.

Many foreign and local managers eventually work through their disharmony to find a new way to interact, which is the focus of Chapter 8, "Convergence: Finding Ways to Make it Work." Sometimes, over time, managers discover different ways of thinking and behaving that moves them beyond conflict and allows them to carry on. Other times, managers are less successful in their efforts and dissolve the relationship.

The last chapter of the section, Chapter 9, "Continue?: Possibilities and Outcomes," reports on potential directions that relationships among managers may take. Although we had few case examples of long-term business relationships, we did learn about potential patterns from managers. Broadly, the outcomes fall into three types and an unknowable possibility: adjusting or accommodating to create a new and stronger relationship and ways to interact; satisficing or compromising to continue the relationship, but without a sense of long-term commitment; or abandoning or resisting a continuation of the relationship. Finally, given the uncertainties and unpredictabilities of working in transition economies, we acknowledge, as do the managers we talked to, that the question—whether and how to continue a relationship—remains open for many.

Chapter 10, "Managing Relationships in Transition Economies," lays out suggestions for how local and foreign managers can improve the chances of their interactions being more steady and positive, ideas that each side can use to help enhance the situation that local managers find themselves in and what foreign managers encounter when they work with them. While this chapter focuses on transition economies as currently defined (i.e., those moving from a planned to a market economy), it also suggests that the ideas here may apply in other developing and emerging country situations—where the contexts and challenges that managers face are similarly chaotic, dramatic, and hard to grasp.

Part I

THE WORLD IN TRANSITION

Part I examines the context that managers who work in transition economies face. A clear impression, based on the thousands of articles that have been written about transition economies, emerges—these economies have undergone tremendous change, especially at the material level. Yet, for many countries, this is a surface change, one that has occurred above a more fundamental base that remains from years of state socialism. The complex environment that managers face in the world of transition economies is the subject of the two chapters in this section.

Chapter 2 examines the fundamental concepts of socialism, which was the bedrock for transition economies for many decades. While these concepts may be withering, their legacy still shapes the mind-set of many managers (and possibly their sons or daughters) who worked under state socialism. The long history of state socialism, especially in Russia and Eastern Europe, continues to influence the psychology and behavior of people long after the demise of communism (Clark 2000). However, the recent dramatic changes that transition economies have experienced are only a small part of an even more dramatic change in the global world of business. Therefore, this chapter also reviews the most important implications of globalization for management in transition economies.

Chapter 3 moves to the level of the organizations in transition economies. It examines the four types of firms that have emerged in these settings. It then considers how these types of firms adjust to second-order, or strategic, change, the type of change that cannot be planned, cannot be easily managed, and for which there is no clear model to follow.

Chapter 2

THE LEGACY OF SOCIALISM, THE INFLUENCE OF GLOBALIZATION

The idea that men are created free and equal is both true and misleading. Men are created different, they lose their social freedom and their individual autonomy in seeking to become like each other.
—David Reisman, Professor of Economics,
University of Surrey, U.K.

KAPITALISM 101

In 1995, in the small city of Boise, Idaho, the ideas of socialism and capitalism faced off in a confrontation that could have been comedic, had it not been such a sad statement of misunderstanding. It started with a headline in the local newspaper.

"Boise State University Brings Capitalism to Vietnam," boasted the local *Idaho Statesman* in July 1995.

"Bully for Boise State University," said the university's supporters.

"Horrible! What arrogance!" said Vietnamese participants in an educational summer program in Boise.

The start-up venture began when 30 Vietnamese faculty members and business managers participated in the Boise State University M.B.A. program in the 1994–95 school year. Those students had spent six weeks in Boise the summer of 1995 taking final classes and participating in company internships.

The headline ripped open wounds and fueled anger in the Vietnamese that astounded their American hosts. The American business people and university experts who heard about the angry reaction questioned how the Vietnamese could feel that way. Such people seemed to believe that although the Vietnamese had won the military victory, their adoption of capitalism showed that the United States had won the bigger war.

The Vietnamese felt insulted, thought that the Americans were (once again) dabbling in their internal affairs and were trying to tell their country what sort of political life to pursue. They railed at anyone who would listen, saying that they did not like the goals of U.S. capitalism and their results—letting people lose jobs, taking advantage of workers, not taking care of old people, making each person work alone, without help. They wondered why Americans thought Vietnamese should want U.S. capitalism, feeling it was wrong for their country.

Most Americans in Boise were baffled. Capitalism and market economics were good ideas; they were fundamental to the economic powerhouse the United States had become in the 1990s. How could the Vietnamese not understand?

Many of us, however, remembering our days in college political science classes on Marxism, might recall Marx's book *Das Kapital,* which described a political system, not just an economic system. But Marxism in the United States makes little sense because capitalism there means an economic system that focuses on supply and demand, not a political ideology, unlike the rest of the world, including China and Vietnam, where the political ideals of socialism still reign. Hanoi boasts one of the few remaining statues of Lenin and a museum devoted to Vietnam's still revered leader, Ho Chi Minh. "Uncle Ho" made communism a reality for Vietnam in the 1940s and 1950s, reuniting the country in 1975, after driving out the French and American "imperialists."

The strong feelings evoked by that simple headline in the opening vignette helped American and Vietnamese counterparts realize how easy it is to misunderstand the context in which each group lives. This chapter, then, provides detail on the socialist system so that foreign managers, in particular, can understand the environment in which their transition-economy counterparts function. Although the focus in this chapter is on the years of socialism, other factors influenced mind-sets. Historical and religious events, in particular the split between eastern and western churches, influenced behaviors that even today continue to reveal the mistrust and hatred among peoples of Eastern Europe, Russia, and the eastern part of the Mediterranean (Clark 2000). Thus, the long-term history of countries exists as an undercurrent along with the more dramatic recent events of socialism and its dissolution.

SOCIALISM AND GLOBALIZATION—CHANGE INSIDE OF CHANGE

The final two decades of the twentieth century saw a widespread decline in centrally planned economies in favor of more market-based approaches, with the economic freedom those approaches imply. The attraction of market-based economies is not surprising when we consider that nations with the greatest economic freedom also have the highest standard of living and those with the least economic freedom have the lowest standard of living (Parker 1998). Yet to understand the implications of transition for both local and foreign managers, we must recognize the environment in which so many have lived. This chapter discusses the history and legacy of socialism, its key elements, and how transition economies have chosen to move toward a market-economy model. In addition, the chapter explores the broader global context facing managers in transition economies. In essence, both sets of managers have met and will continue to encounter dramatic upheaval—foreign managers as they deal with the global context and all it suggests and local managers in transition economies as they face their own internal shift to market economics, which then is tucked into the broader trends of globalization.

ENVIRONMENT UNDER STATE SOCIALISM

The essence of economic transition is the replacement of one set of institutions that govern economic activity by another. Western market economies have built their legal, employment, and educational institutions over decades, if not centuries. Today, former socialist countries have had to adapt or develop such institutions in short order in an environment that is more dynamic and complex than ever. While managers in transition economies are swayed heavily by external influences, the institutions they establish must be acceptable within their own society (Offe 1995; Rock and Solodkov 2001). Therefore, it is not surprising that institutions in transition economies retain some vestiges of state socialism. So, to understand managers in these economies today, we must understand their previous environment.

Anatomy of State Socialism

According to Kornai (1992), the key to understanding state socialism is an examination of the structure of power within socialist societies. The starting point is the undivided political power of the ruling party, which results in a preponderance of state ownership of several key elements of the economy. The next element in the chain is bureaucratic coordination, the forms of which vary from one country to another. These three elements—undivided political power, state ownership of key elements in the economy, and bureaucratic coordination—combine to motivate the actors in the system with the resulting characteristics of plan bargaining, the quantity drive, paternalistic behavior of superiors, soft budget constraints, weak responsiveness to prices, and so on. The final element is a set of the economic outcomes, such as forced growth, labor shortages, unemployment on the job, chronic shortages in the economy, and the system-specific role of foreign trade. The following brief description of the business environment under state socialism uses this framework as its basis.

Locus of Power

The fundamental institution in the power structure in socialist countries was the single-party system, which set rules of behavior and operations as a form of legal power. Any legal system has basic goals: to preserve the social order; to provide a basic model of conduct; to establish property and other rights; and to mediate the views of different societal segments within a set of enforceable rules (Sundaram and Black 1995). Apart from state socialism, three fundamental legal systems exist: common law, used in England and 26 other countries, including the United States; civil law, used by approximately 70 countries in Europe, Latin America, and Asia, including Japan, South Korea, and Taiwan; and Islamic law, derived from the teachings of the Prophet Muhammad as found in the *Koran*. In all three of these systems, managers must comply with the law or risk sanctions.

In pretransition socialist economies, however, laws regarding business transactions were unnecessary since formal constraints on organizations were part of the central planning regime. The Communist Party and the state were interwoven in a way that insured that the party was the dominant force in their common activities (Kornai 1992; Snell and Tseng 2002). The various organizations in society were designed to have an organizational monopoly in their own field: one labor-union movement, one association of engineers, one academy of sciences, and so on. Power and prestige were determined by one's level in the hierarchy of the appropriate organization, with material privileges (e.g., housing, medical care, access to goods and services, holidays) proportionate to rank. Possessors of power legitimized their position through paternalism. That is, the paternalistic role justified centralization and bureaucratic organization of power.

Socialist Sense of Superiority

The conviction that the socialist system was superior to the capitalist one was an important ingredient of the socialist ideology (Kornai 1992). In other words, socialism did not suffer from many of the ills of capitalism, such as errors in allocation of resources due to fluctuations in supply or demand that could result in mass unemployment (as evidenced by the Great Depression of 1929 in the West). Indeed, full (or nearly full) employment was a critical goal of the public sector (state-owned enterprises) in planned economies.

Socialism also sought to prevent the waste caused by competition based on private property. It held that workers, freed from exploitation, could be self-motivated, and therefore, costs of supervision could be eliminated. Socialism's sense of superiority was tied to the idea that capitalism had passed the stage at which it contributed to the progress of society (Kornai 1992).

Ownership

A simple distinction, often made, is that capitalism is associated with private ownership and socialism with public ownership. While this idea was largely true for the means of production in socialist systems, it did not preclude the ownership of some types of property, such as tangible goods. Also, while the state-owned enterprise (SOE) dominated the key sectors of the socialist economy, other types of enterprise ownership existed. These included not only agricultural cooperatives, but also small-scale family farms as well as a wide variety of informal, or underground, economic activities (Dallago 1990).

Prices and Soft Budgets

Producer prices under socialism were set on the basis of vertical (bureaucratic control) mechanisms, whereas under capitalism, prices are set on the basis of horizontal (buyer and seller) market mechanisms. The principles by which prices were set in socialist systems include the following: prices should reflect socially necessary costs; prices should be the means by which producers are encouraged to perform specific tasks; and prices ought to be stable (Kornai 1992). The consequences of this pricing mechanism was a complex system of fiscal redistribution (Kornai and Matits 1990) and a soft-budget constraint. That is, when firms persistently overspent their budgets under the socialist system, they received relief through several possible mechanisms such as direct subsidies, reduced taxation, increased credit, or even, renegotiation of prices. This softening of the budget constraint was accomplished by manipulating the various bureaucracies responsible for the firm.

Investment

Both the pace of growth and the investment priorities that socialist countries gave different economic sectors reflected an underlying impatience to catch up to the developed world. In 1931 Joseph Stalin said, "We are fifty to one hundred years behind the advanced countries. We must make good this distance in ten years" (Kornai 1992: 161). Mao Tse-tung's Great Leap Forward reflected a similar policy of the fastest possible growth. This policy of growth fostered a prioritization of investment in the means of production over consumer goods. Industry was considered the engine of growth, and heavy industry was the primary means used to increase productivity and to encourage technical development. Military demands received priority over civilian needs, and the growth of productive capacity took place at the expense of environmental concerns. Although variation in these priorities did exist across countries, much consistency across socialist and former socialists countries can be detected (see Kornai 1992).

Employment and Wages

A fundamental tenet of socialism is that labor is not a commodity to be bought and sold, but rather a resource to be employed. Under state socialism, the work unit, or labor collective (*danwei* in China), was a central component of the command-and-control production system. The work unit was central not only organizationally but also politically and psychologically. Centralized allocations of workers ignored changes in labor supply and demand. Labor was considered a national resource as opposed to a commodity (Dowling, Welch, and Schuler 1999).

As the principal means of production, the labor collective measured its achievements not only by the increased volume of its production, but also by the size, education, and skill of its labor force (Clarke 1996a). Ideologically, production was meant to increase the well-being of the labor collective with the enterprise manager posing as the paternalistic guardian of the collective. In reality, however, the needs of the labor collective often were subordinated to the production and appropriation of surplus product (Clarke 1996a).

A central belief of the labor collective was that a worker had a right to a job and its associated benefits (Lee 1987). For urban workers, this meant lifetime employment and cradle-to-grave welfare coverage. In China, factories approximated institutions, providing for all of the workers' needs: they fed, housed, hospitalized, and generally protected the working class as part of the wider social contract (Warner 2000). The so-called iron rice bowl and its counterpart in other socialist countries resulted in a perception of the exchange relationship between individuals and the enterprise that differed from that in market-driven organizations.

This perception, called the psychological contract (Argyris 1960; Schein 1965), is a set of individual perceptions concerning the terms of the exchange relationship between individuals and their organizations. It may include beliefs about performance requirements, job security, training, compensation, and career development, and it differs in terms of its transactional versus relational aspects (Rousseau 1989, 1995). Relational contracts emphasize broad, long-term, socio-emotional obligations such as commitment and loyalty consistent with collective interest (McLean-Parks and Schmedemann 1994). Such contracts have a pervasive effect on personal as well as work life. Employees under state socialism were encouraged to perceive their relationship to the enterprise in this way.

Hierarchy in the Collective

Despite the egalitarian picture often painted of the labor collective, the reality was somewhat different. First, the distinction between cadres (individuals engaged in leadership or managerial work) and workers is prevalent across transition economies. Typically, categorization into a cadre was based primarily on technological or other hierarchical grounds. In Russia, for example, engineering and technical workers were viewed as agents of the system since they drew up plans, monitored performance, and maintained records (Clarke 1996a).

Furthermore under state socialism, a kind of labor aristocracy, consisting of reliable and skilled workers who were recruited into the party, existed (Clarke 1996b). These workers enjoyed good pay and extensive privileges, and acted as a bridge between management and labor.

With the transition to a market orientation, a shift in the balance of power has come about. New organizational areas such as marketing and finance have been formed, and the distinction between cadres and workers is becoming blurred (Dowling, Welch, and Schuler 1999). Under these new circumstances, front line managers (shop chiefs) are faced with the potential role conflict of having to decide on which side (management or labor) they stand.

Working around Obstacles

In a planned economy, when managers had difficulty fulfilling an order, purchasing equipment, or meeting a plan, they found ways to work around the system (e.g., deceiving higher authorities about production levels, using illegal hard currency to purchase equipment) (Holden, Cooper, and Carr 1998; Litchfield 1992; Stahl-Rolf 2000). Such behavior stemmed, in part, from the political and economic uncertainty that managers faced; by following orders, they avoided accountability and responsibility, shielding themselves and their careers from damage if mistakes emerged. Working around the system, while hidden from superiors, was something that all levels understood took place.

Labor Discontinuities

To support the mandate for rapid and continuous growth within a socialist environment, the labor surplus (unemployment) was to be absorbed by the public sector. Over time discontinuity developed between labor needs and labor availability. Typically, the majority of surplus labor was unskilled people who lived in the rural villages. The growing economy required people with high skills who lived in the cities. Furthermore, uneven regional development created a high demand in some areas but not others (Kornai 1992). These factors created a chronic shortage of labor. While the overall budget constraint on socialist firms was soft, the constraint on wages was not. The bureaucratic control of employment began with education, where choices open to individuals were severely limited and/or individuals simply were channeled toward a particular type of work. This control extended to establishing upper limits on wages through a variety of mechanisms. Thus, wage costs often were unrealistically low in comparison to what labor actually was costing.

Shortages

There is considerable debate among economists about the causes of shortages and the repressed inflation that occurred in socialist societies. It is beyond the scope of this book to completely discuss the causes of the phenomenon. However, it is important to note that the dominant deviation from market equilibrium in socialist economies is shortage, whereas in market economies the dominant deviation is surplus. In socialist systems, the seller drives production; in capitalist systems, the buyer does so. Within the socialist system, failure to respond to demand led to forced substitution of one good for another, which in turn perpetuated chronic shortage (Kornai 1992).

Economic Security versus Quality

A key goal of the socialist system was basic economic security for the masses. Therefore, under the socialist system, economic security overshadowed satisfying the consumer. The sense of satisfaction a consumer derived in obtaining a product, often after queuing all day long, frequently was dissipated by it not being the product the buyer originally wanted (forced substitution, see Collier 1986) or by the product being of very low quality. Kornai (1992) suggests that the inability of the command economies to achieve high quality products was the result of the following factors:

- The vertical framework of bureaucratic control can only issue production instructions in broad, as opposed to finely detailed, quality terms.
- Central price controls cannot reflect quality differences as accurately as market-based prices.
- Forced growth results in high production volumes at the expense of quality.
- In a sellers' market, the seller can sell its output even with low quality.

Trade

The trade relations of socialist societies were primarily subordinated to the political agenda (Kornai 1992). For example, trade with the West was greatly curtailed because of a desire to isolate the economy from capitalism. Only selected transactions were allowed to occur. Trade with other socialist countries was similarly influenced; economically disadvantageous transactions were entered into in order to support political or military activities. Trade that did occur with the West was driven by the desire to obtain the most modern machinery and equipment to fuel growth. This import driven trade agenda was further fueled by the chronic shortages mentioned previously. It ultimately became impossible to offset these imports with exports of surplus goods.

Bureaucratic Control

A key feature of state socialism was that bureaucratic control facilitated coordination among economic entities (Ericson 1991) at the expense of other coordinating mechanism such as the market, self-control, ethical control, or family control. In a socialist regime, the overriding objective of the firm was to meet the production targets set by the central planners. Bureaucratic control over the firm was extensive and focused on the notion of central planning.

Pretransition managerial behavior was influenced by the bureaucratic controls and by those power relationships inherent in the command-and-control system. As the state gradually relinquished its role in controlling organizations, there was a need for a legal framework to fill the void. However, developing the framework takes time, and the capacity of the weakened state to enforce such laws may be questionable (Peng 2000). In such an environment, then, managers rapidly acquired a great deal of latitude in their behavior as former bureaucratic constraints were removed and as they received incomplete or ambiguous messages from other sources. Business protocol in Russia is often cited as being a result of the legal and regulatory framework failing to keep pace with economic reform, as this tongue-in-cheek example suggests (Dubow 1997: 142).

> If you were the representative of a large Western company and you needed a special permit to begin operations, would you apply to the appropriate ministry, pay the official fee and wait several months (or, more often, years) for permission to come through? Or would you take the minister and his cronies out for a tremendous booze up and give everyone a diamond Rolex? Proper Russian business etiquette would clearly indicate the latter option.

Central Planning

During state socialism, the key institution that coordinated economic activity was the central plan. The central plan fulfilled most of the functions of the market, and planning was seen as one of the key advantages of socialism over the "invisible hand" of capitalism (Peng 2000). However, the strong vertical coordination of central planning came at the expense of horizontal linkages among firms (Meyer 2001). Therefore, central planning resulted in the concentration of responsibility for firms in the hands of a government bureaucracy, which was itself attempting to coordinate a large national economy.

Central planning, based upon the philosophies of Karl Marx and Vladimir Lenin, was an attempt to avoid the vagaries of a boom-and-bust, market-based system. It sought to avoid busts such as the Great Depression of the western economies, which could harm workers' livelihoods and affect employment predictability (Kornai 1992). The controls to achieve the goals of central planning—avoiding overproduction, massive unemployment, or economic depression—were many. Peng (2000: 19) lists seven critical controls and compares them to market practices:

- Creation of firms by the state (versus by an entrepreneur)
- Decision to liquidate a firm made by the state (versus allowing a firm to exit on its own, declare bankruptcy, be merged or purchased)
- Production goals set by the state (rather than by a firm's managers)
- State determines the allocation and distribution of products by matching users and producers; that is, this user buys from this producer (versus allowing the market to determine who buys from whom)
- Decision about prices, investment, technology development and use, and trade are made by the state (rather than by the managers of firms)
- Manager selection, promotion, and dismissal are done by the state (rather than by individual firm managers or boards of directors).
- Workers are assigned to facilities and their pay is based on a centrally determined wage rate (rather than allowing the firms to recruit, set pay scales, and make compensation decisions).

The Legacy of State Socialism

Clearly, the fundamental institution in the power structure of socialist countries was the single-party system. Under state socialism, plans were fulfilled in large part according to state priority, and many countries rapidly industrialized. Although the economic gap between planned and market economies appeared to be narrowing during the 1950s and 1960s (Peng 2000), fundamental cracks began to appear over time. In summarizing the state of legal institutions that exist in most transition economies, Murrell (1996) suggests that the quality of law is quite low, that it lacks internal consistency and completeness, and that laws are only marginally significant in their effect on managerial behavior.

Also, the incentives created by central planning led to severe problems, such as the production of large volumes of standardized, low quality products, lack of concern for demand, and a general disregard for the external environment (Meyer 2001). Virtually all socialist countries suffered from persistent shortages, especially in food and consumer products (Kornai 1980). By the 1980s the failure of state socialism to achieve a high living standard was already apparent (Brzezinski 1989), and in many countries extensive personal networks had evolved as a mechanism of exchange to overcome shortages (Puffer 1996b). It is from this basis that socialist countries confronted the decision to transform to market economies as they encountered an increasingly competitive global environment.

PATHS TO TRANSITION

The steps in economic transition typically involve deregulation, privatization, and the creation of a legal system that protects property rights (Hill 2001). Deregulation involves the removal of legal restrictions to market activity, the establishment of private enterprise, and the way in which private enterprise is allowed to compete. Privatization transfers the ownership of property from the state to private individuals, and often involves the sale of state assets. For a market economy to function effectively, a legal system that protects the rights of owners must exist. Otherwise the incentives to engage in economic activity are diminished.

These economic changes have significant implications for organizations and their managers. While generally following the steps outlined above, the precise nature of the transitions have taken different forms in different countries because of different histories, resources, and cultures. Also, the timing of the transitions can be traced to key historical events. Prior to 1989, 12 countries were all members of a broadly classified socialist system. Because of the break up of the Soviet Union, Czechoslovakia, and Yugoslavia, such countries now number 30 (Peng 2000). While all of these countries have moved toward a market economy, it is important to remember that elements of the old socialist system remain to a greater or lesser extent in each (Campbell 1991).

Approaches to Transition

In the late 1980s and early 1990s, transition economies experienced major change and tended to follow one of two broad approaches (shock treatment or a more gradual approach) in initiating and implementing the move to more market-based economies (e.g., Clark 1999; Leipziger 1992; Parker, Tritt, and Woo 1997). The shock treatment approach, exemplified by the Soviet Union and Poland, initiated both economic and political changes as quickly as possible. Other countries, such as Hungary, pursued a more gradual approach to their economic changes, although they, too, moved toward democratic political reforms. Vietnam and China, on the other hand, pursued gradual economic transition approaches (although there have been fits and starts, particularly in Vietnam, in terms of how the reforms would proceed), but they have left in place their strong single-party political system, dominated by the Communist Party (Boisot and Child 1996).

Poland epitomized the shock treatment approach, which included severe budget cuts, control of domestic credit and wage levels, price liberalization, exchange rate stabilization and export increases. Results from these early steps were mixed. Benefits included a decline of shortages, an increase in the number of private firms, and greater export and import activity. Negative outcomes included a decline in consumer purchasing power and significant increases in unemployment. Nevertheless, some credit the shock treatment approach in helping Poland become a fast-growing, high-flying economy and, for a time, in avoiding recession and the currency crisis that affected Hungary and the Czech Republic (Valencia 2001).

Hungary typified the more gradual approach, which involved less drastic cuts than seen in Poland and fewer restrictions on credit control or price liberalization. The positive results were tempered but included lower inflation, reduced unemployment, increased purchasing power, and higher exports. Other results and changes were more visible, as illustrated by Prague. Like other big cities in central and eastern Europe, Prague in the Czech Republic exhibits the typical changes that illustrate increasing prosperity: many cafes and new restaurants, a new approach to customer relations (i.e., service with a smile), mobile phones, and Internet access are the norm (Goldman 2000). China and Vietnam have likewise pursued more gradual approaches, with a focus on agricultural and land reform (Parker, Tritt, and Woo 1997). This approach was dictated in part by the decision to retain the single-party socialist system (Han and Baumgarte 2000) and these countries' lower emphasis on industry in general (Zhao and Hall 1994).

The results of the fast versus slow approaches recently have received in depth review. Some scholars have concluded that shock treatment, in particular, has had far-reaching social consequences—ranging from large income disparities to decline in health care and life expectancies (Galbraith 2002). Recently, as several of the eastern European economies considered joining the European Union (EU), the fissures and cracks in their newly emerging systems became evident, as did the reluctance of some citizens to join the EU (Stiglitz 1999).

Slower Change and More Problems than Expected

Despite the very different approaches and the evidence of change (especially in large cities), countries moving from planned to market economies often faced extreme difficulties in making the transition. In fact, by the late 1990s and the early part of the new century, some transition economies seemed to be entering a new phase. Many were recognizing the difficulties of transition—the slower than expected pace of change, the potential for social unrest, and the evidence of growing discrepancies between rural and urban areas.

Such realizations are leading some countries toward more conservative policies and a resurgence of reform communist parties. Hungary, for example, has recently begun edging back toward more state ownership and control of firms. Prime Minister Viktor Orban, elected in 1998, replaced free-market-oriented ministers with ministers who were more conservative and socialist oriented. Rather than moving increasingly toward open competition, the government also continued to control prices for certain key industries. Such constraints caused losses for firms like the state-controlled oil and gas company Mol.

The change in Mongolia's ruling political parties also exemplifies a shift away from a strong push toward market and a return to a more socialist orientation. A U.S. project manager for a construction project watched the change in Mongolia's parliamentary make up over 10 years. In 1990, the elected members of parliament were 100 percent communist; by 1994, only about 50 percent were registered communist. Two years later, in 1996, only 10 percent of parliament members were registered as communists. By 1998, some of the repercussions of the shift to a market economy had emerged. The benefits of freedom of movement and access to information and entertainment (e.g., music) stood along side problems, ranging from people's inability to pay for health care to the lack of a support system for older people. By 2001, just 10 years after the transition started, most members of parliament were again registered as communists.

Poland has followed a similar path. By 1999, the private sector in Poland accounted for two-thirds of all economic activity, shortages had disappeared, and more people were working. But most Poles were quite unhappy (Black 1999), with only 16 percent supporting the government. The dissatisfaction stemmed from the government's lack of action. The state had not privatized several key industries, such as steel mills and coal mines; the state-owned enterprises accounted for only 33 percent of the industrial output, 40 percent of employment, and only 5 percent of profit. The rural area accounted for 33 percent of the population, but only 20 percent of workforce employment. Petroleum prices rose 14 times in 1999, school curriculum changed in ways that upset parents, and health care systems were revamped, with few people happy about the results (Black 1999). Furthermore, Poles were frustrated that former communist leaders continued to control significant wealth and politics.

In its September 2001 elections, the Poles replaced the Solidarity-based coalition with the Democratic Left Alliance (the reformed communist party). Furthermore, the Poles' rising ambivalence toward market economics became more evident with their concern about joining the European Union (Valencia 2001). They also showed increasing concern about the widening gap between income levels of city dwellers and rural villagers (Starobin 2001b) as well as about regional income differences. Communities in western Poland, which did more business with Germany, far surpassed those in the east next to Belarus and the Ukraine. Recent comments by Polish economist Krzysztof Bledowski reflected the attitude common among Poles. Seeing graffiti ("Free market, enslaved people") on a shop in Szczecin, Poland, he commented, "It's the spirit of the day. The mood has shifted. Capitalism is not seen by many people as a system for justice, growth, better times for kids, and so on" (Fisher 2002: A1).

Although different factors affect China, some of the same ambivalence and concern about future changes have emerged. As China seeks full World Trade Organization (WTO) membership, it faces requirements that are quite ambitious for its five-year timetable and which may generate internal problems (Powell 2001). Its planned economy model has long followed a philosophy of paternalism (Child and Tse 2001), which translated into governmental actions and a system that traditionally favored some industries and firms over others, a pattern that remains difficult to break (Rock and Solodkov 2001). For example, China has maintained an economic caste system (Powell 2001) that divided companies and industries into groups—those listed on the Chinese stock exchanges in Shenzhen, Shanghai, or Hong Kong and those not listed on the exchanges. The listed firms received favorable financial treatment and access to key assets and resources. The unlisted firms, typically state-owned enterprises, have acted as social buffers thus far with large payrolls, long-term employment guarantees, and benefits that follow traditional socialist approaches.

China's entry into the WTO will generate pressure for open competition within the country and provide motivation for other transition economies, like Russia. The likely result will be that the less-favored firms will lose even the limited governmental protection they have received and will have to compete directly with the stronger firms listed on the stock exchanges. Such a potentially treacherous outcome doubtless weighs heavily on the Chinese leaders who recognize the delicate balance between aggressive market-oriented moves and the probability of social unrest.

Further, there is evidence that China's communist party is weakening, at least in grassroots activities. Professor Pan Wei of Beijing University commented that the party is losing force at the grassroots level. In state-owned enterprises, as well as foreign firms, the numbers and impact of party cells is declining. Such changes join with growing income discrepancies as entrepreneurs and business people build successful companies to fuel the fear among government officials of potential unrest. To prevent major income disparity, the government's solution so far has been to shackle individual entrepreneurs and companies by preventing them from accumulating large blocks of capital. One of the benefits of China's move toward entrepreneurialism has been the return of Chinese who had studied abroad and chosen not to return. Increasingly, these young people see opportunities in China that make them want to return (Kahn 2002).

One entrepreneur, Mr. Li Qinfu, commented that while constraints on capital accumulation will "help social stability . . . in the short term, . . . in the long run it will hurt China" (Smith 2002: A12). He advocated a move toward more democratic policies, despite party difficulties. Such ideas, however, are not likely to be incorporated into the official policy.

In rural Russia discontent and unrest has led to a similar lack of enthusiasm on the part of government officials for moving forward on market reforms. Rural farmers have long resisted the idea of private ownership of property, largely because of the over 150-year history of communal farming in that country. A shift toward private ownership would mean changing deeply rooted mind-sets and beliefs in egalitarian approaches (Stahl-Rolf 2000) that extend well beyond Russia's 50 years of communism. Forcing market approaches in such a setting would create new—and to date unacceptable—modes of interaction among farmers. Also, Russia continues to fight the reality of serious crime and Mafia control (Harper 1999; Klebnikov 2001).

National pride also fuels backlash toward market economic moves. The Bulgarian Rose Company, long one of the world's top two producers (the other is in Turkey) of attar oil, critical for perfume, traditionally employed more than 50,000 people and represented nearly 2 percent of the country's economic activity (Williams 1994). In the early 1990s, the company supplied 80 percent of the attar oil used in the United States. Bulgaria has been opposed to privatizing the firm for fear of losing a mainstay of national pride (Williams 1994).

The move from socialism to market economics has been rockier than expected, fraught with unanticipated setbacks, and frustrating to observers and participants alike. Only in recent years have researchers and others begun to recognize the dangers of such rapid change, even in more gradually shifting economies. Research on firms in central and eastern Europe and Russia (Newman 2000; Newman and Nollen 1998) has found that extreme change at the institutional level may slow, or even thwart, organizational level transformation. Newman (2000) argues that, especially in countries where political and economic change occurred simultaneously (i.e., eastern and central Europe and Russia), significant and fundamental assumptions were shattered. Chapter 3 considers Newman's (2000) ideas in more detail when the impact of extreme change on the four types of organizations in transition economies is discussed.

EFFECTS OF GLOBALIZATION

The similar economic transitions in such disparate places as the former Soviet Union, eastern Europe, and Asia have not occurred in a vacuum, but rather within the context of broader changes that were and are still occurring in the worldwide environment of business. These changes have been described by the perhaps overused, but nonetheless apt, term *globalization* (Kolodko 2002). Globalization is difficult to define precisely. Clearly, however, it transcends economics and involves forms of social, political, and economic organization outside that of the state (Albrow 1997). Parker's (1998) general definition describes globalization as an increase in the permeability of traditional boundaries, including physical borders such as nation-states and economies, industries and organizations, as well as of less tangible borders such as cultural norms or assumptions (Parker 1998: 6–7). This increased permeability from shifts that have taken place in technological, political, and economic spheres. The following types of change illustrate the process of globalization.

Disappearing Boundaries

In addition to economic transition within former socialist countries, traditional economic boundaries among countries have been reduced dramatically with the advent of free trade areas. Regional agreements have become increasingly prominent in the late 1990s with the number of agreements numbering well over 100, up from about 45 a decade earlier (WTO 1999). The European Union (EU), the North American Free Trade Agreement (NAFTA), and the Asia-Pacific Economic Cooperation (APEC) are the three largest trade groups accounting for about half of the world's trade (WTO 1999).

Additionally, the World Trade Organization, formed in 1995, continues to add member nations with a goal of reducing tariffs and liberalizing trade across the board. The result of these agreements is to create a greater degree of interconnectedness among the world's economies. Local economic conditions are no longer the result of purely domestic influence.

To further complicate the environment in which the transition to market economics is taking place, organizational boundaries are also being affected as part of globalization. Conventional organizational forms are giving way to networks of less hierarchical relationships (Kogut 1989) and cooperative strategic alliances with other firms (Jarillo 1988). Firms in former socialist economies must now confront a high degree of global connectedness that weaves complex webs of relationships among states, international institutions, and nongovernmental organizations. In many ways, the goal of the transition is a moving target as the environment of business constantly adjusts to these more permeable boundaries.

Information Technology

A significant force toward globalization, and the one with the most potential to shape the landscape of business, is the dramatic advances in information technology (Naisbitt 1994). The pace of change in communications and computing technology is mind-boggling. We can now communicate a wide range of information (e.g., voice, data, text, graphics) throughout the globe virtually instantaneously.

Furthermore, access to information, resources, products, and markets are all influenced by improved information technology. This new technology now makes it possible to establish a business that is almost entirely unconcerned with traditional boundaries and barriers, including barriers related to economies of scale and scope (Parker 1998). Moreover, the low price of sophisticated systems has placed capabilities in the hands of small business that, only a few years ago, were available only to large multinationals.

Some authors suggest that this technological change will render physical place irrelevant for so-called virtual firms and ultimately will be the

undoing of the nation state (Knoke 1996). At a minimum, the technological revolution changes the nature of the relationship between the state
and firms with regard to the availability and dissemination of information. As firms contend with market forces rather than only command
structures, they must have unprecedented access to information to be
competitive.

The globalization of information technology is not limited to facilitating information access for firms. Two other avenues of influence are
important to consider within the context of the transition from planned
to market orientations. The first concerns managerial skill requirements,
and the second is the influence of technology on popular culture.

Research directed at identifying the knowledge, skills, and abilities
required for a successful managerial career in the twenty-first century
outlined several categories of success factors. Significant among these
were stronger computer literacy skills and the ability to interpret and use
a broad array of data (Allred, Snow, and Miles 1996). That is, while
information technology is a powerful tool that improves access to information, it also increasingly defines the managerial job. For example, by
some estimates as many as 90 percent of white-collar workers in the
United States use computers on the job (Parker 1998). While firms in
transition economies will initially have usage levels much lower than
this, the dramatic decrease in the cost and increase in availability of
technology will demand that more employees become computer knowledgeable.

Entertainment media such as television, film, and the Internet offer a
major avenue for technological globalization. Electronic images are
transmitted to broad audiences without regard for education, status, or
political affiliation. They create a window onto the world that allows
individuals to learn about other societies. Such exposure invites comparisons to their own situations, which has caused some political leaders
to worry about sowing the seeds of discontent (McLuhan and Fiore 1967;
Smith and Bond 1999). The direction of the influence of entertainment
media is predominantly from the West, fueling concerns about the influence of western values on nonwestern societies.

Increased Trade and Investment

World trade among countries has grown at an average rate of over 5
percent since 1990, reaching U.S.$15 trillion in 2000. While the so-called
triad of the United States, Japan, and the European Union combine to
account for a major portion of world trade, trade in developing econo-

mies in Asia such as China, Korea, and Malaysia is growing rapidly, resulting in a shift of the economic center of world trade toward Asia (Parker 1998).

Trade is important for transition economies because it is as much a political as an economic event (Spar 2001). When firms trade in goods and services across borders, they affect societies in each country. Without necessarily intending to do so, their commercial transfers across borders either augment the comparative development of national economies or create dependencies that persist over time. Nation states are acutely aware of these effects and of their possible consequences on the distribution of rewards and power.

In addition to increased trade, the level of foreign direct investment (FDI) also has a globalizing effect. FDI as a percentage of world gross domestic product doubled between 1985 and 1994 (UNCTAD 1999). Most FDI comes from developed countries, and as nations become more affluent, they pursue FDI in geographic regions that have economic growth potential. The role of geographic proximity may be declining as a significant factor in determining the location of FDI. For example, the United States led all other countries in FDI in 1998, investing some U.S.$990 billion overseas, while China and Indonesia were the leading developing countries that received FDI (UNCTAD 1999).

Two fundamental implications can be drawn from these trends. First, multinational firms now manufacture and sell globally on an unprecedented scale, and the expansion of international production continues to gather momentum. Foreign direct investment involves transplanting the means of production, including jobs, technology, and taxes, from one country to another. The impact of this shift is so great that nation states often spend significant energy and great sums of money to attract investors.

The effects of foreign direct investment in transition economies are even more pronounced than are increases in trade (Spar 2001). The creation of wealth through free-market activities, the goal of economies in transition, can obviously be hastened by foreign direct investment. However, as with trade, foreign direct investment is a political as well as an economic issue. Increased foreign direct investment throws into gear the mechanisms that monitor, regulate, and administer investment flows. That is, foreign direct investment means movement of wealth and technology, the control of which means power.

In summary, both the increase in trade and the increase in foreign direct investment have a globalizing effect on the environment for business in transition economies. Further, the influence of these forces

extends beyond their obvious economic ramifications. Trade and investment affect both the domestic and international political sphere, which
in turn affects firms, and ultimately the constraints, demands on, and
choices available to managers.

New Actors on the International Stage

Globalization is more than just economic integration or improved access to information because of technology. A key feature of the new
global business environment is the number and type of new entrants to
the international business arena in recent years. The most rapid expansion
of international business occurred in the latter half of the twentieth century. In the early part of this expansion, the actors on the international
business stage were just the firm and its foreign constituency, but now
they have been joined by home and host country governments, special-
interest groups, international agencies, and economic alliances (Robinson
1984). Additionally, the characteristics of these actors have changed over
time with international agencies such as the WTO and the International
Monetary Fund (IMF) growing in influence and importance.

While U.S. multinational firms dominated the post–World War II period, as of 1999 they accounted for only a little over one-third of *Fortune
Magazine*'s Global 500. As noted previously, technology is facilitating
the entry of small business into the international arena. For example, in
the mid-1990s, 25 percent of all exporting firms had fewer than 100
employees (Aharoni 1994). Additionally, the service sector of the global
economy is rapidly increasing; it now comprises as much as 70 percent
of the gross national product (GNP) of advanced economies. Trade in
services now accounts for about 25 percent of world exports (Parker
1998). Finally, it is important not to omit international gangs from the
discussion of actors on the international stage. Global gangs based in
Russia, China, Hong Kong, Japan, Columbia, Italy, and the United States
manufacture and transport illegal drugs around the world, trade in human
cargo, and use the international banking system to launder billions of
dollars (Parker 1998).

In summary, the cast of international actors has changed over time.
Today, firms struggling with the shift to market economics are more
likely to encounter firms headquartered outside the United States. These
may be small- to medium-sized businesses, and are more likely than ever
to be part of the service sector. Today's international managers must
recognize that the increased permeability of boundaries associated with
globalization also applies to illegal activities.

It is sometimes difficult to disentangle the causes of globalization from its effects. What is clear, however, is that the business environment that firms in transition economies seek to join is itself in a state of massive change that influences traditional boundaries. Thus, a key result of this globalization is that managers in transition economies face a business environment that is more complex, more dynamic, more uncertain, and more competitive than even their counterparts in traditional market economies are used to.

CONTEXT OF TRANSITION

The mechanisms of globalization combine with the national environments of economies in transition to form the backdrop against which managers must try to cope with this change. The following section identifies some of the key contextual elements that influence management in transition economies.

Universality of Capitalism

The failure of state socialism to achieve a high standard of living for its people has reduced the choices among economic systems. As Milton Friedman (1991: 124) wrote, ". . . every country that has achieved a high level of prosperity for the masses has relied on free private markets to coordinate economic activities." Despite state-centered or welfare-based capitalist models in France or Scandinavian countries, the undeniable model for the free market is the United States (Zwass 2002). Therefore, economic transition means more than just adopting free-market principles. For many people it means attempting to model systems, policies, procedures, and behaviors after those found in the United States. The more America resembles Silicon Valley, the more the rest of the world imitates America (Zwass 2002).

WTO Globalization

The WTO is the only organization that has the opportunity to develop into an international institution with control over international trade and investments, working conditions, and even environmental protection. The role of both the WTO and its predecessor the General Agreement on Tariffs and Trade (GATT) in promoting multilateral trade is undisputed. However, the WTO has an added role—to provide a single set of enforceable commercial rules across the globe (Parker 1998). Transition economies, such as those in China and Russia, are seeking membership in the WTO in increasing numbers. The WTO is, however, hampered by the interest of both individual members and special interest groups. The protests at recent WTO meetings involved groups as disparate as the AFL-CIO and People's Global Action group. The members themselves also generate controversy. At the Seattle meeting, for instance, the United States rejected investment and competition policy items brought forward by the EU, and developing countries spoke out against new provisions on working conditions and environmental protection (Zwass 2002). Nevertheless, the WTO remains a key force toward globalization and promises to be an important international regulator of commercial activity in its broadest sense.

Discrepancy between Developing and Industrial Countries

In the past 15 years, the income of the top 5 percent of the world population has risen by 50 percent, while the income of the lowest 60 percent has barely changed (Burbach, Nunez, and Kagarlitsky 1997). More startling perhaps is that in 1998 the richest 200 people in the world had assets in excess of the combined income of 41 percent of the world's people ("The world's richest," *Forbes,* 6 July 1998). The range of per capita GNP is enormous, with Luxembourg at U.S.$45,100 having the highest income, Ethiopia at U.S.$100 having the lowest, and with as many as 1.3 billion people surviving on less than U.S.$1 per day (World Bank 2000). An examination of the World Bank classification of countries by income shows an interesting pattern. All the high-income countries (per capita GNP of U.S.$8,956 or more in 1997), except for Australia and New Zealand, are in the Northern Hemisphere (Daniels and Radebaugh 1998). Most of the world's wealth (about 80 percent) is located in these northern, high-income countries, which represent only about 15 percent of the world's population (World Bank 2000). The economics of globalization has pushed the less-developed countries into even deeper misery (Burbach, Núñez, and Kagarlitsky 1997) and has raised the issue of finding a more just distribution of wealth. This consequence of globalization has been the centerpiece of debate and legislation regarding the role of the nation state in the world economy (Zwass 2002), and promises to be a major influence on the environment of business for the foreseeable future.

Transnational Corporations

The international division of labor is determined as much by competition among transnational corporations as it is by the concerns of nation states (Zwass 2002). For example, the most international of firms, Nestle, has 87 percent of its assets, 98 percent of its sales, and 97 percent of its employees outside its home country of Switzerland (UNCTAD 1999). Many transnationals, such as Microsoft or Vodaphone, dominate important sectors of the economy. The strategies of these firms are directed, of course, at profit maximization. Because of their global resources, these transnationals are in stronger bargaining positions than are governments in transition economies. So it is not surprising that transnationals are often able to extract concessions from governments in transition economies. These concessions most often are concerned with equity control, preferential tax treatment, and infrastructure development (Peng 2000). However, they also can extend to more fundamental legislation like labor laws.

Western Financial Assistance

The tradition of financial assistance from the West, begun at Bretton Woods in 1944, continues today for economies in transition. The key international institutions in this endeavor are the IMF and the World Bank. However, as the missions of the institutions shifted from post-war reconstruction to development, so too did the relationship of these institutions with their members. In the mid 1970s the IMF's attempts to influence the stability of exchange rates of member states was abandoned. It is now primarily the lender of last resort that bails out countries in financial crisis. This assistance, however, is increasingly tied to broader policy issues. For example, the bailouts of South Korea and Indonesia in 1997 and 1998 included a requirement that these countries restructure their financial systems for increased transparency (Parker 1998).

The positive influence of the World Bank and the IMF on world economic development is unquestioned. However, opponents of globalization suggest that power is shifting from democratically elected governments to anonymous institutions, which are concerned with economic interests at the expense of the self-determination of nations (Stiglitz 2002; Zwass 2002). For example, William Greider (1997) noted that the IMF and World bank "serve as the paternalistic agents of global, capital-enforcing debt collection, supervising the financial accounts of poor nations, promoting wage suppression and other policy nostrums . . . instructing and scolding aspirants on the principles of neoclassical economics." Thus, a key issue for transition economies is that the enormous financial assistance provided by the IMF and the World Bank (and their associated policy requirements) still requires performance from the transition economies.

SUMMARY

This chapter describes the complex tapestry that forms the context in which the transition to market economics is occurring. These contextual factors influence managers both directly and indirectly. The direct effect of this context is in establishing the environmental demands and constraints placed on the managers in these societies. Indirectly, the broader environmental context influences the strategies and structures firms employ to function effectively. These firm-level effects on the managerial role are discussed more completely in the following chapter.

The dramatic changes that have been occurring in international business have been encapsulated in the term *globalization*. Globalization transcends the economic shift toward capitalism to include the increased permeability of boundaries among trading partners and among organizations. The pace of globalization is fueled by the rapid change taking place in information technology. At the same time, a key feature of the new global business environment is the existence of new participants. Technology has facilitated the entrance of smaller firms to the global stage. Additionally, international institutions such as the WTO, the IMF, and the World Bank play increasingly important roles.

Against this pattern of globalization, managers in transition economies still exist in an environment that contains the vestiges of state socialism. The indelible mark left by socialism includes:

- Centralization and bureaucratic organization of power
- A drive for production quantity over quality
- Paternalistic behavior of superiors
- Soft budget constraints
- Weak responses to prices
- Mechanisms to compensate for chronic shortages
- A disregard for the external environment.

The mechanisms of globalization have created an environment in which transition economies must accept the following realities. First, the failure of socialism has left only one viable economic ideology—American style capitalism. Second, globalization has increased the need for and the influence of international institutions such as the WTO, the IMF, and the World Bank. Third, the most pressing issue facing these institutions is the increasing gap between the wealthy, developed nations and third-world countries. Finally, financial assistance, through foreign direct investment of transnational corporations or international institutions, comes at some cost to self-determination.

Managers in transition economies face an external environment that is a composite of the new global context in which all firms must operate combined with systems that, to a greater or lesser extent, contain the vestiges of state socialism. Thus managers are often the recipients of multiple, and sometimes inconsistent, signals about their jobs and functions.

Chapter 3

ORGANIZATIONAL CHANGE
IN TRANSITION

Nothing is permanent but change.

—Heraclitus, 500 B.C.

One day on my first visit to Vietnam, I lunched alone at the university where I worked. The foggy canteen had smoke spilling from coal stoves in the kitchen and dogs roaming under the tables, scrounging for scraps. Women in black pants and thin cotton shirts squatted over wooden planks about the size of three bricks pushed together, hacking at vegetables and meat.

I sat on a wooden stool with my knees at chest level. The rickety table had a plastic tablecloth speckled with rice from the previous diners. As a canteen lady wiped the tablecloth, I took a gray paper napkin and began the ritual of cleaning the wooden chopsticks and aluminum soupspoons that sat in plastic holders on the table. I drank my canned beer and started on my lunch—fried spring rolls, rice, scrambled eggs, mushy lettuce and cucumbers saturated in vinegar, and peanuts. I stayed away from the fish heads, inchworms, and pork fat.

That day, a third-year student joined me.

"May I sit?" he asked. "I like to practice English."

"Of course. What are you studying?"

"I want to be a teacher. To teach accounting at the university. I learn to be a teacher."

"Why not work for a company?" I asked. I knew that the university teachers were making about U.S.$40 a month. Foreign firms, hungry for well-trained,

English-speaking Vietnamese with accounting degrees, were offering U.S.$500 a month in 1994.

"I want to be a teacher," he said again. "I will help students learn about market economics. That is good for my country. I can help Vietnam become strong if I am a teacher. If I work for a foreign firm, I help myself only."

As an American professor, I could not remember the last time my students at home had talked of pursuing careers that would help anyone beyond themselves or their families. But this young Vietnamese man—who was not unique—sought a career that would pay little but had a bigger payoff. He was making a choice for his future and his career.

I remembered him a year later at a student-faculty party on a balmy October evening. I stood on the balcony of the house where I lived in Hanoi, chatting with a student. The three-story stucco building was a renovated French villa, built in the early twentieth century and taken over by the Vietnamese in the early 1950s, when they drove the French colonialists from Vietnam. I always thought it ironic that the villa, which held the communist party propaganda printing office in its basement, housed visiting professors from abroad, who taught market economics to university professors and business people, on the upper two floors.

During the party, one of the students told me about his career plans. His small eyes drilled into me; I had a hard time looking away. H. smiled a half smile, almost as if he were sharing a joke with himself. He was about 27, intense and ambitious; he leaned into me, almost leering, as he told me about how Vietnam was changing and how he would take advantage of the changes.

"We are the generation to bring capitalism to Vietnam," H. said. I bristled at the word. After my experience with the capitalism headline in Boise earlier that summer, I looked around for microphones and thought about moving inside the building, or at least acting like I'd not heard the word.

"My father is a ministry official, and he agrees. The young people, my generation, will change Vietnam. We must change our country. We must learn how to compete." H. lifted his beer in a toast to Vietnam, to learning about capitalism, to taking advantage of his age and energy.

"I work for a Dutch bank," he said, "so I can learn from foreigners. I get training and make money. After my M.B.A., I want to work some time more for a foreign firm. Later, I will start my own company so I can hire other Vietnamese people. I know I must work hard, even harder and more than I work at the bank. But it is good to start a company and make money.

"Also, I want to get a Ph.D. and a position at a university. Then, I can still do my company work on the side—and work for a university, or another state-owned company, or one that is equitized, if there are some then. They are not so hard to work for, since they change little in Vietnam. So, that way, later in life, I will not work so hard."

Interestingly, H. has indeed followed a path almost exactly like the one he laid out for me—after getting his M.B.A., he worked for five years for a nongovernmental financial organization that focused on loans for small businesses. He parlayed that knowledge into starting his own, Web-based investment and consulting firm, and has started to hire employees. All the while, he has been pursuing a low residency doctorate degree in Europe, and he's found a part-time lecturer's post in Hanoi. By 2003, he should have the degree, his firm will be a year old, and he'll still be in his thirties.

The vignette reflects the ways that young Vietnamese people viewed the types of enterprises that would be operating in their country by the end of the 1990s and into the next century. As young people whose environments were changing dramatically, many wanted to sample the variety of enterprises becoming available to them. They wanted to be part of the market economy and to take advantage of the changes they saw. But they also wanted to contribute to Vietnam. And, they wanted to have a safe and comfortable option—a state-owned firm—where they thought they would have the security of a paycheck and the ease of a slow pace and low performance expectations as they aged. That such options exist in a transition economy is what makes it so exciting and complex and difficult for foreigners to grasp.

Given the range of firms, the changes they encounter are vast. This chapter discusses the types of firms, change, and the way the types may react to it. Following Peng (2000), four kinds of firms that commonly emerge in transition economies are identified, and the influence that type of firm may have on the jobs that managers hold is examined. Then the focus shifts to a consideration of organizational change common among organizations undergoing transformation (adaptive and strategic change). Particular attention is paid to the ways firms adapt to strategic or *radical change*, which Newman and Nollen (1998) argue is the type of change faced by firms in transition economies. Those ideas of organizational change are examined in light of the four different types of firms in transition economies, and finally, the influence of this context on managers who work in or with these firms is considered.

FIRM TYPES EMERGING IN TRANSITION ECONOMIES

In transition economies, four types of organizations emerge after economic reform: state-owned enterprises; privatized, or reformed, firms; entrepreneurial, start-up firms; and foreign companies (Peng 2000). Each type has different features that constrain and influence how managers may act in those settings.

State-Owned Enterprises

While the state-owned enterprise (SOE) predominated in socialist countries, it is not an organizational form that is confined solely to that economic environment (Aharoni 1986). Even in the United States, for example, the government owns portions of the health care and educational systems. As an organizational form in transition economies, SOEs are unique only in state ownership (Peng 2000). However, this simple distinction leads to a number of characteristics that have profound implications for managerial behavior.

The primary objective of the SOE is to meet the centrally planned requirements of the state, which typically means reaching annual production or output goals. Profit maximization, the domain and objective of a market economy firm, is not a priority; nor is it even acknowledged as a goal by SOE managers. While a competitive firm must be concerned with the entrance of potential rivals into the market, the state bureaucracy protects the SOE from such threats. Because the SOE is state financed, it has only a soft budget constraint that allows it to continue to be viable regardless of its financial performance. Objectives such as stable employment and reaching production levels drive decisions; competition does not. Furthermore, while a competitive firm must contend with fluctuating demand for its products, no such stress exists for the SOE: demand for its products is fixed within the central planning cycle, and prices are arbitrarily set.

Therefore, SOEs and their managers are exposed to a set of expectations very different from those of their counterparts at competitive firms. Chapter 2 itemized some of these expectations ranging from production goals, to allocation and distribution of products by producers, to making decisions about prices, investment, and personnel. Additionally, a difference in the demands, constraints, and choices available to managers is apparent in SOEs. For example, in a study of managers in Chinese SOEs, Boisot and Xing (1992: 169) found that, in striking contrast to studies of western managers, "Nearly 30 percent of the paper that lands on the desk of our sample originates in the supervisory bureaucracy. Much of it will take the form of new, detailed instructions or regulations covering all aspects of the firm's activities—purchasing, personnel matters, quality control, energy use, etc." Boisot and Xing (1992) concluded that the Chinese firm is not an extension of managerial activity, as suggested in classic definitions of competitive firms. Rather, the Chinese SOE is designed to constrain choices in management behavior. In addition, given the constraint on expectations and the clear, yet limited objectives, SOE managers are not expected to pursue behaviors that require risk taking or initiative.

Despite the major push by transition economy governments to encourage state-owned enterprises to become more market driven, or even to equitize or privatize, thousands remain. Russia has made significant progress—with more than 130,000 privatized enterprises by January 2000 (with about 14,000 SOEs remaining). By 1996, Hungary had privatized about 80 percent of its large SOEs, Poland about 55 percent of its large ones. Other countries have had more mixed results: Vietnam, for example, had equitized about 400 SOEs by June 2000, with more than 5,000 SOEs remaining in place. The fact that so many SOEs still remain clarifies why young people in their thirties anticipate that the slower-paced life in SOEs may still be available to them in 10 to 15 years.

Privatized, or Reformed, Firms

One of the key elements in moving from a planned to a market economy is the transformation of state-owned firms into privately owned ones. While state ownership is waning across transition economies, the exact nature of reform varies. For example, in China and Vietnam, which are still governed by the Communist Party, terms such as *corporatization* or *equitization* are used instead of the politically sensitive term *privatization* (Peng 2000). Besides the use of proper terminology, the fact is that, even in officially reformed companies, the state maintains a great deal of influence. Peng (2000) suggests that former state-owned enterprises typically take one of four forms: employee controlled; manager controlled; owner controlled; or investor controlled. Each of these forms influences managerial behaviors through what role the managers play and managerial demands, constraints, and choices.

Employee-controlled firms arise when nonmanagerial employees become equity owners, typically through a buyout of shares (Ben-Ner 1988). This form of ownership is atypical in capitalist societies, yet appears in several transition economies. For instance, in Macedonia the vast majority of companies (340 or 27 percent) were privatized in the late 1990s by employee buyouts (Drakulevski 1999), and employee ownership is a dominant form in Romania (Thompson and Valsan 1999). The employee-owned structure succeeds most often in small firms, where employees can easily understand and decide on business issues.

The goals of the employee-controlled firm differ from those of the SOEs. The SOE demands, such as meeting production targets or reinvesting profits for long-term development, may be less critical in employee-owned firms than is paying above-market wages, for example. Thus, the expected job functions that managers of employee-controlled firms receive from their employee-owners are likely to stem from different motives than those of the former state-owner. Also, the variety of interests of large numbers of employee-owners increases the opportunity for contradictory expectations about job tasks for managers. Given the potential for conflict and ambiguity that managers in employee-owned firms may encounter, it is not surprising that in some transition economies, restrictions have been placed on employee participation in management.

Manager-controlled firms resemble employee-controlled firms, with the exception that ownership is vested in a small number of senior managers. Common in market economies as well, the process moves managers from agent to principal, ensuring (or enhancing) their commitment to financial performance. While managers as owners are motivated to improve firm performance, they may also be interested in servicing large personal debt as a result of a buyout (Long and Ravenscraft 1993). Additionally, manager-owners are in positions of great power and are likely to become entrenched (Finkelstein 1992). As a result, manager-owners are likely to derive perceptions of what their job functions are largely from their own internally conceived expectations of what managers should be. Also, in the case of manager-controlled firms, a number of managerial demands and constraints are removed. Demands such as attending meetings or following bureaucratic procedures may be unenforceable, and managers are able to largely define their own work. Unless some manager oversees, coordinates, and ultimately clarifies expectations for the manager-owners, many of the management behaviors these managers learned under the old command-and-control system may persist.

Owner-controlled firms typically have a simple structure with a single individual or family owning and controlling an enterprise. Often, owner-controlled firms face situations of limited capital and financing ability. On the other hand, vast conglomerates have been established in former planned economies by those taking advantage of the disequilibrium that develops during transition. By using financial leverage and the ability to organize, small numbers of individuals have gained control of vast assets. The so-called oligarchs in the former Soviet Union are a case in point. Their empires were created by exploiting the political and economic turmoil following perestroika. More recently, however, questions have begun to emerge about their ability to endure. The following description demonstrates the potential for influence of owner control on managerial tasks:

> The typical oligarch is notoriously unable to organize his own time or office, let alone delegate to managers. He sees business opportunities in terms of political contacts rather than new products, markets, or services. He is an opportunist who cannot look beyond the short term. His understanding of capital markets, even of balance sheets is close to nil. ("Face Value" 1998: 76)

This is not to say that all owner-controlled firms cannot be well managed, as Chinese family owned firms in Hong Kong or Korean Chaebols such as Samsung and Daewoo have shown (Ghauri and Prasad 1995). However, this extensive individual or family control (often with close connections to government) results in a high degree of centralization with its attendant demands and constraints on management behavior.

A final form of privatized firms in transition economies is the investor-controlled firm. Such firms are a familiar and dominant form of large organizations in the West. While investor-controlled firms succeed in North America and Europe, questions arise about whether former SOEs can migrate directly to this form. For instance, China and Vietnam opened stock exchanges in only the last few years, before that private investment in firms was impossible. Such a lack of outside investors in early stages of transition typically forces insiders to take control through management or employee buyouts. This results in a two-stage privatization process, whereby initial employee and management buyouts are followed at a later date by outside investors and managers (Peng 2000).

Entrepreneurial Start-Up Firms

A third type of firm that has emerged in transition economies is the newly formed enterprise, or entrepreneurial start-up. While private ownership did not officially exist under state socialism, a small and informal private sector operated in virtually all socialist countries prior to major economic transitions (Rupp 1983; Tan 1999). In Poland, for example, a private sector accounted for 5 to 10 percent of the economic activity even before transition had begun.

In some countries, the combination of the lure of capitalism and the removal of restrictions on private ownership saw a flood of entrepreneurship in the 1990s. One of the most interesting aspects of these firms from the perspective of their influence on managerial behavior is the origin of the entrepreneurs. Peng (2001) identifies four categories of entrepreneurs in transition economies. These are farmers, "gray" individuals, former cadres, and professionals. A fifth category can be added: the children of the former cadres and professionals, who form a unique group, with less need to unlearn old habits and ways of thinking.

Farmers were organized into collectives in most socialist countries. However, as government regulations relaxed, a great deal of small scale and unregistered private farming emerged. Over time, some of these enterprises grew and became more formally organized. For example, the largest private company in China, the Hope Group, founded in 1982, was originally a private farm (Au and Sun 1998).

On the other hand, some farmers chose to pursue alternative paths as transition began. Since farmers tended to be less subject to state control, they could easily migrate to cities to take other jobs in the new private sector. These factors, combined with the inefficiencies of collective farming, made farmers among the first group of entrepreneurs (Peng 2001).

The restrictions against private ownership under state socialism prevented legal entrepreneurial activity. Therefore, an unlawful, or "gray," economy developed, which was widely accepted by society. With the relaxation of regulation against private ownership, the rapid accumulation of wealth thorough gray activities became possible. These gray individuals were the entrepreneurs who responded to what Schumpeter (1911) called "economic discontinuities," providing new products and developing more efficient markets and processes—and making lots of money.

The range of gray activities is broad, sometimes involving questionable activities such as tax evasion and bribery, but also extending to organized crime (LaFraniere 2001; Minniti 1995). Estimates of the size of the gray economy range from about 12 to 15 percent in the Czech Republic and Poland to around 30 percent in Bulgaria and Hungary to perhaps as high as 50 to 60 percent in Russia and Azerbaijan (Schneider and Ernste 2000). While clearly not all managers involved in the gray economy are criminals, they are typically outsiders (sometimes ethnic minorities) who did not function well in the mainstream society (Peng 2001).

What at first seems an unusual source of entrepreneurs is the former Communist Party leaders and officials, or cadres (Rona-Tas 1994). Peng (2001) points to two reasons why these individuals are key candidates to engage in private sector activities. First, most educated people joined the party, not because of ideological motives, but to promote their careers. Furthermore, better educated people were more able to understand

and take advantage of free market opportunities. Second, these people accumulated power under state socialism that they could convert to high value assets. They did so by taking advantage of their positions to acquire state property and/or by tapping into their personal networks to gain access to valuable information or to manipulate the gray market. Soulsby (2001) found that Czech Republic Communist Party members who adjusted, or complied, after the Russians squelched the 1968 Revolution in Czechoslovakia became those quickest to adjust to transition. The compliers used their flexibility to become successful in the new economy.

The story of Vagit Alekperov, founder of the Russian oil firm Lukoil, now one of the eight largest oil companies in the world (Klebnikov 1996), illustrates the journey of this type of entrepreneur. Alekperov, a director of production in the oil town of Kogalym, was about to be fired when his boss at the ministry got embroiled in a failed coup by hardliners against Soviet president Mikhail Gorbachev. As a result, Alekperov unexpectedly became the acting oil minister. At that time, government investment was declining, and the industry was falling apart in the new economy. Alekperov turned Russia's oil assets over to Rosneft, the state holding company. Alekperov then appointed a friend, Alexander Putilov, as the director of Lukoil. With this maneuver, Alekperov gathered Russia's best oil properties and brightest engineers under one enterprise, and established Lukoil with Putilov as a principal shareholder (Klebnikov 1996).

The emergence of this class of entrepreneurs, party members who pursue private business ventures, has been less prevalent in some countries. As recently as March 2002, the Vietnamese government acknowledged that it would *begin* to allow Communist Party members to start up and own businesses. Each such removal of constraints and regulations in transition economies spurs additional entrepreneurial activity.

Another source of entrepreneurs is professionals such as engineers, lawyers, and professors. These people have the advantage of education to understand the technical side of business, and unlike former cadres, these entrepreneurs have been sanctioned officially and often are widely supported by the public. For example, in 1991 a group of defense scientists founded Vimpelcom, a high tech start-up that has become Russia's largest cellular phone provider (Peng 2001). While the scientists may have lacked the networks or connections typical of cadres, they possessed legitimacy in operating their firms that the other entrepreneurs lacked.

Recently, a new group of entrepreneurs is emerging in transition economies. These, the children of the *nomenklatura,* have adapted to the new circumstances of their career prospects very rapidly (Kets de Vries 2000).

Because they are not so entrenched in the old way of doing things, they see the value of being able to adjust to the new system, and they recognize the opportunities transformation presents. The young son of the Vietnamese ministry official, portrayed in the opening vignette, exemplifies the ambitious, unfettered generation who will have a more positive experience in the transition to a market environment.

The following profile of a young Russian entrepreneur illustrates another example of this class of entrepreneur:

> This young man started his business career while he was still a student at the university. When he learned that the state travel agency charged higher prices for hotel rooms to Russian tourists than they did to those from the West, he built a network of contacts that allowed him to exploit the discrepancy in room prices, and in the process, he had his first exposure to Western business practices. (Kets de Vries 2000: 69)

A final note on the emergence of entrepreneurs involves the history of risk taking. In their study of paradoxes between the United States and Vietnam, Vu and Napier (2000) suggest that risk taking is a response to an uncertain and chaotic environment, which characterizes transition economies. In such settings, where managers have little control, Vietnamese say that they seek ways around the chaos to get things done. When they take risks, they put their own stamp of stability on the environmental picture. Choosing which risks to take allows the risk taker to feel that he or she has some control over an unstable situation.

In summary, two general themes are apparent with regard to entrepreneurial start-ups (Shekshnia 2001). First, there seems to be a high correlation between educational level and entrepreneurship. This may suggest that the start-up firms will eventually absorb the countries' educated elite, leaving the less educated to run SOEs or privatized firms. Second, most entrepreneurs set up ventures that are unrelated to their previous professional activity and are often ventures in the service sector. The fact that much entrepreneurial activity takes place in the service sector should not be surprising since socialist states typically neglected this sector in favor of heavy industry.

Foreign Companies

Besides being export firms, foreign firms have two basic choices for establishing a presence in transition economies: as wholly owned subsidiaries or with some sort of collaborative alliance. Collaborative alliances typically take one of three forms: informal cooperative alliances, formal cooperative alliances, and international joint ventures (Lorange and Roos 1992). The informal type of arrangement is usually limited in scope and has no contractual requirement. Formal arrangements typically require a contractual agreement and often allow broader involvement by the foreign firm. Joint ventures are separate legal entities with joint ownership. The majority of firms entering transition economies have opted for, or have been required by government regulation to use, equity joint ventures. In some countries, such as Vietnam, the firms have no option but to have a local partner (only recently has wholly owned subsidiary become an option in Vietnam, for example). Even McDonald's, the world's largest franchiser, set up a joint venture when it entered Russia (Peng 2000).

Joint ventures are collaborative arrangements that result in new organizational structures, the form of which must be determined by the organizational preferences of two, often very different, partners. An additional complexity in transition economies is that the role of government in establishing the agreement tends to be expanded and that the government is often the direct partner.

Managers in an international joint venture in a transition economy occupy a precarious position on the boundary of two organizations. As such, they are subject to the expectations of both the foreign firm and the local partner. Thus, the expectations that joint venture managers face are often in conflict as a result of organizational, institutional, and culture differences. Managing this conflict is a key factor in the success of a joint venture. For instance, managers in the Vietnamese joint venture of Asea-Brown Boveri (ABB, the Swiss-Swedish merged firm) laid off workers, giving them what the foreign managers considered fair warning and fair severance, based on their norms and Swiss law. However, the Vietnamese government interpreted these actions differently and ultimately penalized the firm, which generated bad press and damaged future good will on both sides.

In summary, four types of organizations—state-owned enterprise, privatized, or reformed, firms, entrepreneurial start-ups, and foreign companies—have emerged following economic reform. Each of these organizations faces the contextual changes mentioned in Chapter 2. This dramatic change is the focus of the next section, which describes elements of the radical change that confront these firms and their managers.

ORGANIZATIONAL CHANGE

Scholars and managers have investigated change in organizations for years. Much of what is written, of course, examines change in business firms based in western industrialized settings (e.g., Argryis 1977; Greiner 1972; Lane and Lubatkin 1998; Lane, Salk, and Lyles 2001; Levitt and March 1988). However, some authors have addressed change specific to transition economies (e.g., Clark 1999; Denison 2001; Luo 1999, 2001; Peng 1994, 2000; Robinson 2000). Generally, this literature classifies change into two broad types: first and second order. First order change is the set of incremental changes that typically can be planned and managed (Fox-Wolfgramm, Boal, and Hunt 1998). Adaptive learning (Senge 1990) applies in this type of change and involves adjustment rather than wholesale revision or transformation of an organization. First order change demands doing more or less of what has been done, is reversible, and requires incremental instead of new learning on the part of organization members. An underlying assumption, of course, is that the environment will change in directions that are consistent with what has happened in the past. Even describing this type of change sounds naïve and wistful in light of what we have observed in transition economies.

Second order, or strategic, change occurs in situations of turbulence or crisis (e.g., Greenwood and Hinings 1988, 1993, 1996; Greiner 1972; Meyer, Goes, and Brooks 1993). Such radical change appears in transition economies, which epitomize situations of turbulence, with their own special twists (Newman 2000; Newman and Nollen 1998). Second order change requires generative learning (Argyris 1977) that involves new ways of operating and seeing things. In transition economies, this learning translates into making a profit versus filling production orders, testing new ways of doing things through constant experimentation, and finding ways to solve problems that are unlike previous approaches.

Second order change leads organizations to signal managers that they need to operate in fundamentally different ways. That is, organizational changes of this magnitude mean managers individually, as well as collectively, must make adjustments in the way they perceive their jobs and in the way they behave. In addition to learning the language of the free market (*profit, customer service*, and *credit*), managers must also understand the underlying concepts. A manager of an infrastructure project in Poland described hiring a manager who "knew all the right words, said all the right things," yet whose actions did not match the western business concepts he purported to understand. The firm eventually had to let him go because his performance did not match his promise.

Organizations in transition cannot turn back. Strategic change in crisis, once begun, is irreversible. Despite the myriad recent articles and discussion by citizens from Russia or Mongolia, reminiscing about the better days, there is no chance to return to the prior order (Fisher 2002).

Newman (2000), in particular, argues that the radical change of transition economies and the resulting institutional shift from a planned to a market economy fundamentally shook the norms, values, and assumptions regarding economic activity that managers and leaders previously held. The shock in some countries was greater than in others. For example, in Russia, which had no historical experience with capitalism (going "from czars to communists"), organizations shifting to market economies faced more shattering impacts. Russian managers had little experience with private ownership, with the risks involved, or in dealing with outsiders in market economies.

In contrast, some central and eastern European economies had been market-based between the world wars so that an awareness of market economy concepts existed in older generations. And, some countries on the border of western Europe, such as East Germany and Poland, had had significant experience with their western counterparts, even before the transition. Similarly, parts of China, such as Shanghai, have had a long history of business interaction with the western world, making its transition somewhat less formidable. In fact, managers in Shanghai today talk of the relative ease that organizations there, compared to those in inland China, have had in finding ways to shift to more market-driven perspectives (Boisot and Child 1999). However, while individual managers might have had some exposure to capitalism, the organizational structure, goals, and strategies were based upon centrally planned economic policies. For example, Vietnam was closed to the United States through an embargo for nearly 20 years, and had limited contact with Asian and European businesspeople. It had no economic models except for Soviet planned approaches and its Russian state-owned enterprises. As a result of different environmental experiences, the extent to which organizations faced change varied across transition economics.

As some research is beginning to show, for managers in many transition economies, the change was too fast and resulted in a backlash. For example, Newman (2000), in studying Czech Republic firms, found that they exhibited a strong reaction to the radical change in their environment. The research showed an inverted, U-shaped relationship between the degree of turbulence in an environment and an organization's ability to absorb and succeed in it (Newman 2000). In countries where change was more drastic—where, for example, political and economic change was pursued quickly and harshly—Newman (2000) claimed that organizations made major changes, but then reached a point where they could no longer adjust well. In fact, change in some organizations stalled or moved back toward previously used approaches. Even countries, like

Hungary (Pearce and Branyiczki 1993), that pursued more gradual change were shaken by the institutional upheaval that transition brought. The nature of the change (whether shock treatment or more gradual) in these countries still influenced the responses of the organizations and, as a result, the reactions of managers working in them.

Drawing upon organizational learning and change concepts, Newman (2000) suggested several dimensions to predict the likelihood of a (relatively) smoother transition and the probable approaches or responses that organizations will follow in implementing their transformations. The relative smoothness of transition will be dependent on the amount of *institutional upheaval,* which, according to Newman (2000), is the degree of change in the fundamental context or environment of a given country or economy, specifically in terms of its institutions (e.g., legal, political, social). SOEs, privatized, and start-up firms will all face tremendous upheaval, in part because they have been isolated from any other contexts for a generation or more. Foreign firms, with operations elsewhere (often in more stable parts of Europe or North America) will find the change dramatic and new, but will be likely to better weather the upheaval because of their diverse operations.

The following discussion combines Newman's ideas with Peng's four types of firms to consider how SOEs, newly privatized firms, entrepreneurial start-ups, and foreign firms might react to the turmoil of extreme or radical institutional upheaval. The enterprise type (Peng 2000) is juxtaposed against Newman's (2000) dimensions and are classified as the characteristics that will influence an organization's ability to cope with radical change and the response likelihood (high, medium, or low) that an organizational type may pursue, particularly when it is unsure of future steps (Table 3.1).

Organizational Characteristics that Influence the Ability to Cope

The impact on organizations of institutional upheaval is tempered by several organizational characteristics. First, the extent to which an organization has the *capacity to absorb* change (Cohen and Levinthal 1990) and the degree to which the organization is *embedded in old processes* will affect its managers' reaction to upheaval. State-owned and newly privatized organizations are likely to have the least capacity to absorb a major change because their systems are well-entrenched and embedded in the ways of operating in a planned economy. Newly privatized companies are likely to be less embedded in old processes, however, simply because they have begun the process of change.

Although start-ups may lack capacity to absorb change, they are by their nature less embedded in old methods and are in the process of creating new ones. Thus, their managers have less to "unlearn" in adjusting to institutional change. Furthermore, as mentioned previously, these entrepreneurs tend to be younger, less committed to older methods and ideologies, and they may have a broader perspective as a result of having visited or studied outside their countries. Foreign firms likewise, are less invested in former planned economy modes of operating, unless they have been in planned economies for many years. They may also have a greater capacity for absorbing the upheaval if they have experience in other chaotic environments, such as newly developing or other emerging economies.

Under conditions of extreme change, organizations draw upon *available resources and capabilities* (technical, financial, human resource) to adapt (Newman, 2000). The relevance of those resources and capabilities and the availability of appropriate approaches is limited in SOEs and privatized firms. SOEs have an excess of certain tangible capabilities and resources (e.g., human resources, production capacity) but lack management talent and knowledge about market economy concepts like marketing, quality, or information systems. Newly privatized firms are in the process of shifting resources (e.g., laying off excess employees, restructuring production facilities) but are not likely to have the full set of capabilities or resources for the new economy. Furthermore, privatized firms are, at best, only in the process of developing approaches to help them manage in the new conditions.

Entrepreneurial start-ups are in a somewhat different situation. They lack tangible resources such as employees or production capacity, but they may be able to move more quickly since they do not have to shed excess resources or previously used approaches. For example, a young Vietnamese M.B.A. graduate started a firm that developed products and services, ranging from laminated cards (for identity cards, credit cards) to travel tours for foreigners, in response to whatever market he saw had potential. Unconstrained, the firm jumped into many different areas, setting its direction more on opportunities than on goals at the early stage. However, the ability to adapt to change, at this stage at least, may be less a characteristic of the firm and may depend greatly on the energy of the owners.

In general, foreign firms have fewer problems since they typically already operate extensively in market economies and have a more

Table 3.1
Transition Economy Organizational Change (adapted from Peng [2000] and Newman [2000])

	State-Owned Enterprises	Privatized Firms	Start-up Ventures
Institutional upheaval	H	H	H
Absorptive capacity	L	L	L-M
Embeddedness in old system	H	M	L
Relevance of existing resources and capabilities	L	L	M
Relevance of organizing templates	L	L	M
Clarity of cause and effect	L	L	L
Reliance on obsolete routines	H	H	M
Strategic confusion	H	H	H
Mimicry	H	H	M

Foreign firms	Comments
M	All experience same changes but foreign firms are shielded because of external operations
M	Few firms have experienced such change, except for some foreign firms in developing or emerging economies, so none can absorb easily
L	SOEs strongly embedded and wedded to old systems; private firms shifting; start-ups and foreign firms have no loyalty for old systems
H	Foreign firms and start-ups looking for new ways have resources and capacity, particularly in managerial talent and intangibles, to move forward
H	Foreign firms and some start-ups have the new templates for market economic operation; private firms just learn; SOEs have none
L	No one knows what will lead to what; new game with no rules to follow; all affected since none have experience
M	SOEs and private firms have no new templates or routines so will use existing ones; start ups and foreign firms also testing water and use their existing routines, which may be more appropriate but still not perfectly suited
M	No clear sense of "what next" for any; foreign firms may draw on experience in developing/emerging economies but all groping for directions; SOEs and privatized firms may take on riskier than expected strategies
L	Likely few clear examples of "successful" firms to mimic but SOEs and privatized firms will look for and follow any that appear somewhat successful; start ups have no one to follow so lower mimicry; foreign firms likely to follow existing strategies

appropriate mix of resources, capabilities, and approaches for operating. However, in their case it is important to consider another view of capacity to absorb change. This view comes from research of how firms, especially international joint ventures, learn from each other (e.g., Lane, Salk, and Lyles 2001; Lane and Lubatkin 1998). Specifically, when firms are more similar in certain characteristics (e.g., knowledge bases, organizational structure and compensation policies, dominant logics in terms of what and how business is done in a given industry), learning across firms is more likely. In transition economies, foreign firms in joint ventures with local firms may have some similar characteristics (e.g., technical knowledge bases) that may encourage the local firm's ability to absorb change. The likelihood of widespread similarities, however, is small since the local firm's dominant logic of how business operates would have been formed in a socialist context.

Even though foreign firms and entrepreneurial start-ups may have a greater capacity to absorb change, Newman (2000) argued that the links between actions taken and the results will still be unclear. Foreign firms may draw upon their experiences in other rapidly changing environments, but the extent and nature of change in transition economies still raises issues they have not previously encountered. SOEs and newly privatized firms are on completely new ground. SOEs operated with confidence in the planned system (e.g., meeting a production plan led to continued operations and success). In this new era, firms are without clear ideas of what will generate success or rewards.

Organizational Responses

The organizational responses depend, in part, on the degree of certainty managers feel about understanding the cause and effect of their actions. In turbulence and second order change, where managers face completely new conditions, no one knows what to expect. Until the transformation of transition economies began, no models of how countries, regions, institutions, organizations, and individuals would undergo such a massive change existed. The only comparable shift in institutions and values in the twentieth century might have been India's move from being a Raj to a democracy. Yet this shift involved only three regions that had been tightly controlled by Britain (India, Bangladesh, and Pakistan) rather than an expanse stretching from East Germany to China and Vietnam, from Siberia to Nepal, with a multitude of cultures and forms of communism. So no models, no formulae, no templates existed to help policy makers or managers know what the causes and effects of actions would be.

With no pertinent models or templates to follow, the responses of organizations in transitional economies are likely to follow one of three less than satisfactory (and, in fact, generally messy) courses (Newman, 2000). First, organizations may grasp for and apply to their actions *comfortable yet obsolete routines*. Next, they may engage in *strategic confusion,* having no sense of direction or concept for the future. Finally, organizations may seek and *mimic* what they presume are successful examples. That is, they copy practices that they hope will remove uncertainty, whether to improve their quality (e.g., total quality management), their employee-manager interactions (e.g., transactional analysis, participative management, team building), or their financial performance (e.g., mergers, acquisitions, and layoffs).

SOEs and privatized firms are likely to pursue any of these responses, since they have been shaken thoroughly and are seeking direction from any source. Foreign firms are less apt to try to mimic other firms than are start-ups, SOEs, or privatized firms, in part because they have views and knowledge of conditions and situations outside of the transition economies (and realize that there are no exact replicas of situations and thus no firms to mimic.) Foreign firms are also likely to attempt to apply existing routines in the transition situation. Peng and Luo (2000) found that transition economy firms seek to use some of the same patterns of activities that they used in the past, which may not be completely effective. For instance, managers try to maintain or strengthen ties with government and other firms (i.e., use networks) as a way to build market share even in the more competitive environment. But this is not enough to generate long-term performance. Firms also need capabilities relating to quality improvement and advertising to perform well (Peng and Luo 2000). Managerial ties are more likely to be related to market share than return on assets (ROA) because networking (e.g., banquets, gifts, and entertainment) involves an outflow of cash and there maybe a time lag between the networking activities and return on assets. In SOEs where governance is weak, managers may find focusing on market share is easier or more similar to activities they used in the planned economy system.

Clearly the type of firm and its reaction drives the experiences that transition economy managers—and their foreign counterparts—face as they do business. For example, SOE managers experience greater resistance to change since their firms are more likely to be embedded in old systems. Conversely, foreign and start-up firms are more likely to seek and try new ways of operating since they have less history with previous, old systems. Likewise, their managers should be more open to change since they chose that type of firm. In addition to the context of their firms, the characteristics of individual managers may also influence their modes of behavior and interactions.

SUMMARY

This chapter describes the four types of firms that commonly emerge in transition economies (Peng 2000): state-owned enterprises; privatized firms that are moving toward being market driven; start-ups, or entrepreneurial ventures, led by local managers who are less constrained by planned economy modes of thinking or acting; and foreign firms, whether alliances, wholly owned subsidiaries, or joint ventures. The chapter also reviewed the type of change—second order, or radical, change—that transition economies and the firms in them have faced in the last decade and will continue to encounter in coming years.

Characteristics of the firm (Newman 2000) likely determine its ability to adapt to change and the nature of the responses that it will use. The types of firm facing the most upheaval and showing the least ability to absorb and adapt to change are most likely to be SOEs and newly privatized firms. Start-ups and foreign firms may have approaches or characteristics that allow them to respond better. Foreign firms, in particular, often have experience in other volatile environments (e.g., other developing countries), have operations in more stable environments (which allow them to weather difficulties in transition economies without seriously wounding the whole firm), and bring expertise to the transition economy partners through their expatriate managers. Finally, differences in firm types will also influence the ways that managers respond to their business situations and to their foreign counterparts. That is, managers roles are determined, in part, by characteristics of the firm. For example, state-owned enterprises, which are more likely to remain committed to earlier ways of operating, might also contain managers who are less adaptable. These firm level factors combine with the individual characteristics of local managers to influence the context in which interactions with foreigners takes place. The individual backgrounds that local and foreign managers bring to the situation are the subject of the next chapter.

Part II

THE MANAGER IN TRANSITION

Transition economies and their participants face tremendous change in their environments and in their organizations. The participants in those environments and organizations are, of course, the managers—both local and foreign—who try to deal with the changes and to make the best of a dynamic and sometimes unpredictable situation. Part II examines the managers, in particular those from transition economies, who seek to carry out business in such conditions and proposes a model of how these managers interact with their foreign counterparts. Chapter 4 examines manager characteristics and provides a foundation for the development model presented in Chapter 5 that describes how managers interact with one another.

Our interviews with managers from both transition and western countries largely supported what we found in the literature about the characteristics of transition economy managers. For example, some managers continue to be uncomfortable with market economic concepts and implications, are often resistant to change, are leery of taking risks and making autonomous decisions, and are less prone to use participative management than are their western counterparts. The literature has less to say about foreign managers who engage in business in transition economies. However, as part of the equation in making successful (or not) business transactions, foreign managers also have traits and characteristics that may influence interactions. Our interviews provided information about how those foreign managers appeared to locals, as well as to themselves.

For instance, foreign, and perhaps especially North American, managers tend to hold ethnocentric ideas about transition economies and managers and find it difficult to believe that transition economy managers have such difficulty with "obvious" ideas like market economics.

The characteristics of managers and the ways they view each other offer the background for the stage model of interactions presented in Part III. Those stages—Contact, Critique, Converge, and Continue?—reflect manager perceptions about one another, stemming in part from their characteristics. The chapters in Part III, then, illustrate the stages presented in Chapter 5 and draw upon the characteristics of mangers that discussed in Chapter 4.

Chapter 4

INDIVIDUAL MANAGER CHARACTERISTICS

> It has been said that man is a rational animal. All my life I have been searching for evidence which could support this.
> —Bertrand Russell (1872–1970)

A foreign manager who worked in East Germany in 1990 just before formal reunification and then in Albania in the late 1990s encountered conditions and expectations that mirrored each other. In both cases, the foreign firm sought to reinvigorate key facilities (e.g., a lignite mine and utility facilities) and to increase their productivity. The foreign manager's assessment in each situation was that the facility could become quite productive, given some basic changes. One of the most important changes was to reduce numbers of employees. In the East German lignite mine, it was necessary to reduce numbers from 8,000 to 1,500; in the Albanian case, the plant needed to drop from 10,000 to 2,500 employees. The foreigners delegated the human resource tasks to local managers, but neither the East German nor the Albanian managers had experience with layoffs, no training for such a situation, and thus, no idea of how to carry out the reductions. In addition, their planned economy mentality established full employment as a revered goal. The local managers also assumed that more people must mean more productivity, so they argued that reduction in employment would reduce productivity and be unfair to employees. They resisted cutbacks. In the end, according to the foreign manager, his firm's managers, not the local managers, carried out the reductions. The productivity levels increased, and local managers seemed amazed.

Previous chapters discussed the implications of both environmental and organizational level factors. Now the discussion moves to individual level issues that affect managers working in transition economy organizations. Since the focus of this book is on the ways that local and foreign managers interact, it is important to understand the individual characteristics that influence the roles of transition economy managers, as well as their foreign counterparts. Only such knowledge about each other allows managers to identify, understand, and manage the complex interpersonal interactions they are likely to encounter. Understanding the complexities of the environment and firm level change in transition economies is difficult enough. Adding individual differences about business knowledge, culture, and demographics to that mix makes understanding even more complicated. However, individual differences can lead to stressful, confusing, and frustrating interactions, sometimes frustrating enough for one or both parties to give up. Foreign managers who work in transition economies thus need a basic understanding of such differences since local managers represent the pool of raw human material that implements change in transition economies (Gobeli, Przybylowski, and Rudelius 1998; Holden, Cooper, and Carr 1998; Tan 1998). Understanding both the systematic differences in individual characteristics and the interaction process itself is important. The following sections identify key individual characteristics that feed into the process of interaction dealt with in Chapter 5.

CHARACTERISTICS

In addition to the environmental, institutional, and organizational factors that influence managers in transition economies, several individual characteristics contribute to the dynamics of interpersonal interaction. It is when these characteristics, which have developed over lifetimes of working in different economic settings and living in countries with different social values, come into contact in an interaction that their effect is felt.

For example, an early survey ("Managers Talk" 1994) of 150 local and 150 foreign managers working in the Czech Republic, Hungary, and Poland foreshadowed some of the differences in the perspectives between some foreign and local managers that continue to exist. The western managers had believed that their main goal would be to transfer knowledge about finance and sales and marketing to the local managers, but they found that local managers were the weakest in organizational and management knowledge and that it was difficult to transfer that knowledge. They found the greatest obstacles to be the transition economies' lack of infrastructure, the constant changes in laws and regulations, and the differences in the economic and business mentalities between locals and foreigners. Finally, they found local managers unwilling to take responsibility for their jobs and slow in decision making.

On the other hand, local managers felt foreign managers created obstacles to communication between the groups by not taking local differences into account when working with local managers. In addition, they found foreign managers inflexible and lacking in awareness of the cultural differences. However, local managers viewed those same foreign managers as professional with much practical experience and an ability to make quick decisions.

Our research, conducted almost a decade later, found remarkably similar results. We considered three broad aspects of individual differences that underpin these differences in perspectives of local and foreign managers and that are consistent with the process perspective on the interaction that is presented in the next chapter. These are differences in business knowledge and skills, cultural differences, specifically as they influence work motivation and work attitudes, and demographic differences.

BUSINESS KNOWLEDGE

We define business knowledge as the understanding, held by individuals, of concepts and practices commonly used in the western market economic world. Business knowledge can be explicit, or codified, and observable. Tacit knowledge, on the other hand, is implicit and unobservable, and it involves the level of understanding of the differences in thinking, of limitations, and of conditions of operation in those economies by foreign managers who work in transition economies. Also, it is important not to assume that foreign managers hold all of the relevant knowledge; local managers also have a range of understanding, knowledge, and facility for working successfully. The knowledge of local managers, because of lack of formal management training in socialist societies, may be more tacit (in the bones expertise) than explicit. This section considers the knowledge of local managers, which ranges in extent, and the way that they reveal their knowledge (or do not). A discussion of foreign managers' knowledge then follows.

Local Manager Business Knowledge

Given the common logic of the planned economy system, much of the knowledge and experience that transition economy managers have is similar across countries. Both local and foreign managers we talked with agreed that the general level of understanding of market economic principles and practices and the ability to apply western business concepts is still relatively low among many local transition economy managers. Even after a decade of transition and even though many local managers have learned the vocabulary of market economics, fewer are completely comfortable with or able to carry out western business practices. Nevertheless, local managers in some areas, especially in larger cities, and in some types of enterprises (e.g., foreign or start-up firms) or certain industries (e.g., high tech versus rural based, such as farming) appear farther along on a knowledge continuum. In this section, some of the dimensions of the state of business knowledge are discussed.

Untrained in and Unaware of Market Economics

Local managers continue to have a low level of knowledge about what market economics means and of market-based management practice. Farmers and managers in rural areas are often mentioned as among those with the lowest level of business knowledge. For example, a manager of food processing facilities in the United States told us that in rural Russia, Hungary, and Poland, even as recently as the mid-to-late 1990s, farmers were uninformed about how to prepare, ship, and market their products. He found that, of the farms he visited over several years, less than half of what the farmers produced made it to market. In addition to an inadequate transportation infrastructure, the farmers had no storage facilities, and added no value to their product (e.g., did not wash potatoes, grate or bag them). Instead, they simply carted them (often, literally, by horse and cart) to farmers' markets and tried to sell what they had. Most of their products spoiled as a result.

Some local managers, especially early in the transition process, admitted their surprise at some of the fundamental aspects of market economies. For example, Vagit Alekperov, the Russian founder of the Lukoil firm, was surprised at the entrepreneurial flexibility and adaptability of western firms and managers. In particular, he was amazed to realize that if crude oil prices fell and oil firms lost money in that market, many still did well because they were diversified, in petrochemicals for example (Klepnikov 1996).

This lack of knowledge is understandable when we consider that most transition economy managers' administrative training, if they had any, was involved with how to run a firm in a centrally planned economy. Many, according to foreign managers, continue to lack even the vocabulary to communicate effectively about business issues. The following description of the typical Russian executive indicates the effect of this lack of exposure to management training.

> Not only do most Russian executives lack basic economic training, they are also unfamiliar with fundamental psychological concepts. Frequently, they treat their employees like robots and have little respect for the person. (Kets de Vries 2000: 74)

However, transition economy managers often have remarkable educational backgrounds. Their high school education typically surpasses North American standards in its range and exposure to language, the classics, science, and mathematics. University education, particularly technical, engineering, and scientific has been strong for years. From one of our informants:

> [The Russians I meet] say "I've been to school, I have my Ph.D., no one's going to tell me what to do." That's the attitude they have. They're educated people. You know, you take a cab from the airport to the hotel and you could talk about music, about concerts or ballet—to a cab driver. Try this [in North America]!

Because of this educational background, local managers sometimes feel superior to foreigners, mostly because of the quality of their technical education or the depth and history of their culture. Indeed, one of the surprises for many foreigners we interviewed was the widespread and very high levels of technical knowledge, in engineering and the sciences. For example, when local and foreign managers disagreed, the local managers sometimes played up their qualifications and resisted advice or requests from foreigners as a result. In fact, the simple act of admitting that they needed new knowledge and skills, that the managers were no longer the experts they had been, has been difficult for many (Schrage and Jedlicka 1999).

Management Education

As the decade of transition progressed, as local managers received training and education (in and out of their home countries), as they encountered more foreign managers, and as they gained more access to communication and information from and about the West, they gained business and related knowledge. Many have become proficient in the ideas and language of western business practices. Yet, sometimes, foreign managers are deceived by what they imagine to be more knowledge or understanding than exists in reality. Several interviewees gave examples of hiring local managers who "had the vocabulary in the interview," but of having to fire those same managers later when the foreigners discovered language facility could not compensate for inability to understand and work with a balance sheet or a budget or for knowing how to hire, reward, and develop people.

Managerial behavior is influenced very directly by the extent to which managers have been exposed to formal management training. Obviously, the kind of education that individuals receive is a key factor in establishing their perceptions of their roles in society and in organizations. For example, we might expect that individuals who have been exposed to formal management education are more likely to see management as a unified profession. Conversely, individuals who come to management with a technical training background are more likely to see their roles in terms of applying specific knowledge and are more comfortable with specific job titles rather than general ones such as manager or executive (Stewart, Barsoux, Kieser, Ganter, and Walgenbach 1994). In transition economies the extent to which individuals perceive themselves as managers depends, in part, on if and when they have had formal management education.

In the late 1980s and early 1990s, the need for management training led to several approaches within transition economies. Some transition economies developed various rules or regulations for education. Some countries created business schools, offering short-term programs for individuals interested in learning the basics of business in a market-oriented economy (Kozlova and Puffer 1994). In China, for instance, the number of M.B.A. graduates soared from 86 in 1989 to over 5,000 in 1999 (Child and Tse 2001). In Vietnam, the first M.B.A. graduates from an international program appeared as late as 1995. Some governments required that all managers have university degrees, that they all be educated in management, that any management training that lasted more than a month include some form of an in-company internship, and finally, that managers be "requalified" every three to five years (McNulty 1992). Additionally, Eastern European countries began replacing traditional economic doctoral education (weak in math and statistics) with more western approaches. Some countries (e.g., Hungary, Croatia, Bulgaria) have been more successful than others (e.g., Poland, Slovakia, and Slovenia), while still others (e.g., Romania) have not made much progress (Svejnar 2000).

However, the impact of the boom in management education in these economies may be less than some might expect. Sheila Puffer's (1996c) comments on management education in Russia suggest that there is a lot of ground to cover:

> It is easy to be pessimistic about market-based management education in Russia. Too many people need to be trained, including those who cannot easily let go of the old ways of doing things and those who want to do new things immediately without taking the time to learn the right ways. Too few faculty are qualified to teach market-based management. Too few resources are available including books, buildings, and computers. And there is too much social and political resistance to a market economy to make management education easy to deliver and to receive ready acceptance.

Educators often find that the language of market-based management is completely unfamiliar to transitional economy managers. In the early years of transition, managers simply had no conceptual framework of ideas common to market economies. In the early 1990s, many foreign educators and managers commented that transition managers had no sense of what profit meant or how to make it. Even more fundamentally, managers had little idea of why making a profit was important in a market economy. Explaining pricing was likewise hard since transition economy managers had no experience in or understanding of the impact that pricing has on demand or of how supply could affect price (Schrage and Jedlicka 1999). Furthermore, in some cases, transition economy managers, familiar with an idea or concept, have no easy way to express it. Sometimes, they are reluctant to discuss topics because of political or related sensitivities. For example, there is no good word in Vietnamese for the concept of "organizational politics." The word *politics* in Vietnamese traditionally refers to party politics. However, organizational politics thrives in Vietnam. The Vietnamese people are experts at it, but it is a topic that is not openly discussed. As a result, no clean or direct translation or word exists for it in Vietnamese.

Networking Skills

Both foreign and local business people recognize the use of networking. It is a skill that locals have used for many years and that foreign managers see as an expertise (tacit knowledge) that is increasingly important. Even high school and college aged Americans learn to network. In planned economies, networks were crucial for survival in many ways. Holden et al. (1998) describe the skills of Russian managers in building relationships and using networks to achieve their own and enterprise goals. Their findings corroborate comments from the managers we interviewed and our own observations. The planned economies gave birth to well-honed networkers, trained to understand how organizations work, who the key players were (in government, politics, business, etc.), and how to use information in achieving career advancement and gaining access to housing, education, and other privileges. Managers worked their networks both inside (e.g., with subordinates and peers, trade unions and party representatives) and outside (e.g., with local party bosses, regional authorities and officials, and ministries) their firms and developed those skills.

From our discussions with foreign and transition managers and from reading current literature, we see that networking skills continue to be important. Peng and Luo (2000) found that managers in Chinese firms who used their ties to government and to other firms during transition were able to help increase the market share of their firms. On the other hand, those managers still needed to develop skills and mind-sets that focused on quality and on managerial capabilities, which move beyond the networking skills they drew upon from their pretransition days. Some foreign managers who work in Russia mentioned the need for networking with security or police groups to protect business firms. Finally, a foreign manager, watching changes in China over the last decade, commented that as the Chinese get information from television and the Internet, they are able to find and interpret information for themselves rather than having to rely on a network or their superiors to provide information. One of the areas of possible change, then, in transition economy management may be the nature of networks and how managers use them.

Foreign Manager Knowledge

Much of the attention among scholars and journalists who monitor the transformation process as it affects businesspeople within the various countries focuses on the business or management knowledge (or lack thereof) among local managers. The underlying, unspoken supposition is that local managers are the ones who need to be taught management knowledge. It is important to remember, however, that while management concepts have a long history around the world, what we have come to understand as management in modern organizations was defined in the West (in the United States in particular) after World War II. Following the war, the United States became the dominant economic power and remained so for the next 20 years. During this period the concepts of modern management emerged and flourished. The assumption that U.S. management practice was the influence behind its economic success led to those practices becoming the accepted models for the world. Thus, the history of the concept of management itself has an indelible western (American) imprint (Boyacigiller and Adler 1991). In addition, most management education was similarly influenced, with many foreign institutions adopting western models of business education. Therefore, the explicit knowledge that managers need is, by definition, a western market orientation to management. Also, the idea of management as a concept that can be taught is a peculiarly western notion, which was perhaps first articulated in the early twentieth century by Henri Fayol (Gray 1987). Fayol believed that university professors could teach principles of managing one's own affairs, managing others, and managing an entire enterprise by exposing students to increasingly more advanced courses. Thus, another basic assumption is that the transition economies wanted market-oriented management training and that it could be taught.

Despite being steeped in western management philosophy, foreign managers may lack knowledge that can influence the interactions they have with their local counterparts. As we talked with managers from both sides, the foreign manager's knowledge level emerged repeatedly. Many foreign managers spoke of having what they called "aha" moments, when they learned something unexpected about working in transition economies or about themselves. The missing knowledge on the part of foreign managers seemed most often to come from their lack of exposure or experience in transition economies and their failure to be open to new ways of thinking and acting.

Lack of Knowledge and Experience

Some foreign managers admit that before they worked in China, or Russia, or Poland, they had no idea of the details of the market or management issues there. In 1998, a U.S. manufacturer of wood products for residential units began to assess markets in China. Given China's population and need for housing, as well as the relative ease of construction of his product, the general manager expected that the best market would be low-income housing. In fact, once he arrived in China and did more research, he discovered that the better market was for very high-end housing—villas in the U.S.$150,000-plus range. His first "aha" moment came when he learned that more millionaires live in China (over 60 million) than in the United States and that they were desperate for high quality, status housing. His firm switched its market focus, and after four years, developed a strong business.

A second surprise for this same manager was the treatment he received from some of the government authorities who had to approve his firm and allow it to operate in China. Some of the questions they asked on his initial visits, according to him, were annoying and "showed effrontery."

> . . . the Chinese made disparaging comments about wood houses being "temporary housing," of less quality and value. I reminded them that the Forbidden Palace in Beijing is made of wood.

Then the foreign manager realized such comments stemmed more from a lack of experience with wood on the part of the Chinese officials and from his own lack of knowledge about building materials in China. The manager had assumed that the Chinese officials and engineers would understand wood products; only when he visited China did he realize that all buildings built in the last 50 years were of concrete (or brick) and that the Chinese had no experience with wood.

In another example, an American firm preparing a proposal in Russia first approached each institute separately to solicit bids, pitting plumbing firm against plumbing firm and electrical supply firms against each other. Government authorities demanded that the foreign firm negotiate only with certain joint stock firms, each of which had a collection of suppliers, rather than going to individual suppliers. The Russians and Americans deadlocked for a time. Eventually, the Russians allowed the American firm to approach individual supplier firms. While the American manager initially found the practice simply irritating and frustrating, he recognized that the Russians had no other model and still had not fully comprehended the concept of competition. In their view, having foreign firms negotiate with different (although identified) joint stock companies was competition and also acted as a way to spread the work, which fit their prior socialist notions.

CULTURE

Culture consists of systems of values, attitudes, beliefs, and behavioral meanings that are shared by members of a social group (society) and that are learned from previous generations (Kluckhohn and Strodtbeck

1961; Thomas 2002; Tongren, Heckt, and Kovach 1995). Values are learned in terms of beliefs about what is good or bad, right or wrong, ugly or beautiful, and so on. Culture is programmed at a very deep level of consciousness in terms of how societies have solved the fundamental problems of interacting with other people and with their environment. Thus, culture is an important factor influencing manager motivation and attitudes.

Individualism and collectivism are perhaps the most useful and powerful of the dimensions of culture to help explain a diverse array of social behavior (Earley and Gibson 1998; Triandis 1995). Individualism refers to cultures that value autonomy and equal status among individual members, while collectivism values the group more. In addition, Markus and Kitayama (1991) describe vertical and horizontal culture orientations. The vertical dimension of culture reflects an acceptance of inequality, while the horizontal dimension emphasizes that people should be similar on most attributes, especially status (Triandis 1995).

This distinction between vertical and horizontal individualism and collectivism is helpful to understanding transition economies as well. In general, vertical collectivism and horizontal individualism may be the most common cultural profiles around the world.

Vertical collectivists see themselves as part of a well-defined social group (in-group), and members of the in-group are different in terms of status from other groups. These cultures are characterized by patterns of social relationships that emphasize communal sharing according to need and authority ranking, or the distribution of resources according to rank (Fiske 1991). They typically have social systems that do not reflect the values of individual freedom or equity (Rokeach 1973). Inequality is the accepted norm and serving and sacrificing for the in-group features prominently.

In horizontal individualism the self is autonomous, and people are generally equal. Such cultures are characterized by patterns of social behavior that emphasize equity in resource sharing according to contribution and distribution of resources equally among members (Fiske 1991). They are characterized by social systems that emphasize both the value of equality and of individual freedom (Rokeach 1973).

In a general sense, transition economies appear to fall closer to the vertical collectivist end of the continuum, while market-based economies tend to lean more toward the horizontal individualism end of the spectrum. These dominant profiles of cultural variation may affect management behavior along two paths. On one path, managers make role choices about what to do and how to behave guided by their culturally based value orientations. Managers are not necessarily aware of these subconscious influences. Instead, they simply make choices that they feel are correct. For example, a manager who worked in Mongolia throughout the 1990s said that his firm hired highly educated Mongolian men and women to become managers and one to become the chief engineer. While the managers performed well with their foreign bosses and peers, they had serious difficulties managing their Mongolian subordinates. Their culture, reinforced by the socialist system, had embedded in them the notion of equality among all to the point where Mongolian managers, appointed by foreigners, could not see themselves as being "above" their Mongolian colleagues and thus could not "manage" them. They were comfortable as subordinates (and even peers) to the foreigners, but not as bosses of their fellow Mongolians.

The other way for cultural influence to emerge relies on environmental pressure to shape managerial action. That is, management behavior is less the product of conscious decision making than a reflection of the roles that society accepts as legitimate. Many of the pressures that affect organizations and managers emanate from the institutions (e.g., legal, political, educational) of a society. However, because culture and the institutions have evolved together over time, they are inevitably linked. Patriarchal management behavior may have evolved because society demanded it. Also, perhaps organizational paternalism developed because state paternalism existed "up the line," that is, the expectation became that someone higher up in the hierarchy would always take care of someone lower down. Child and Markóczy (1993) provide an example of how culture may influence managers in transition economies:

> In short, defensive, conforming behavior will have been learned under a system where protection from censure and the securing of resources both depended heavily on the maintenance of good personal relations with higher level officials and, to some extent, with political organs within the enterprise itself. (Child and Markóczy 1993: 617)

The assumed universality that results from the U.S. dominance of management theory is problematic because the United States, like all cultures, has deeply embedded values that influence the way people think. Three examples (Boyacigiller and Adler 1991) demonstrate the biasing effect of culture on managerial practice. First, the United States is the most individualistic culture in the world (de Tocqueville 1835; Hofstede 1980). Individualism has to do with the extent to which Americans define themselves according to individual characteristics (or alternatively by the characteristics of the groups to which they belong on a permanent basis) and with the extent to which individual interests dominate. Central to the idea of U.S. individualism is the importance of individual freedom and choice (Triandis 1995). It is not surprising that U.S. managers focus on rational decision making with a goal of maximizing individual utility.

A related characteristic of U.S. managers is the belief that they are in control of their own circumstances and can influence their environment and future events to a great extent (Kluckhohn and Strodtbeck 1961). Such a belief stands in marked contrast to the learned helplessness that is characteristic of managers in former socialist countries and which is discussed below.

Finally, U.S. culture is characterized by a low-context communication style. That is, most of the meaning of a message is contained in the explicit communication as opposed to the context in which the information exchange takes place. The relatively low context orientation of the United States is consistent with a reliance on written agreements rather than on personal relationships (the United States has the world's highest number of lawyers per capita) and with thinking of organizations as composed of jobs whose requirements can be documented explicitly. These three examples suggest that western managers approach their jobs with an orientation that is very specific to their background and one that can be very different from their transition economy counterparts.

Effects of Culture

Cultural backgrounds influence the behavior of managers in terms of both motivation and work-related attitudes. Risk taking, self-efficacy (working past obstacles), and attitudes toward others are all conditioned by culture. Western attitudes about management and human resources are among the most difficult ones for local managers to accept since these attitudes are inconsistent with the managers' past conditioning both through culture and as a result of adapting to state socialism. To understand these effects, a discussion of the psychological concepts of motivation, learned helplessness, and healthy paranoia is necessary.

Motivation for Behavior

Motivation involves the reasons that people take or persist in a particular action. Culture guides the behavioral choices that people make because it determines what behavior and outcomes they value. That is, cultural values reflect individuals' needs. Those values also prescribe the behavior required to satisfy those needs (Erez and Earley 1993). We should, therefore, expect that members of different cultures will respond to different motivating factors in their intercultural interactions. For Americans, being different and getting individual rewards may be central motivating factors, for example. However, these same factors could have a negative effect in a culture such as those in many former socialist countries that values equality and cooperation. Western managers have been socialized to express their inner needs, to claim their individual rights, and to withstand undue social pressure. In contrast, the socialist ideal involves being receptive to others, adjusting to the collective needs, and restraining inner needs or desires.

While most people may be motivated by self-interest, the role that others play in how people define themselves is crucial. That is, individuals are differently motivated depending on whether they view themselves as independent of or interdependent with others.

Learned Helplessness

A psychological concept related to motivational differences, and with specific implications for managers under state socialism, is learned helplessness. Learned helplessness is the belief that individuals have no control over the rewards and punishments they receive from interacting with their environment (Garber and Seligman 1980). Dunbar (1983) suggested that learned helplessness reflects the nature of organizational behavior in a state-run and regulated market place. That is, the success of managers did not depend on company profitability or competitiveness since firms operated as monopolies in a shortage economy. Therefore, because managers learned that they were helpless to affect their own performance, they based their behavior on an achievement through association perspective (vicarious achievement) rather than on a personal achievement motive.

Healthy Paranoia

The concept of healthy paranoia was developed to explain minority-majority relationships in the United States (Ridley 1984), but it has also been applied to understanding organizational life under state socialism (Dunbar 1983). Against the background of totalitarianism and a planned economy that existed in state-owned enterprises, healthy paranoia was characterized by a natural suspiciousness and interpersonal guardedness. Healthy paranoia became normal behavior for socialist managers. Additionally, Dunbar (1983) suggests that the arrival of self-proclaimed business consultants from the West exacerbated the problem of out-group suspicion that was fostered under state socialism. This carryover from state socialism may have significantly influenced the interactions with western managers that occurred during the transition to more market-oriented systems.

These three psychological factors manifest themselves in individual attitudes and behavior that are consistent with the individual's culture and history. Following are salient examples of management behavior influenced by culture.

Motivational Effects

In planned economies, managers operated under conditions in which they were told what and how much to produce and when and where to deliver their products (Robinson and Tomczak-Stepien 2000). Under such conditions of plans and orders, they reacted, rather than taking initiative (Stahl-Rolf 2000). Even local managers who were more market oriented encountered the same situation. A manager for Bao Viet, Vietnam's largest insurance company, helped other Vietnamese firms undergoing equitization. He commented that Vietnamese managers needed at least two years to digest the idea that they can—and should—make their own business decisions (Cohen 2001).

Managers in socialist systems reported to political operators who monitored employees for "anti-state activity" (Litchfield 1992). While the countries that changed their political systems no longer face such political scrutiny, economies that retrained a socialist system and a communist party continue to have political constraints within organizations. Until only recently, China did not tell foreign firms and joint venture partners which employees were party members or whether party cells existed within the firm. In Vietnam, local and foreign firms hire (and pay for) party cell leaders who monitor company activities and employee behaviors.

With such scrutiny, local managers kept low profiles to blend in with their colleagues and to not stand out. Since taking the initiative to start or the responsibility to complete some task was standing out, managers typically refrained. Furthermore for so many years, managers and employees in state-owned enterprises held jobs that were more the art of marking time than of performing; they had no need for initiative. One manager who has worked in Beijing since the mid-1990s found the attitude especially frustrating:

Another issue is the work ethic of Chinese managers. As you know, western mangers are trained to focus on tangible results. We "must produce" or we are replaced. This is not the case with a manager in a SOE. Many of them spend less than half of the day actually working in the sense of producing something. They may instead feel quite at ease reading a newspaper or sipping tea in the presence of a boss because they don't work under a time schedule to "produce tangible results." The results they are expected to achieve are more relationship and power oriented.

Information Sharing and Risk Taking

Some foreign managers reported local managers were reluctant to share information, rather they insisted on keeping, or owning, it. One manager reasoned that this might be more of "a European than transition economy trait," since he saw it as a common characteristic among managers in Italy, France, and Germany. When managers attained positions of power, they felt "anointed" and thus did not want to share the wealth or the information their positions brought with others in the firm. Others saw a similar attitude in Russia, where Russian managers were surprised to hear that foreign managers share information with employees. One foreign manager working in Far East Russia said the attitude of local managers was one of "I've reached a high status, and I'll keep this information." Such an attitude might also be a holdover from communist days, when information was power.

Holden, Cooper, and Carr (1998) found that Russian managers, most of whom had few legitimate opportunities to decide their own fates, were generally unable or unwilling to take risks as a result. A North American educator who conducted training in Uzbekistan reported that even the idea of customer feedback was difficult for manager trainees to accept. To them, it meant that they were not the experts, that they might have made a mistake, and that asking customers how to improve suggested that the managers had done something wrong (Schrage and Jedlicka 1999).

Even when transition economy managers overcame their risk avoidance and did take a risk, they got few others to buy in. Several foreign managers commented that spreading the notion of risk taking or entrepreneurial thinking was difficult in transition economies. One foreign manager for a food-processing firm spent a year trying to encourage such thinking, and felt that he failed. He tried to help potential suppliers understand what the firm would need should it buy from them. He worked with about 20 farmers and cooperative managers in a rural area of Russia, training them on site and then bringing the group to the United States where they were trained for several months on growing techniques to increase yield, on ways to add value to their product, and on processing requirements (hence on what the farmers as suppliers needed to do). The American manager also showed the Russians the type of equipment they would need to invest in (take a risk on) to produce a product that his (or any) American firm would purchase.

During this time, the U.S. manager found only one Russian who he thought picked up the concepts—technical, agricultural, and business—and was able to apply them in Russia. This one manager, a unit leader for one of the cooperatives, located and secured the capital he needed to pursue more sophisticated practices. The local manager convinced the six managers who worked for him of the benefits of a more advanced approach to agricultural management, but he was unable to convince any of the farmers.

Attitudes Toward Employees

Transition economy managers' attitudes towards employees are com plex (Holden, Cooper, and Carr 1998; Jones 1995; Luthans et al. 2000; Snell and Tseng 2002). On the whole, strict hierarchy continues to dominate: a manager reigns in a plant or shop. Holden, Cooper, and Carr (1998) argue that, under a socialist planned economic system, Russian managers, or "bosses," (and other Eastern European as well as Chinese and Vietnamese managers) expected to be authoritarian and paternalistic. Foreign managers who work in Russia continue to report the same dominating, domineering attitudes when they interact with managers and their employees on site.

Other evidence of the complexity of work attitudes emerged in a study of employee involvement in Croatia and Slovenia, where local managers pursued employee involvement in two ways (Martin, Martin, and Grbac 1998). Some managers wanted no involvement from their employees. Others wanted involvement but found it hard to encourage because of ingrained cultural influences. In particular, the verticality (i.e., hierarchy) that existed in these cultures discouraged employees from giving opinions or being involved in decision making. Involvement also was difficult because employees did not take or expect to have the autonomy or authority to make decisions, even if managers delegated or encouraged them to do so.

Furthermore, the desire to avoid uncertainty may have led employees to defer to managers, who they expected to be powerful and able to deal with uncertainty better than they might. In an environment characterized by uncertainty, which transition economies are, employees will avoid uncertainty by avoiding involvement in decision making.

Attitudes Toward Others

Managers in transition economies appear to view people and the world outside their immediate situations in different ways. Some use their own firms or countries as a point of reference, a source of information, or a benchmark for performance, essentially disavowing an "outside." Gobeli (1998) illustrated such local naïveté and inward focus in an example about Bulgarian managers. At a management-training program in Bulgaria several years ago, a group of engineers was touting a medal they had won recently for the design of a prototype machine. One of their counterparts asked if the contest had been held just in Bulgaria or outside its borders as well, showing the insular thinking common among managers in the former Soviet Bloc (not uncommon within the United States as well!). The medal winners admitted that the contest had been held only within Bulgaria, essentially discounting its value when considered in an international setting.

Perhaps partly because of the poor advice and mistakes made in the early transition years, but likely also because of years of inward focus, some managers from transition economies hold an attitude of disdain for outsiders. Holden, Cooper, and Carr (1998) noted the "xenophobic populism" of Russian managers, who believed that outsiders were unable to fathom Russia's history and problems. They dismissed external suggestions and support on the assumption that foreigners had nothing to contribute since Russia (or China, or Poland, or Vietnam) had a "unique" set of problems and, therefore, working with people from outside the country was wasted effort. As one group of secretaries said to a Russian manager about their new foreign boss: "Why should we deal with him? He's a foreigner!" The Russian manager interpreted their comments as meaning they thought the foreigner a fool.

DEMOGRAPHICS

A final aspect of individual differences that should not be overlooked is demographic characteristics. Demographic characteristics themselves are probably not particularly influential. However, demographic differences often represent fundamental differences in values, attitudes, and beliefs, which can be extremely important. Two aspects of demographic differences can be identified. First, as indicated in Chapter 3, there are four types of managers: former SOE operatives, former communist cadres, professionals, and the children of the *nomenklatura*. Each of these groups is likely to be very different with regard to age and education, with the attendant differences in values, attitudes, and beliefs. A second demographic issue is that expatriate managers from western countries are likely to be more similar to each other—mid-career, middle-aged, and male (Thomas 2002)—with broadly similar experiences and attitudes.

These differences may account for the fact that, over the decade of transition, many educators and managers reported that some transition economy managers seemed more willing and ready to learn new techniques and knowledge than others. This may stem from age (i.e., younger managers are more eager), from a newly developed orientation toward individualism and materialism (Ralston, Egri, Stewart, Terpstra, and Yu 1999), or from "idiosyncratic circumstances" and experience with competitive markets (Newman 2000). Also, those who have worked for western firms, thus learning through immersion and from role models how to operate in a market economy (Newman 2000) will constitute a distinct group.

SUMMARY

This chapter identified individual manager characteristics that, when coupled with organizational factors and the legacy of state socialism, form the backdrop against which interactions between western and transition country managers take place. Understanding the differences that exist in knowledge, motivation, attitudes, and beliefs forms a basis for building a model of interactions that is presented in the following chapter.

Transition country managers are likely to be highly educated, but not in western market-oriented management. They typically have a cultural profile characterized by vertical collectivism, which has been reinforced under state socialism. In contrast, their western counterparts have an almost implicit knowledge of market-oriented management practice. That knowledge is coupled with a cultural orientation that emphasizes individual freedom and equality. Western managers believe in their ability to control their own fates, a marked contrast to the learned helplessness prevalent in managers under socialism. And, western managers engage in very explicit communication, while often ignoring the rich context of the country in which they are operating. Finally, transition country managers likely represent a range of backgrounds and paths toward management. Their western counterparts are likely to be much more similar because of restrictions on who takes up such assignments. The next chapter examines interactions of managers from different backgrounds, based on an understanding of the factors of individual differences.

Chapter 5

DEVELOPMENTAL MODEL

Actual social change is never so great as is apparent change. Ways of belief, of expectation, of judgment and attendant emotional dispositions of like and dislike, are not easily modified after they have once taken place. Political and legal institutions may be altered, even abolished; but the bulk of popular thought, which has been shaped to their pattern, persists.

—John Dewey, American philosopher and educator
From *Human Nature and Conduct* (1922)

A project manager in Vietnam mused about time spent working in that country during the 1990s:

"It's funny how things changed over the years I worked with Vietnamese colleagues. At first, when we foreigners showed up, the Vietnamese treated us like gods, almost. People wanted to hear what we had to say, to learn and to work with us, even though they were really wary. They'd grown up hearing government people talk about the evil foreigners, so a number of people didn't want to spend much time with us—especially away from work—but they wanted to learn. They thought that since we came from the 'outside world' we knew it all. Then they moved to a point where they became less cautious, wanted more from us, wanted to know why and how we did things. They still accepted what we said; they just wanted to understand our reasoning.

"Later, things shifted again. Much of it was subtle—people didn't respond as enthusiastically as before, or they said something wouldn't work because of the 'special conditions' in Vietnam. Other times it was more blatant. The local managers became more confident, believed they had learned what they needed from the foreigners, and just wanted us to give them money and leave. The attitude was, 'We've gotten from you what we want, so you can just leave now. It's our country and our organization, we don't want outsiders telling us what to do.' This shift in behavior and attitude was tough to get used to—some of the foreigners couldn't adjust to being questioned and challenged.

"But those of us who stuck with it (or had to since our projects weren't finished) tried to adjust. And slowly, the Vietnamese behavior and attitude changed once more. Our Vietnamese colleagues seemed to realize that there was a lot they could learn. Perhaps just as important, we started to realize that we could learn from them. It was sort of a stage of becoming colleagues rather than mentors or of feeling like we weren't needed. We all recognized that we had to work together, had to complete the job, and wanted to do it well. So we found ways to work together—each of us adjusting.

"We're now at a point where our work is coming to a close—at least on this project—and we have to decide and find a new future path as partners. We might just stay in touch, or we might find some way to collaborate that is quite new and unusual. But we made it through the rough spots and know that if we want to continue, we can."

As suggested in earlier chapters, the discussion about management in transition economies, in the general as well as the academic press, has focused much on change at the macroeconomic level, with a recent shift to the organizational level (e.g., Clarke 1996a; Peng 2000) and manager levels (e.g., Drakulevski 1999; Hraba, Mullick, Lorenz, and Vecernik 2001; Illes and Rees 2001; Puffer 1996c). Even so, research has tended to focus on the transition economy managers or foreign managers and how to do business, rather than on how the groups interact as they try to work together. The intent for this book was to fill the gaps in information about how local (transition economy) managers have changed. That is, we entered into this project seeking insights and information to help foreign managers understand the mind-set and behavior changes that the transition economy managers were undergoing as their countries experienced dramatic changes.

We originally assumed that local managers were increasingly using foreign practices to run their companies. This assumption was based on the range and depth of change in transition economies since 1989, including the inflow of foreign firms and managers, of training and education in western business practices for locals both inside and outside the transition economies, and the governmental focus of those countries on changing policies to encourage market-oriented practices. A decade after the transitions began, we expected a dramatic shift toward foreign approaches on the hiring, evaluating, and motivating of employees and on how managers conducted relationships with their partners (foreign and local), customers, and other key stakeholders. We hoped that, by understanding how the local managers' mind-sets and behaviors had changed over time and how they viewed their own roles in the new environment, we would be able to develop guidelines to help foreign managers, both the old pros and the novices.

We systematically began to look for examples of how transition economy managers' values, attitudes and beliefs, and behaviors had changed so that we could understand their current roles, how they approached their jobs, and how they might differ from foreign managers. With such an understanding, we aimed to give foreign managers insights on what they needed to know now, in the new environment of transition economies, to operate successfully with those local managers and employees. However, during our interviews, we began hearing a somewhat different story than we had anticipated. Foreign and transition economics' managers agreed that tremendous change had occurred at a surface level—in terms of visible change (e.g., prosperity, access and use of technology, job opportunities). However, they talked little about changes in behaviors, attitudes, or the ways that local managers went about their managerial work.

Based on the literature, media reports, and general observation, we assumed initially that surface-level changes in the transition economies indicated that deeper change—in the thinking and behavior of managers, employees, and citizens—was also happening in those transition economies. However, what we found was that the most dramatic change seemed to be occurring in the perceptions about and interactions between local and foreign managers rather than in management style. Some of those findings, while surprising at first, made sense as we examined them in the context of the environmental, organizational, and individual factors presented in previous chapters. Several key findings emerged.

The foreign managers we interviewed spoke frequently about their expectations and the limitations they faced in finding ways to work with their local counterparts to succeed in doing business in the transition economies. They also mentioned the resistance of local managers toward their foreign colleagues, which was stronger than they expected it to be and changed in nature over time. The degree of resistance seemed to be influenced by factors such as local manager age, the industry in which he or she worked, and the location of the site within a country (e.g., urban versus rural). Nevertheless, the resistance continued to exist in the interactions with foreign managers at several stages over time. Interestingly, but not surprisingly, given the changes in the interactions over time, foreign managers also showed resistance toward their local counterparts, although that resistance seemed to emerge almost unexpectedly from the point of view of the foreign managers. These observations led us away from developmental models that explained the change in individuals in transition economies toward a developmental framework that captured the interactions between these local managers and their foreign counterparts.

The model of changing interactions that emerged from our observations and experiences and from those of the managers we interviewed is a key element of this book. The most dramatic impetus for the model came from observations—such as those in the introductory vignette in this chapter—of foreigners who had become stuck in roles and ways of behaving toward their local counterparts that no longer fit the perceptions and stage of development that the locals held. Thus, the model initially developed inductively, and was later tested against the experiences of both foreign and local managers as we began to gather material for the book. Overall, the model presented in this chapter, and expanded in later chapters, held up well in discussions with managers from foreign and transition economies, who had experiences in different time periods, different industries, different locations, and different types of work.

STAGE MODELS

As we began to conceptualize a model of the sequential development of the interaction between foreign and transition economy managers that was consistent with what managers were telling us, we found it useful to draw on other stage models for help in classifying and defining the stages. Elements of our model have been drawn from Tuckman's (1965) developmental sequence in small groups, from a model of adjustment to new cultural environments (Lysgaard 1955; Oberg 1960), and from organizational life-cycle models (e.g., Adler and Ghadar 1989; Milliman, Von Glinow, and Nathan 1991). Interestingly, each of these models proposes four fundamental developmental stages.

The stages of the group development model (Tuckman 1965) suggests that small groups are initially concerned with orienting the members through testing and by establishing dependency relationships *(forming)*. This stage is followed by a period of conflict and polarization around interpersonal issues *(storming)*. Groups then progress to a period when cohesiveness develops, standards of behavior evolve, and new roles are adopted *(norming)*. They finally attain a stage in which the interpersonal structure is resolved and can be the tool of task activities *(performing)*.

According to the early models of adjustment to new cultures (e.g., Lysgaard 1955; Oberg 1960), individuals progress at regular intervals through four phases: honeymoon, culture shock, adjustment, and finally, mastery. In the honeymoon stage, everything is new, exciting, and interesting; the new environment intrigues people in much the same way it would if they were tourists. At the culture shock stage, individuals become frustrated and confused because the environment is not providing them with familiar cues. At the adjustment stage, sojourners begin to understand cultural differences, learn the ways to get things done, and begin to settle into the rhythm of daily living in the foreign country. Eventually, individuals may achieve the mastery stage in which they are able to function in the new culture almost as well as they did at home.

In an interesting application of this developmental model, Feichtinger and Fink (1998) drew on collective culture shock to explain the effect of changes in the social and cultural systems that individuals experienced in transition countries. In this model, exaggerated expectations following the fall of communism correspond to the honeymoon phase in the individual level model of adjustment. However, in later work (Fink and Holden 2000, 2002), the notion of a honeymoon period is replaced by a more tangible set of variables that indicate the possibility of early acceptance and satisfaction with the change that individuals encounter. Collective culture shock follows and results from the unfulfilled expectations and the unjustified idealization of the new free-market system that (a) reduces orientation and clarity about the appropriate frame of reference; (b) results in a lack of trust and self confidence; (c) promotes apathy, passivity, and lack of initiative; and (d) fosters defensive mechanisms, withdrawal, and a resurgence of old values.

A number of organizational development models have been built on Vernon's (1966) four-stage international product life-cycle model. Notably, Adler and Ghadar (1989) relate the stages of firm development to the firm's perspective on culture. In the first, or high-tech, stage of firm development, cultural sensitivity is unimportant to the success of the firm, and an ethnocentric perspective prevails. The second, or internationalization, phase is characterized by a polycentric perspective in which culture becomes critical to the firm's success. The third, or multinational, stage sees culture as only marginally important to success, and consequently, it is often ignored. Finally, in the global phase a high degree of cultural sensitivity is required to enhance competitive advantage. Similar four-phase approaches have been used to explain the fit required between human resource management (HRM) policies of the firm and internal and external environments (Milliman, Von Glinow, and Nathan 1991) and the degree of adaptation required of HRM systems in international environments.

The concept of a four-phase developmental model fit well with the stories we were hearing about the interactions between foreign and transition economy managers. Each of the stage models reviewed above illuminated certain aspects of the phenomenon we were observing. However, to understand the dynamics of the cross-cultural interactions that occurred within each phase, we needed to draw on some fundamental psychological principles. The following section reviews some of the basic concepts that we used to enrich our four-stage developmental interaction model.

CROSS-CULTURAL INTERACTIONS

Our understanding of interactions between foreign and transition economy managers is grounded in the psychological concept of social cognition. In general social cognition is concerned with the role that mental representations play in how humans process information about people or social events. It is relevant here because these mental representations can be about members of a foreign group (e.g., transition economy managers) and, therefore, affect the processing of information about members of that group. To make sense of a complex environment, humans categorize others in terms of shared characteristics, such as physical appearance, religion, political views, lifestyle, and country of origin. Through the assignment of a set of characteristics to a particular national label, humans create a mental representation, or schema, for that nationality. This categorization of others and ourselves results in a sense of who we are and how we should act toward others (Tajfel 1981). It is this categorization of social environment into "them and us" that underlies much of the psychology of interacting with individuals from another culture.

Norms and Scripts

One result of belonging to a particular cultural group is the adoption of its norms. Cultural norms, like other norms, are acceptable standards of behavior that are shared by a group of people. They suggest what is expected of a person in certain situations. Although individuals may vary in the extent to which they adopt the norms of groups with which they identify, the norms are a powerful influence on behavior (Asch 1963). Therefore, individual behavior is influenced by the cultural norms of society, but only to the extent that a norm exists for a particular situation and only if societal sanctions for noncompliance exist. The norms of behavior required and promoted by state socialism were discussed in some detail in previous chapters.

Culturally based scripts are related to normative behavior. Scripts are mental representations that humans have about themselves in a given situation (Abelson 1981; Gioa and Poole 1984). Scripts are concerned with actions and a sequence of events. Once they are developed, they are used in interactional situations based on situational cues. They consist of a particular action plan, or behavioral sequence, that is indicated for familiar situations. When individuals find themselves in familiar situations, they need not think in detail about how they should behave. They react more or less automatically based on situational cues. Therefore, behavior may be a semireflexive response influenced by cultural norms that were learned over time. Business people in the West have a variety of scripts for common business situations, such as management meetings, negotiations with a supplier or customer, or presentations to security analysts. The scripts held by local managers for interacting in a business setting are likely to be based on a very different set of prior experiences from those of their foreign counterparts.

Selective Perception

Perception is the process by which individuals interpret the messages received from their senses, thereby giving meaning to their environments. Because the environment presents individuals with more information than they can effectively deal with at any one time, they screen out much of what is presented to them by their senses. As people are socialized into a particular socio-cultural system, they learn how to perceive, because they share certain expectations and understandings of situations. When individuals perceive people and their behavior (as opposed to objects or events), a key element of their perception is whether or not they categorize those people as members of their group (in-group members) or not (out-group members). An important effect of categorizing others as out-group members is that, once categorized, they are subsequently perceived as being more similar to each other than to in-group members (Linville, Fischer, and Salovey 1989). That is, people see the individual variation that exists in their own cultural group, but perceive other cultural groups as homogeneous.

Another way people filter information presented by their environment is through selective avoidance. When faced with information that is contrary to their existing views, they tune it out by diverting their attention elsewhere (Kavanaugh 1991). If the information, behavior, or comment does not fit what they expect, they ignore or discount it, rather than trying to understand or learn from it.

Therefore, cultural differences can influence perception in several ways. First, people are socialized by their culture to perceive things in a particular way. Second, they tend to filter out information that is incompatible with their views. Finally, they perceive members of other cultures as more similar to each other than members of their own cultural group.

Expectations and Stereotypes

Selectively perceiving others is based on learning to perceive in a certain way because of socialization into a culture. However, perception also relies on some expectation of how people in the other culture will behave. These expectations and stereotypes about others, in this case perceptions of local and foreign managers about one another, are often based on very limited information.

Stereotypic expectations of a cultural group result from the natural cognitive process of social categorization, discussed above. However, these expectations are based on simplifying or filtering the information provided by the environment. As a result, stereotypes invariably emerge and include feelings about the cultural group as well as expected behavior. Research on stereotypes indicates that people can hold intense stereotypes about other national cultures even though they have never met a person from that culture (Katz and Braly 1933). Because stereotypes are based on very limited information about others, such as very basic physical or social evidence (i.e., skin tone or country of birth), they do not always provide accurate expectations of behavior. Regardless of their accuracy, however, stereotypic expectations have several characteristics that are important in understanding interactions across cultures.

First, when an individual is placed as a member of a category, such as a national culture, the associated information about the category is applied to that person. The outcome is a stereotype. Once formed, these stereotypic expectations of others tend to become self-perpetuating (Snyder 1981). That is, people interpret information about the national culture to be consistent with their stereotype and behave toward members of that culture in ways that confirm their expectations. New information about a member of the culture is often discounted as not representative, thereby maintaining the stereotype (Hamilton 1979). For example, Russian managers are often categorized as being autocratic (Puffer 1994). When confronted with a very liberal Russian manager, people may consider him as atypical and still maintain their stereotypic expectation of Russians.

Second, since people learn stereotypes, they develop more complex mental pictures about their own national cultures than they do about the culture of others. Because they know more about their own, it's easier for them to realize the extent of variation within it and to expect variation. However, stereotyping also leads to differences in how people evaluate new information. In other words, when people receive new information about a group they know little about, and may have very simple stereotypes about, they tend to evaluate that information in a more extreme manner—both positively and negatively. When they receive additional information about their own culture, which they know well, they tend to be less extreme in the way they assess the information. As a very simple example, consider a person seeing someone else run a red light. If an American sees a Caucasian white male do this, he might say to himself, "he's drunk, distracted, late for a meeting, or rushing his wife to the emergency room." If the same person saw a small Asian woman run a red light, he might use a more limited set of explanations, such as "she's an immigrant and doesn't know how to drive." Thus, the more information people have about a cultural group, the more likely they are to accept (evaluate accurately) new information about it.

Finally, national stereotypes may also fit what is called social dominance theory (Sidanius 1993). That is, there may be a hierarchy of nationalities that is generally accepted based on status. High status may be attached to a particular nation because of economic dominance or of other desirable characteristics. According to the theory, the extent to which a national group has high status will influence the attitude of others toward the group, as well as its members' attachment to it. In general, the recent economic dominance by the West suggests that many people will hold some western nationalities in high regard and that members of these national cultures will be strongly attached to (some even to the point of arrogance) their national culture because of its high status.

Differences in Attributions

Attribution is the search for and assignment of cause for observed behavior. To attribute behavior, people rely on cues from a situation that indicate the extent to which individuals are in control, such as whether or not the behavior is distinctive to a situation, consistent over time, and if the same behavior is displayed in similar situations (Kelley 1972). Sometimes, however, the situational cues are not clear about the cause of behavior. In cases where observations about an individual's behavior do not clearly indicate the cause, others rely on information they already have about that individual to make a judgment. In cross-cultural interactions, people might rely on their stereotypic expectations of another culture to fill in the gaps (e.g., Russians are by nature autocratic). In other cases, they may project their own behavior on the situation (e.g., What would cause *me* to behave that way?). In either case, cultural differences influence beliefs about the cause of the behavior. In the first case, culturally based expectations of another culture influence attribution. In the second, people's own culturally based behavioral norms or scripts influence their judgment of causality.

Attribution about the cause of behavior is also influenced by whether or not the behavior is being exhibited by a member of one's own cultural group. Because people derive a sense of who they are from association with their cultural group, they are favorably biased toward that group. Therefore, they are more likely to attribute desirable behaviors by members of their in-group to characteristics or skills of the individual. Conversely, they are more likely to attribute desirable behaviors of out-group members to chance or external causes (Hewstone 1990). That is, if members of one's cultural group exhibit positive behavior (perform well on a task), one is more likely to think it is because of their ability or effort. In contrast, when one observes the same behavior by members of another cultural group, one is more likely to think it was caused by luck or other favorable circumstances.

INTERACTION SEQUENCE

The fundamental psychological principles just presented underlie cross-cultural interaction. By drawing on these principles, it is possible to outline a basic interaction sequence that occurs between foreign managers and their local transition economy counterparts in a variety of day-to-day activities. The interaction sequence assumes, as a starting point, some behavior on the part of a manager from a transition economy, although the starting point could be either party in the relationship. First, the manager might behave according to some culturally based script for the situation, or because of some expectation about how her/his behavior will be perceived, he/she adjusts the behavior. This script can be influenced by behavior that was learned to be appropriate under state socialism, as well as by the characteristics of the manager (age, education, previous managerial experience, etc.), and by the organizational context (e.g., SOE, joint venture, entrepreneurial start-up).

There are an almost infinite number of situations in which a cross-cultural interaction like this might take place. However, many situations in business settings, such as business meetings, employee interviews, negotiations, and so forth, are familiar enough to evoke a semireflexive type of behavior. Aspects of the situation determine the extent to which it evokes a preexisting behavioral sequence or script. If a script does not exist for the specific situation, as it may not for a particular foreign business context for transition economy managers, the individual gives more thought to how to behave, what he/she may want to achieve from the behavior, and how such behavior might be perceived. Next, the foreign manager seeks to interpret the meaning of the actions of the local manager. This interpretation consists of two-stages. The first is the identification of the behavior. This identification, as discussed in this chapter, can be influenced by culturally biased selective perception. That is, the foreign manager perceives only what the manager has learned to perceive at a given point in time. Ability to perceive accurately improves over time as experience is gained and as the manager is exposed to more examples of behavior. The identification stage also involves categorizing the other person as a member of an out-group. This categorization is influenced by the extent to which the transition economy manager's behavior matches the foreign manager's expectation. If the local manager's behavior is consistent with the foreign manager's expectations of transition country managers, the foreign manager automatically makes the categorization, giving it little thought. If, however, the local manager behaves in an unexpected way, the foreign manager must give the categorization more careful consideration.

The second part of the sequence involves attributing the identified behavior to a cause. This attribution is influenced by the culturally based expectations that the foreign manager has for the behavior of managers from transition economies. Both the extent to which situational cues about the cause of the behavior exist and the level of knowledge and understanding of the foreign manager about transition economy managers influence the accuracy of the attribution. If the foreign manager has very well-developed prior conceptions of local managers, the evaluation of behavior is likely to be less extreme and more accurate. If the observed behavior is ambiguous, providing little information about its cause, the foreign manager relies more heavily on preexisting information, such as stereotypic expectations, to make a judgment. In other

words, when foreign managers aren't sure about the behavior they observe, they attribute it to the stereotype they already hold for a member
of that group. For example, poor performance is sometimes attributed to
a stereotype of Russian managers as inherently lazy, which is derived
from a common saying, "We pretend to work, they pretend to pay us."
The uncritical use of stereotypes is particularly prevalent in early stages
of the development of the relationship.

So, the foreign manager's attitudes and behavioral response depend
on how he or she attributes the behavior of the transition economy manager. To the extent that the attributions made are tied to a familiar cause,
the response behavior of the foreign manager may itself be scripted. For
example, the foreign manager may respond to good performance with
public praise in a semireflexive manner. This response may or may not
be acceptable in the local culture, affecting the next response of transition
economy manager. If, however, the behavior of the local manager does
not fit an existing category for the foreign manager, he/she may be unable
to use an existing script to guide behavior. In this case, the manager may
be forced to invent a new behavior. The ability of people to adjust old
scripts or create new ones is a significant part to successful cross-cultural
encounters. Chapter 10 discusses these types of skills.

This behavioral sequence plays itself out day after day in interactions
between foreign and local managers, between managers and subordinates, between negotiators, and among work group members. The stage
of development of the relationship between transition and foreign managers may change, but the fundamentals of the interaction remain the
same.

These psychological principles are difficult or impossible to observe,
and even the participants are often unaware of them. Therefore, to allow
us to examine these fundamental principles in interaction sequences
within the model we describe below, we focused on three indicators of
the underlying processes that the managers we interviewed articulated.
These are (a) their perceptions of the level of trust in the relationship,
(b) the accuracy of their expectations of the behavior and attitudes of
the other participant in the relationship, and (c) their description of the
nature and flow of information between themselves and others.

THE MODEL OF INTERACTIONS

The indicators of trust, expectations, and information flow vary in
systematic ways with the stage of development in the relationship between foreign and local managers. This section briefly describes the

stages in our model, which are developed more fully in subsequent chapters. Based on our observations of the characteristics of each stage, we have labeled the stages Contact, Critique, Convergence, and Continue?

Contact

The first stage of the model involves the initial contact between foreign and transition economy managers, a period of getting to know each other. At this stage, both sets of individuals are primarily concerned with establishing both interpersonal and task-related boundaries. They do this by testing the relationship through a series of interactions similar to that described above. Ideally, each individual seeks out the other, anticipates change, is clear about the expectations that foreign and transition economy managers hold about the environment, people, and outcomes, and is realistic about the resources and sources of information that exist to make the project go smoothly (Fink and Holden 2000, 2002). In reality, however, at this stage each party is likely to have very underdeveloped or stereotypic mental representations of the other. Therefore, their perceptions and expectations of behavior are likely to be naïve and typically inaccurate. Foreigners, for example, may expect managers of transition country X to exhibit certain stereotypic behaviors, such as avoiding risk. Conversely, the transition economy managers may expect foreigners to be experts at all aspects of business, regardless of specialization. Each group may also fall into the trap of projecting its own behavioral norms or scripts onto the other party, therefore expecting both groups to be more similar than they really are. Each group then would be likely to attribute behavior based on its own cultural norms.

Responses to unexpected behavior may be muted or considered interesting or exotic as boundaries are tested. However, such behavior will be salient to the observer because attributing its cause will require more active thought. The scripted behavior of the parties will stem from their previous interactions, and since many managers may have interactions only with members of their own culture, their range of expectations will likely be limited. For example, foreign managers may use tried and true managerial techniques that have worked well for them in the past (e.g., in North America) and be frustrated when they do not work elsewhere.

The flow of communication will also be based on initial perceptions, particularly perceptions of status relationships. That is, transition country managers may defer to their foreign partners because of the economic hegemony of market economies and the transition economy managers' learned helplessness. At this early stage, the expectations on both sides may be that foreigners are teachers and the transition economy managers are learners.

Trust will initially be low, in part because trust involves the expectation of future behavior, which takes accurate knowledge of behavior to develop. Low trust may also be enhanced by the healthy skepticism of transition economy managers that was fostered under state socialism. And, the motives and goals of the two parties will often be different, but this may not be apparent at this stage.

Critique

A second stage of development is characterized by a review and critiquing of the behaviors and interactions between the foreign and transition economy managers. Sometimes conflict—whether overt or under the surface—begins to emerge with regard to interpersonal interactions. The manifest or subtle friction may lead to emotional responses to both interpersonal and task-related interactions. In addition, both parties may resist—again either in obvious or subtler ways—adjusting to the other. While transition economy managers desire the improvements they hope will come with a change toward a market economy, they fear the negative consequences that may come with it (Neilsen 2000). Their healthy skepticism, nurtured for years under socialism, now results in resistance to change. In the process, the foreign managers may lose status as the all-knowing experts. The transition economy managers may exhibit behavior, such as avoiding direct conflict by ignoring or not carrying out tasks they are asked to do, that confuses their foreign counterparts.

Thus, at this stage both parties will encounter some behavior that contradicts their stereotypic expectations. However, in many cases, they will discount this behavior as atypical, maintaining their stereotype of the group. They will experience the shock of confronting the reality of their task and interpersonal interactions. They may start questioning their perceptions and may be confused about the cause of the behaviors that they observe. Each group starts to realize that the other may have different goals and motivation. Effective communication flow may become blocked. The scripted behavior of both parties, based on their home country norms, may create confusion and conflict. Disorientation and stress, lack of trust and self-confidence all exemplify and fuel the frustration that emerges. Transition economy managers may employ defensive mechanisms such as withdrawing, being passive, or being confrontational in asking why things must be done in a certain way. Foreign managers may similarly withdraw, explode, or give up.

Converge

Progressing from the critique stage requires that managers find new standards of behavior and expectations. Initially it means both sides may adapt expectations and behavior to be more like that of their counterparts in the interaction. In this stage, both groups make what amounts to superficial changes in behavior or attitudes, often without any real understanding of the basis of the changes other than that they seem to work. Foreign managers may give in to the environment and adjust their expectations of performance, for example. Transition economy managers may suspend their distrust enough to accommodate activity they see as in their best interest.

Stereotypic expectations begin to break down and trust starts to (re)develop. For example, foreign managers may start to fully appreciate the high intelligence and educational level of transition country managers. Both groups may move toward mutually beneficial (or at least nonconflicting) goals. The flow of communication now begins to be two-way.

Continue?

In the final stage of development, the interpersonal aspects of the interaction have been largely resolved. In a sense, managers step back and analyze where they have come from and where they wish to take the relationship. Constructive conflict about task activities may still exist, but the managers can resolve these issues without the emotional conflict of previous stages. Both parties become capable of making better causal attributions for behavior because they know and hold more accurate perceptions and expectations. They are able to see the individual differences that exist among members of the opposite group. There is less reliance on semireflexive scripted behavior, and individuals give more active thought to how their own behavior may be perceived and how the other party is likely to respond. There should be a more active two-way communication flow, and significantly higher levels of trust begin to emerge.

At this point, the counterparts consider whether to continue their relationship, and if they wish to continue, what the nature of the relationship will be. They have at least four options: continuing activity in a positive manner; muddling through a relationship to complete a project; abandoning the relationship; or finding a new form and method to proceed. We found that this last alternative—that of a new way—is very likely, given the unpredictable environment and uncertainties about the future in transition economies.

ASSUMPTIONS AND CAVEATS

This stage model is a method of understanding the links between the effects of individual, firm, and environmental characteristics on the outcomes of interactions in transition economies. That is, the attributes of individuals combine with characteristics of the firm in which they must function, which itself exists in the context of a changing environment, to affect managerial behavior. However, this behavior is also affected by the stage of development of the relationship between foreign and transition country managers. While this stage model is consistent with other four-stage models of development, its particulars are largely induced from our empirical investigation, the detailed findings of which are presented in the following chapters.

Like other stage models, this one rests on several assumptions. First, any model that tries to be general will not neatly fit each individual case. Although an individual manager or situation may vary from the description, the model is broad enough to be useful for managers who work in a variety of transitional economy settings.

Second, development tends to vary in pace (some relationships move through stages faster than do others) and end points (some relationships skip stages or start at different stages from other relationships). Our research involved talking with managers who had worked abroad prior to the economic transformations, at its beginning, and many years into the changes. Their views concerning the stages of interactions varied. This model is a succinct depiction of common phases that appeared; it does not propose or prescribe any one best approach.

Finally, unlike many descriptions of activities in transition economies, this model proposes that the development of the interaction is bidirectional. Like others, we initially assumed that most change in action and behavior would occur in transition economy managers and be parallel to the shifts in their countries' policies, absorption of market economic ideas and actions, and the like. However, our research indicated that significant change occurs with regard to the interactions and relationships that develop between local and foreign managers. Moreover, we suggest that foreigner managers also change in the process.

SUMMARY

This chapter reviews several stages models that we have drawn upon to help us understand the reports of managers working in transition economies that we gathered in our research. These models related to the developmental sequence of creating small groups, adjustment to new cultures, and organizational life cycles. Then the chapter explores some basic psychological concepts that form the basis for interactions of people from different cultures. By combining these ideas, the chapter details a conceptualization of a four-phase developmental model of interactions between foreign and transition country managers. Our model is proposed to mediate the effect of individual, firm, and environmental factors on outcomes. The final section then draws attention to some of the limitations of stage models, including ours.

Part III

THE RELATIONSHIP
IN TRANSITION

Chapter 5 provided the overall model for the stages of interaction that foreign and local managers appear to experience over time. The following chapters go into more depth on each stage and provide examples and illustrations from managers we have interviewed as well as some from our experiences.

Chapter 6 examines the reactions and interactions that managers have as they make initial contact. Those interactions emerge through managers' comments and reactions relating to several key elements—the extent and nature of the trust they have for each other, the nature of their communication, and their expectations about each other and themselves. The remaining chapters examine similar elements as the managers work through the subsequent stages of their interaction—through tension as they critique the way they interact and solve conflict (Chapter 7) and through the process of finding better ways to work together (Chapter 8). Since we do not have examples and evidence from many long-term (more than three years) relationships between transition economy and foreign managers, Chapter 9 provides more discussion on possibilities for relationships and their future interactions, rather than specific data. It is often at this stage that managers appear to review and reflect more on the nature and state of the interactions and begin to decide where to go with them. It is also at this stage when unusual or unexpected outcomes and interactions may emerge. Thus, we also suggest that managers allow for possible unanticipated forms of relationships or interactions (Holden 2002). The section closes with Chapter 10, which offers suggestions for ways managers can strengthen their interactions and relationships.

Chapter 6

CONTACT: GETTING TO
KNOW YOU

Assumptions are the termites of relationships.
                              —Henry Winkler, actor (1945–)

The senior manager in charge of international operations for a large American food processing plant had high hopes for his firm in the newly opening eastern European markets. His firm was one of the world's largest processors of potatoes for the fast food industry. In discussions about areas for expansion for the firm, Poland came up as a good prospect. In the early 1990s, Poland was rapidly embracing market economics, had a trained labor force, and had a tradition of growing potatoes. Also, its location provided ready access to the huge European market.

Thus in the early 1990s, when the manager set off to try to find a Polish plant for purchase, he did so with optimism. He had been involved in international business around the world—in South America, Australia, Turkey, and Europe—and felt confident entering discussions with Polish government officials about an acquisition.

After visiting several sites, the manager found one that had potential, although it was a run-down facility, with out-of-date equipment. Still, it had the attractions of location, employment base, and access to western European markets. Then he began to negotiate with the governmental ministry in charge of industry privatization.

According to the American manager, the government officials demanded an unreasonably high price for the plant and equipment. He tried to understand their perspective and acknowledged that the Poles, new to market economic concepts, did not know or understand ideas of equipment depreciation or what it would take to update the facility. He sensed that the objective of the Poles was for more money since that is what they understood the market economy to mean. After six weeks of bargaining, the American gave up, never reaching agreement. Later, as he reviewed the situation, he understood that he had expected far more sophistication in the deal-making process. Also he suspected that he might have come across as an aggressive American trying to manipulate the Poles into a deal and cheat them in the process.

When his firm entered China to explore a possible venture in the mid-1990s, his approach was completely different and more effective, but also much more expensive. One of the firm's largest customers was entering China and needed a reliable source for potatoes. Therefore, the American manager's firm considered China to be a required future site; it had to make the business work.

The company's initial steps were not commercial at all. Instead, the manager said the firm wanted to "build the relationship" at the grassroots level—with farmers and with potential processing partners. The firm provided free training to farmers on how to increase potato yield; its managers spent time in the fields getting to know the farmers. They also spent time getting to know government officials. The process of building the relationship took a year. However, when discussions began about pursuing a commercial venture, they were smooth and quick. By the time negotiations started, a fundamental trust and understanding had developed, and the two sides moved forward effectively. The final result was the construction and operation of a now successful processing plant.

These two incidents described in the vignette reveal the importance of initial contact on the ultimate development and outcomes of business relationships. This initial stage of the interaction between foreign and local managers in transition economies involves establishing both interpersonal and task-related boundaries. A myriad of factors shape the characteristics of this stage, including the individual manager characteristics, organizational factors, and the environment in a given transition economy, which were discussed in prior chapters.

This chapter describes the characteristics of the initial phase of business relationships in transition economies. As in any initial contact, this tends to be a process of getting to know you. Each type of manager brings a range of expectations and emotions—from euphoria to reluctance, from curiosity to caution. During our interviews, managers on both sides of the relationship often described the initial contact, or stage, as full of contradictions and confusion. The following section discusses the dimensions that describe this stage of relationship development in terms of the level of trust, information sharing, and expectations about each other, drawing extensively on comments from managers we interviewed.

TRUST

True for any relationship at its start, the level of trust that each side has for the other may be limited. On the whole, our interviews revealed that both local and foreign managers approached a new business venture with the other with a great deal of caution. We found that individual managers often had a sense of curiosity, mixed with some enthusiasm about what could be gained and learned, and also a fair amount of wariness. In our interviews, three initial approaches to trust emerged: expect trust but don't be surprised if it doesn't develop—in other words, take a wait and see approach; withhold trust; and assume there is no trust and work to build it before getting into a business venture.

Wait and See

Some foreign managers entered transition economy ventures with an assumption of trust rather than of distrust. They assumed that their counterparts wanted them there and that a deal could be worked out. The manager who went to Poland (described in the vignette) is an example of one who assumes trust. This assumption was often based on a belief that local managers wanted the knowledge and skills that the foreigners brought and, therefore, that a critical bond and eventual trust would stem from that need.

Some foreign managers did indeed feel that they were treated well and were trusted by local managers. This feeling stemmed from their belief that they brought expertise from the world beyond the borders that had closed Russia, the eastern bloc nations, Vietnam, or China for so many years. Likewise, some local managers rarely questioned the comments and views of foreign managers in the early stage of creating a relationship, especially if they had little previous contact with outsiders.

However, there often appeared to be initial reluctance to trust on both sides. Foreign managers sometimes encountered attitudes of local managers that surprised and frustrated them. When the foreign managers didn't understand or were wary of the attitudes, they were less likely to trust their counterparts. For example, foreign managers reported that local managers could use the vocabulary of market economics but that they put a different spin on it. Instead of building long-term value for a firm, reinvesting in the firm, or creating a partnership, local managers sometimes conveyed a short-term view of "getting something done now" or "getting what I can from a deal."

The "get what you can now" attitude struck foreign managers as coming from a lack of information or understanding about how market economics works. As a result, some foreign managers gave the local managers the benefit of the doubt and perceived the attitude more as a "reinterpretation" of concepts. For example, when foreign managers sought equipment or services from local managers, sometimes they encountered what they considered unrealistic quotes. One manager needed a translator in the Czech Republic; the translator started with a request for U.S.$150 an hour, and after realizing the foreigner would not pay it, worked his way down to U.S.$10 an hour, which the foreign manager knew was closer to the local market rate.

A corollary seemed to be an attitude of "anything goes" (McCarthy, Puffer, and Naumov 1997). After years of few institutional guidelines or of finding ways to work around restraints, Russian entrepreneurs (and some managers), showed an attitude of optimism, opportunity seeking, and short-term profit taking, for example. The attempt to gain as much money for a specific task as possible was a typical example of this attitude as well.

A Russian manager attributed the "getting something done now" attitude to the legacy of state socialism when he compared attitudes toward investment:

> In the western world where free market was established a long time ago, people got used to the stability. If they invest money, they can take it back any time, even in 10 years or more. In Russia, we have had some investment history too, but as we don't have a confidence in tomorrow, our people want a quick result if they invest money. Western managers don't understand this. They think, as our company was opened recently, we should just wait [to have a successful business].

Interestingly, most foreign managers we interviewed were not upset by the local managers' attitudes of "getting it done now" or "getting what I can" and attributed them primarily to lack of knowledge on the part of local managers. On the other hand, some mentioned that it was a "waste of time" to work through every transaction having to deal with a "get it done now" or "get what I can" attitude. In either case, though, foreign managers seemed to decide to wait and see what would develop before allowing themselves to trust their counterparts.

A manager working in China felt that until the end of the 1990s, the Chinese he worked with also exhibited a "do it now" attitude, wanting to complete a deal with foreigners as soon as possible rather than planning or expecting future business. Some foreigners found this intriguing, given that in many transition economy cultures, "building relationships" was touted as necessary before doing a deal. Thus, for some foreign managers the attitude of "getting what I can now" smacked of a one-time deal approach, which conflicted with what they had heard about long-term relationships.

However, some (perhaps the more jaded) foreign managers also commented that doing a deal now with a local manager sometimes led to unpleasant fraud and deception. Therefore, many foreign (as well as local) managers developed an attitude of wariness toward overly anxious transition economy entrepreneurs. One local Chinese manager lamented that such tactics fed wrong impressions to foreigners who, once burned, might be reluctant to work with other Chinese.

Likewise, a Russian observed that some countrymen came across as "wolves" and that might put off or worry foreigners:

It is not the easiest time psychologically for foreigners in Russia. I have such feeling . . . for [Russians] who come from other cities, they are like wolves, they whack into it, they want everything, and immediately. They don't have this delicate feeling that a person from Moscow or St. Petersburg, in these real capitals, has.

Some local managers were also reluctant to start a relationship from a position of high trust. Their wariness doubtless stemmed from years of state socialism and the healthy paranoia that reduced their willingness to trust anyone. This apparent unwillingness to trust, make long-term commitments, and be open with information may have had deeper causes and be unique to certain locations. A foreign accounting manager in China encountered reluctance to make long-term commitments, which she saw as related to culture but became, for her, a strongly held stereotype:

They do not understand [looking to the long-term, bigger deal]. They only look at a small deal. They don't build up a long-term relationship[, and this short-term view] is not counterintuitive within China today, but it's counterintuitive, in terms of [Asian] culture in a way. In Japan, for example, and . . . much of Asia, there is more a tendency to look over a long term, but I think maybe the environment here is really endangered.

Interestingly, China is often presented as a society in which long-term relationships are valued; perhaps, given other conditions (i.e., nontransition), those values still hold. However, in the current environment of rapid change, uncertainty, and transformation, the future is more unpredictable, making it more difficult for managers and others to commit (Nguyen, Giang, and Napier 2001).

Of course the differing backgrounds of each party account for many of the characteristics of this early stage of the relationship. In the early stages of transition, local managers were at a serious disadvantage on one hand (i.e., lack of knowledge and experience with market economics) and at an advantage on the other (i.e., working with foreign managers who do not understand the culture or how to do business in a new China). Initially, each is naïve and sophisticated in different ways, and as a result, misunderstandings emerge.

A young Chinese manager was more blunt about underlying reasons for caution and suspicion in commercial transactions.

> After Tiananmen Square, the government came up with new rules regarding students. If you went to school for four years, you have to give back four years. One of the teachers told us, "don't worry." Our government may change the rules tomorrow. By the time you get out of college, the rules may be changed. They don't make laws visible. You don't know what laws are. For example, you show up at the bank to do some transactions. They tell you no; you couldn't do it. Why not? I did it yesterday. No, the law has changed. When was the law changed? 1995. But I did it yesterday. We didn't enforce, but we enforce it today.

In his view, perhaps the history of unpredictable government reaction justified the healthy paranoia common within socialist economies. Both foreign and local managers seemed to move cautiously as they got to know one another—not expecting immediate trust, but hoping that it would develop. In many cases, they were pleasantly surprised, although the trust building may have taken several years.

One local manager of a hotel in Russia said that in the early 1990s, his international hotel brought in about 25 foreign managers to oversee everything from finances to bed making. By early 2002, only five or six foreign managers remained. This pattern, he claimed, was common throughout large foreign businesses in Russia. His view was that the foreigners had developed trust in the local managers' abilities and that the Russians had come to trust the foreigners' knowledge and skills. As each side saw the Russians absorbing the management practices that the hotel's international manager sought to transfer, trust grew.

Withhold Trust

Several interviews with foreign managers, who were at the initial stage of interaction, revealed that they felt they could not trust local managers.

Their attitude seemed to come from two perspectives. First, some managers attributed their lack of trust to their view that local managers lacked knowledge and didn't know how to carry out tasks. As a result, the foreign managers couldn't trust that those activities would be done, or done in the manner that they were accustomed to. For example, one manager of a project in Far East Russia had numerous discussions with Russian managers about his international construction firm's pricing policies. The company was doing work for major international oil companies and for U.S. government agencies. For each sector, the U.S. firm charged fair, not exorbitant, rates. The Russians questioned what seemed to them to be the low prices that the American firm charged its customers, asking the foreign manager, "Why not get all you can? Why not charge as much as the customer will pay you? You can make more money." The American responded by explaining that his firm had worked many years with the oil companies and the government agencies and that the firm wanted to continue to work a long time for both customers. Gouging them would accomplish none of that. According to the foreign manager, the Russians were baffled.

Like the managers who took a wait and see approach, he attributed the Russian comments to lack of knowledge about doing business in a market economy rather than to dishonesty. However, in this manager's case, he never came to fully trust his counterpart.

A second perspective of some foreign managers was simply outright distrust of their local counterparts that went beyond assuming local managers lacked knowledge. A construction company owner who immigrated from the Soviet Union to Canada as a young man returned to do business there regularly since 1984. Despite his cultural and linguistical knowledge, despite having family and friends still in the country, and despite his business success, his attitude about business transactions in Russia is completely clear: don't trust anyone. He said:

> nobody trusts anybody. That's the difficulty there. . . . You know our western way, especially the North American way of doing business, is on trust. . . . When I make a phone call to a supplier, he doesn't doubt me. He starts shipping before I even get the documents to him. . . . If you do that [in Russia], chances are you won't get paid.

Certain situations became lightening rods for their suspicions. Several foreign managers mentioned that in eastern Europe and Russia, as well as in China, they were often advised by their potential business partners (suppliers, customers, alliance, or joint venture partners) to "just trust me." As our previous examples have suggested, that statement does not engender confidence among many foreign managers. Often foreigners interpreted this comment as "Believe me that I can do this; I may work around the corners, I may have to do things in ways that you wouldn't like, but I can get it done."

One senior manager of an international infrastructure firm saw trust in a slightly different light, yet reached the same conclusion—"I'll wait till I see a reason to 'trust' before giving it." He believed that some transition economy managers wanted to be trusted rather than to show that they deserved the trust by performing. Without repeated evidence, he was unwilling to risk trusting local managers.

Some foreign managers cited their impressions and fears that their counterparts were involved in behind-the-scenes activities or were influenced or affected by underworld forces, particularly in Russia. While none had direct proof that their own counterparts were part of organized crime, the media certainly promoted that likelihood (e.g., Harper 1999; Klebnikov 2000). Many managers had impressions that local business owners and managers faced pressures they couldn't discuss. For example, one foreign manager noted that his Russian distributor casually mentioned that the cost of security for his firm had increased and hinted that he was referring to payoffs to the police. In this environment, foreigners were less willing to place full confidence in their counterparts because they sensed that the local managers could not control all of their business conditions.

In other cases, foreign managers felt that too much evidence of corruption existed to move forward on deals. One manager explained that his firm would have had to add a 35 percent extra payment (what he thought of as a bribe) on top of a bid. He refused to do this, and did not bid on the job in Far East Russia. While such requirements may have been declining, some foreign managers continued to be cynical about trusting counterparts.

Local transition economy managers also frequently approached their foreign counterparts with a suspicious attitude. They reported that too often they felt as if they were treated as children, that foreigners held an unspoken attitude of "just watch us, we'll show you how to do it" or of "we came from countries where everything is going well, and we know how to do business." The result was a forced parent-child relationship in which the local manager was relegated to an inferior status even if the foreign manager did not intend to do so. Some foreign managers we interviewed even used the analogy of local managers as children, unskilled and uneducated in the ways of doing business in a global world.

While such managers used the analogy in a way that was forgiving of the local managers' actions or lack of knowledge, clearly the attitude was sensed by the local managers. They reacted accordingly with an attitude of "how can we trust them when they don't respect or trust us?". One frustrated young Russian manager made the following observation:

> When a Russian [young person] is trying to say something [to a foreign manager], especially when he doesn't have so much experience in that field or special education, he will not be considered seriously. [The foreigners will say] "we don't think you can do it. Wait for some time. Better, we will teach you."

According to this manager, the foreigners he worked with did not believe that local managers, especially young ones, had knowledge or skills to carry out a job, so they discounted whatever local managers offered. As a result, trust did not develop.

Both foreign and local managers in transition economies commented that older local managers, particularly those over 50, tended to be more distrustful of foreigners. Growing up and working for most of their careers in an era when capitalism and the market economy were reviled, these managers resented foreigners. In one case, an American manager encountered local managers who commented that America had everything Russia once did but no longer has: a flag, a history, and music. The Russians missed the sense of power and culture they believed their country had, embodied in symbols like the flag and artistic endeavors. These local managers thus started with an entrenched attitude of distrust, built over decades, had to be unlearned or unfrozen before trust could develop.

Experience may also be a primary driver of this attitude of mistrust. In Vietnam, when one of us first met university colleagues, those most suspicious of and resistant to foreigners were the Vietnamese in their 30s and 40s. Having been children during the "American War," these young instructors and managers had been conditioned to believe all foreigners, especially Americans, were evil.

Assume No Trust and Build It

Foreign managers whose views were tempered by experience in developing countries were usually enthusiastic about the chance to work in transition economies. They also tended to be realistic about the risks and frustrations inherent in working in such environments. Several used earlier experiences to fashion a balanced and pragmatic perspective for their approaches to working in transition economies. For example, the senior manager profiled in the chapter vignette used his failure in Poland to revise his approach for China.

Another firm used a measured approach to building trust by showing, through its investment in people, that it expected the relationship to continue and succeed. The firm hired younger, unqualified local staff for senior positions. These local managers then worked with a western manager-mentor for 12 to 18 months. The training program, according to the international firm's managers, exhibited trust in younger people, even when they did not have the requisite educational qualifications or status in the firm. It provided for trust and relationship building in a format that was safe for the firm (since the expatriate managers stayed on site), for the new young managers (since they worked along side experienced mentors), and sent a signal that the firm anticipated it would have local managers who would eventually manage the facility.

An American manager who worked in a battery plant in the Czech Republic used yet another approach. As he reviewed health and safety issues in the plant, he discovered several dangerous features involving the machinery and the production process. When the foreign manager made recommendations ranging from machine guards (to prevent injury to hands and fingers) to respirators (to reduce the likely impact of chemicals and toxins), he couched the recommendations in terms of protecting employees rather than of ways to meet regulations or improve productivity. His approach challenged the expected stereotypes— that the locals were wrong in their approaches and that he (the expert) would show them the right way—that his counterparts might have held. The western manager sought to make no judgments (or at least to exhibit none in front of the local managers) and hoped that the local people would attribute his actions and recommendations to positive, helpful motives. In other words, rather than putting employees and the local managers on the defensive by telling them they were failing to meet international safety standards, he used his interactions to build trust.

Clearly, a repercussion of low initial trust is the cost and time required to build it. A foreign accounting manager in China talked about the tenuous nature of trust:

> They [the Chinese] will do things for you if they like you. If they don't like you, they won't do it, and they just say they can't do it. Building relationships is building trust. When [an American aircraft firm] first came here, it took a long time to build the first airplane because [the Chinese] didn't trust Americans. They were asked to do things the way the Amer-

icans wanted, but rather than doing it, the Chinese ran around and asked everybody "do you think I should do it?" It took a long time to build up that trust. Trust is very important.

COMMUNICATION AND INFORMATION FLOW

Closely related to trust is the nature and way that information flows within a growing relationship. In interactions between managers of transition economies and market economies, communication and information flow is often not smooth. Not only are there cultural differences, but there are also fundamental differences in ways of thinking about business relationships and economic systems.

At this stage of the relationship, each side is in the process of learning how the other thinks. As a result, there are often mishaps as the process exposes misunderstandings and discrepancies in how each perceives the other.

Because both managers are unsure of the way the other will react and of what various forms of communication mean, they are likely more tentative in their information sharing. The managers we interviewed consistently agreed that information flow and communication is not smooth or open at this stage. A young Russian manager put it this way: "If I look at the level of communication, there was not any. But it's difficult psychologically for Russians to talk to people who think that Russia is a backward country. It's difficult for me too."

Managers' concerns about communication at this stage tended to follow similar patterns: Will the information be used against me so that the other side can manipulate me in some way? Is the information I receive accurate? Are they hoarding or withholding important information? The following sections illustrate some of the reactions at this early stage of creating a relationship.

Will the Information Be Used Against Me?

Foreign managers, in particular, often feared that information they provided would be used against them. One manager of a major construction project in Mongolia commented that, given the back channels that were used among local managers, he feared that some of his firm's information (especially about personnel, pricing, and other financial information) would be funneled to competitors. As a result, he, like managers from some of the larger firms we interviewed, commented that he was wary of sharing information on a wide scale.

Another warning signal for foreign managers emerged when they realized the extensive, and often behind the scenes, discussions that occurred between their local counterparts and service providers. For instance, an environmental consultant working in the Czech Republic discovered that even buying photocopies required long discussions about the cost of each page. Rather than having fixed prices for services like secretarial, translation, office, and technical, each service provider wanted to negotiate prices that the consultant found unrealistic. He reasoned that the local managers, who tried to be intermediaries, were still unfamiliar in dealing with foreigners and with market economy practices. As a result, they sought to gain as much financially as they could, for themselves and for the service providers.

Accuracy

A second typical comment from foreign managers was the feeling (often without tangible evidence) that a counterpart manager was "steering" a project or its negotiations from behind the scenes. A foreign manager sent to assess the value of a potential joint venture operation felt that the local Georgian government agent who sought to sell the plant was orchestrating the deal. The foreigner sensed that the local manager had primed people in meetings about what to say to ensure a positive view of the plant. The foreigner discovered that interviewees he spoke to had been paid and that technical consultants or suppliers of services were also paid, quickly and at a lower rate than the foreigner would have expected. He believed that the local manager promised future work to the providers if they worked with him on the potential deal. "It was a chess game for the local manager," he said. "There seemed to be deal making going on—at the government agencies, at the sites, everywhere." As a result, the foreign manager felt that the information he received was suspect and that nothing was as it appeared.

Withholding Information?

Several foreign managers commented on the way local managers seemed to hoard information (even some younger local managers voiced the same sentiment). Other managers commented that the local managers seemed to spend time "seeking resources," whether people, information, or materials for production—just as they had done in the pretransition era.

Other evidence of holding onto resources or information emerged in

China. One manager, commenting on Chinese managers from state-owned enterprises moving to foreign firms, said:

> the two cultures clash like fire and water. The western manager is pushing to meet a deadline or a goal while the Chinese manager is more focused on husbanding his and the company's resources to gain more power . . . the power then [should] lead to more business opportunity and more power.

Other managers commented that in countries outside North America hierarchy plays a major role in information sharing. Slamming his fist on the desk in front of him, a young Russian manager spoke vehemently about older Russian managers who held on to their jobs for status and authority and rarely shared information down the line:

> It's a fear to lose his authority and proof of authority . . . therefore very rarely can you see people from old management who [are] ready to share their concerns with subordinates.

Restriction on information sharing is not surprising, and it fits the pattern of healthy paranoia found under state socialism. Foreign managers reported on the related authoritarian style among their counterpart managers, who often exhibited aggressive behavior toward employees. Therefore, local managers appeared more reserved than their typically more open, less hierarchical western counterparts.

EXPECTATIONS ABOUT LOCAL MANAGERS

All foreigners who worked in transition economies went with expectations about how their counterpart transition economy managers would think, behave, and react. Sometimes their expectations were confirmed; but more often, they discovered surprises as they began to create a relationship with local managers. The reactions to initial expectations of local managers voiced by the foreign managers we interviewed can be grouped into five categories: concerns about the level and type of understanding about western business practices; the perceived uncertainty of some transition economy managers about ways of operating (in emerging market economies); surprise at the education level of local managers and their reaction to western education; the extent of continued government involvement; and the degree to which two-way learning (not just foreign to local manager) occurred.

Many of the reactions stemmed from stereotypic and ethnocentric ex-

expectations that foreign managers held about the level of sophistication of local managers. Because these expectations were founded on small amounts of information of questionable accuracy, they were often wrong. The foreign managers who appeared to have the best initial interactions with their counterparts were able to approach them with nonjudgmental expectations.

Level and Type of Understanding about Western Business Practices

Due to the publicity about transition economies since the early 1990s, the widespread change visible in the cities of transition countries, and the increased emphasis on foreign investment and trade with western countries, many foreign managers expected a high degree of sophistication about western business practices from transition managers.

A housing manufacturer, with extensive experience in Japan and Taiwan during the 1990s, heard about China from experienced business colleagues. In 1999, he decided to visit China to explore doing business there. He was unprepared for what he found. Based on his experiences in Japan and Taiwan, and on all the written reports he'd seen, he was surprised to find less business awareness than he had expected. Furthermore, he was stunned to find a perspective on the part of the Chinese that, in his view, bordered on arrogance about doing business with him and his company.

In contrast, other managers were surprised to discover that some transition economy firms were quite capable of doing business with foreign firms. One foreign manager, whose firm sells lubricants to the automotive industry in the United States, had a major customer in Russia. That customer was very demanding in ways that mirrored some of the U.S. customers. That is, they expected fast turnaround, accurate orders, and very short production time. The Russians further surprised the U.S. manager when they offered to pay for large orders with a credit card!

In other areas, foreign managers were surprised at the general naïveté among local managers about business conditions within their own countries, such as how competitive their firms or countries were. For instance, in Vietnam foreign managers continued to find a belief among local managers that low wage rates were the main advantage Vietnam offered to investors. In reality, as neighboring Cambodia, Laos, or eventually, Myanmar (Burma) become more integrated into the regional economy, they will become the low wage sites, displacing Vietnam. In addition, Vietnamese managers often did not acknowledge the obstacles that waffling government policies had caused in the last decade, making the process of investing and doing business in Vietnam difficult.

Finally, several managers expected, and found, discomfort among local managers with some of the market economic practices that foreigners introduced. Several managers who worked in Mongolia, Poland, Hungary, or Vietnam commented that the local managers were uneasy with notions of employee layoffs, employee evaluation, and performance-based compensation.

Caught Between the Old and the New

Many foreign managers reported that transition economy managers often did not understand or fully incorporate market economic concepts, even several years after transition began. What emerged in some situations, however, was not resistance toward the changes but rather a sense of being in limbo. Transition economy managers seemed caught between pressures to make changes and a form of paralysis based on lack of knowledge or residual socialist norms.

Managers in a Vietnamese, state-owned university, in which the hierarchy and power structure remained based in communist party and collective patterns, encountered the conflicting pressures of "using western practices" and yet being forced to meet local expectations. In this case, the local expectations included involving senior university managers in activities in which they did not make direct contributions. Outsiders often thought this involvement economically unjustifiable. Yet, the Vietnamese managers in the middle had to balance the outsider's expectations or concerns with the internal power structure requirements.

Similarly, local managers in Russia described their management process as no longer "Soviet" and not quite western, but something in between that had yet to be described or understood. They straddled their former modes of operating and tried to blend them with the new expectations. The transition economy managers remained in a quandary about how to move forward. Too many diverse changes are hard for people to absorb and make it difficult for them to determine how to progress. A human resource manager in a large hospitality company in Russia expressed this view of management and the country in late December 2001:

> Soviet management style, I wouldn't say that it was authoritarian . . . it would be too much to say. . . . I mean managers that I met, they could make the "ideas to possess crowds," to say it in words of that time. But it was bad that the imagination of those managers was very limited. There

were some moral boundaries, which weren't appropriate for the moment [i.e., the managers crossed boundaries between right and wrong]. Because of that, the Soviet Union died deeply inside, because in a cultural sense, the society couldn't digest the political power we had. I mean that the political and social structure couldn't digest pop aesthetics, sexual revolution, mass communications, and so on.

Education Level and Reaction to Western Education

Several foreign managers were surprised by and highly impressed with the quality of the technical (engineering and scientific) education that local managers had received in their own countries. Conversely, some local managers were annoyed when their foreign counterparts initially assumed that planned economies had low levels of education.

The low levels of productivity, despite the high levels of training, that foreign managers found did not surprise them. What did surprise some, though, was the extent to which the transition economy managers in some countries were also aware of this low productivity. One manager noted that Hungary in the late 1990s was "more advanced in its transition stage, sensitive to economic influences," and that its wage rate of about 30 percent that of western European countries gave it an advantage. The Hungarians, he discovered, were concerned about losing that advantage since they realized that global competition could not rest upon wage rates as a long-term advantage.

Another observation related to local managers' views about opportunities for education abroad. Many foreigners assumed that the desire for western education would be high throughout transition economies, particularly since local managers would (they assumed) want to understand market economics. Some countries, such as Vietnam and China, do indeed have ambitious young managers wishing to study abroad. However, for those two countries in particular, there is an appallingly high rate of attrition. That is, most students who go abroad never return. The U.S. Embassy in Vietnam claims that the country holds one of the highest nonreturn rates in the world. As a result, even securing student visas is extremely difficult for Vietnamese. Because of the poor return rates, foreign firms that want to support local managers by providing education abroad risk losing employees, and the home country risks losing highly talented young people. Interestingly, the trend may be shifting for China. Increasingly, young people are recognizing that the entrepreneurial opportunities may be greater in China than in the United States, and more are returning (Kahn 2002).

On the other hand, some countries rarely send young people to study overseas. One manager who worked in Russia and Poland commented that, unlike Japan after World War II, transition economies in eastern Europe and Russia have not sent large numbers of young people abroad for education for fear of losing them:

> Maybe it has something to do with culture. The Japanese went home [after their education] because they thought of themselves as second grade [class] citizens in the U.S. They didn't really want to be here. In Russia, it's different. You have to be very careful whom you bring in to train, because if you train them, they will stay in the U.S. They want to stay in the West. To escape. Not to go back there because the whole system has been destroyed and not rebuilt yet.

Continued Government Involvement

Vietnam and China, given their continued single party systems, wrestle with the balance between opening the economy and maintaining the political system. As a result, foreign managers (particularly in Vietnam) have faced constant shifts in policy. Other countries battle government control as well. In Russia, for instance, one of the foreign managers we interviewed found that his major distributor was unable to predict sales resulting from advertising because he never knew how much advertising would actually occur in a given time period. In this case, although the distributor bought advertising spots on television, the government sometimes decided to replace the paid advertising with other programming. Other foreign managers were surprised at the continuing prevalence of the socialist mentality, especially in some organizations in countries such as China where government controls are strong. A foreign manager working in China expressed it this way:

> I believe that there is a distinct "socialist" mentality and an "other" mentality. You can use the term "communism," but I think "socialist ideology" more accurately reflects that description. We tend to think of communism as East German *Stasi* or the iron fist of Stalin. That was China 20 plus years ago and is a part of history, but is not reflective of today. The "other" [mentality] can be capitalism or a market economy. The socialist mentality is pervasive in state-run companies or in government institutions, bureaucracies, universities, etc. Foreign companies, joint ventures, and "forward" thinking Chinese companies attract people from the "other" mentality.

Two-Way Learning

Finally, some foreign managers commented that they realized learning could go both ways, even in the early stages of creating a relationship. For example, as foreign managers began to learn the environments in which they wanted to do business, they saw obstacles that could kill a deal, whereas their local counterparts saw those same obstacles as ones to work around. Local managers understood, from their pretransition days, that they needed methods to work "around the edges," of ways to get work done that foreign managers in many countries would not be aware of.

In Vietnam, for example, where foreign managers saw a path as being from *A* to *B,* Vietnamese managers (sometimes with a snakelike weaving of their arms) suggested that maybe another route—one outside formal channels—would work better at first. Often there was a liaison or co-ordinator of those informal outside discussions. As foreigners began to understand the methods in a particular country, they often realize the need for a "cultural interpreter" to handle the coordination tasks.

Some local managers commented that benefits came to both sides when foreigners realized they could learn from their local counterparts. As one young Russian manager saw it, an unexpected outcome could be managers reaching a goal, what he called "to a common pleasure":

> [The Russians] learned to be purposeful, since western management is so oriented towards a positive result. In Russia . . . before [transition], a positive result wasn't so important. . . . A consistency in achievement of a positive result, an insistence, and an ability to name your goal and go to it . . . these are the most important things that I as a Russian manager learned from foreign specialists. At the same time, foreign specialists have appreciated the ingenuity, talent, and creativity of Russians in achieving this result . . . it enriches such cooperative activities and lets managers reach a goal to a common pleasure.

EXPECTATIONS ABOUT FOREIGN MANAGERS

Interactions between foreign and local managers flow or jerk along, in part depending upon what each side expects about the other. This is especially true in the early days of getting to know each other. Just as the foreigners had assumptions and expectations about the local managers, the reverse was also true. This section discusses some of the typical expectations (accurate and not) about foreign managers. Three expectations were particularly apparent: a belief that foreigners were naïve about local business practices; a perception of foreigners as romantics; and the negative stereotypes common of out-group members.

Naïveté and Lack of Local Knowledge

Our research suggested that local managers often viewed foreigners as being naïve about or lacking knowledge of local business conditions. They often perceived these traits as overbearing, which created friction. Sometimes the foreign managers were unaware that they were behaving in a naïve way; sometimes they realized that they did not understand local conditions or that they were not functioning well and became frustrated. As one Russian manager put it:

> The idea is that western managers can "better sell but they buy worse in Russia," because they have different standard of price and they think that price that they pay for something is a good price. But we think that it's too high. And besides, they can't check into proposals that are made to them [for accurate information]. Generally they buy something by mistake if they try to [buy] on their own. From personnel to equipment, they don't know how everything is happening here.

Aspects of local customs often frustrated foreign managers. The facts of life in transition economies became issues that created much stress for foreign managers, even something as mundane as traffic. From a Russian manager who worked with a U.S. manager:

> [My foreign manager] was getting frustrated because the Russians drive very quickly. The traffic lights haven't changed but a car flow [starts] and other drivers are beeping. . . . It was offending for my supervisor because in his own country, he was always a number one. He was offended when someone starts going before him at a crossing.

Romantics

In the early years of the 1990s, transition economies attracted their share of adventurers—curious about what was happening in Russia, or Vietnam, or Hungary. Local managers sometimes classified those early arrivals as romantics (those looking for adventure or quick deals), or pioneers and idealists (looking for ways to help the newly transforming economies). Some came for the trophy aspect, the "I've been in Romania before anyone else" status. Others were just curious, as a Russian manager discovered:

the first people who came to Russia, they were absolutely crazy "romantics," because it was crazy to go to Russia at that time. . . . They came not because of professional development, but for a "Trophy." When I started working [at this international firm], we met several New Zealand managers who came here and said, "We just want to know what's going on in this area, even not in a professional sense, but in a general 'what is happening here' sense."

The situation in Vietnam mirrored that in other transition economies. In the early 1990s, foreigners who arrived were the few transferred by their firms (i.e., to open a sales office, to set up a law firm's branch) or those seeking business opportunities (e.g., to set up a real estate development firm or a training and recruiting firm). Still others came to support Vietnamese government ventures that were developing infrastructure and regulatory or human capacity for the market economy (e.g., developing the forestry industry, creating a new legal system, working with universities to train faculty members and build programs). A few came looking for ways to make big money. In Vietnam, they tended to be the *Viet Kieu*, returning Vietnamese who had fled the country following the war with America. They had become successful and wanted to return to help remaining family members and to do business. People who returned to home countries to make big money, including making money from aid funds (Wedel 1998), were a phenomena in other countries as well.

Many of the early arrivals to transition economies had been successful elsewhere, holding corporate jobs in North America, Australia, or Europe. They sought some way to contribute in what they perceived to be an interesting country. Many underestimated the difficulties and risks of doing business in such unpredictable and chaotic environments. Some succeeded, and some gave up and left. The reaction of a Russian manager is typical: "Disappointed 'romantics' said, 'It's impossible to live here; it's awful here; it's bad here, although there are some positive sides." Others left as conditions improved when they felt the conditions were becoming too soft: "Those 'romantics' cooled down here, as everything started to get a shape of a civilized business."

Negative Stereotypes

In many cases, most often in Asia where western foreigners stand out more, local managers and employees sometimes exhibited behavior that indicated the negative stereotype they held about foreigners. While foreign managers sometimes expected that their backgrounds (e.g., being able to speak the language, having a heritage from the country) might be helpful, sometimes the opposite turned out to be true. A Chinese-American woman whose family runs a real estate development firm in Shanghai found that being bilingual was an advantage, but that her Chinese appearance was not:

> When working with my clients, because I look Chinese, [I have problems]. The local people here have a very funny way of looking at Chinese girls. They know there are a lot of prostitutes here in Shanghai. Even most prostitutes have daytime jobs. Some of them have a master's or Ph.D. degree. [They can be] very highly educated prostitutes, and expensive, too. So when I go out with my clients showing properties or for . . . dinner, the local Chinese give me a funny look. That makes me very uncomfortable. During a client dinner once, I even had somebody come toward me and ask me for a night!

Similarly, foreign managers quickly learned the slang that classified people into in-groups and out-groups. In an example from China:

> Banana is for people like me. Yellow [Chinese looking] outside and white [from America] inside. Egg is the other way around. Like my boyfriend, he is white outside and yellow inside. You can be any color egg. In China, we have the soy egg (it's brown and yellow) or the rubber egg (they call that thousand-years egg). We have some overseas Chinese. They are just yellow. We have another egg white group, too. They are new in town.

The manager went on to clarify Chinese views of non-Chinese:

> They are afraid of them. They are like ghosts to [the Chinese]. In Chinese ghost stories, ghosts are black-skinned. [And they don't like black people]. Even in the [United] States, when you go out to downtown LA at midnight, when you see black people, you grab your purse. . . . You will be very cautious here, too. [For Chinese], it really depends on which country you are coming from. They don't treat Mexicans as nice as Americans. They have their priorities.

SUMMARY

In the early stages of a relationship, transition economy and foreign managers are somewhat tentative as they establish interpersonal and task-related boundaries. Some assume that trust will come, that they can build it, and are nonjudgmental upon entering a relationship. Others, who may have had earlier unpleasant experiences in similar countries or situations, may hold extremely negative assumptions, stereotypes, or beliefs about counterparts, making it difficult and even more time-consuming to build a relationship. Their approaches to information sharing and communication closely reflect attitudes of trust. Managers—both local and foreign—often base communication and information sharing on previously established status relationships or stereotypic expectations. Managers often worry that information will be kept from them, used against them, or used to manipulate them.

Foreign managers' expectations of transition economy managers often involve low levels of knowledge about western business practices or an inability to make decisions. These often flow from inaccurate expectations about the level and sophistication of local education. Foreigners also sometimes misjudge local managers' views on going abroad for education. North Americans, especially, expect that all locals want to study abroad where they believe western education to be better. Finally, foreign managers are often surprised that they can learn from their local counterparts.

Locals also have expectations about their foreign manager counterparts, including their naïveté and lack of knowledge about the local situation. These expectations have developed over the years as many foreigners ("romantics") come with enthusiasm and profit in their eyes only to realize that doing business in transition economies is more challenging than they expected.

The results of our investigation, presented in this chapter, suggest that this early stage of the interaction between forcign and local managers in transition economies is characterized by a testing of the relationship, but with behavior based on past experiences and stereotypic expectations. Low initial levels of trust are common. The flow of communication is based on initial perceptions, particularly with regard to status. As individuals test the basis of the relationship, opportunities for conflict develop. The manifestation of this inherent conflict is the subject of the next chapter.

Chapter 7

CRITIQUE: SURPRISES AND FRUSTRATIONS

When there are two conflicting versions of a story, the wise course is
to believe the one in which people appear at their worst.
                              —H. Allen Smith, journalist (1907–76)

A consultant, who had years of experience in Russia, stormed into the office in
Hanoi one morning. She'd been hired to train small- and medium-sized business
owners in human resource management issues—how to hire, select, train, ap-
praise, and pay people using market-oriented approaches rather than the
seniority-based system they were used to. She worked closely with a Vietnamese
cotrainer, who also had many years of experience teaching, training, and consulting for Vietnamese state-owned and private firms.

The consultant had joined the project because of her extensive experience
living and teaching in another country going through transition, where she'd
gotten rave references from her foreign supervisors and from the Russian managers she'd worked with. But the cross-cultural and adjustment problems she
experienced in Vietnam mounted over the months. She rattled off her most
recent complaints about teaching with her partner and dealing with training
course participants:

"I've taught this course 12 times—in Russia, in the Ukraine, and in the United
States. It's always worked before. But here they want answers, they want me to
tell them the right answer, even when there isn't one. They want structure, they
want to know where this course is going, where a discussion is going. I want
to encourage discussion and thinking, and they don't see that.

"And my partner! The other day, he asked me to write on the board for him—what does he think I am, a secretary? Then one day he tells this story about 'beautiful ladies' in a company and how important it is to have them around—doesn't he *know* that stuff is illegal to talk about? He lectures and uses slides, so old-fashioned. I'm trying to use new methods, new ways to reach the students with metaphors, with cases, and he wants to lecture! And today, he didn't think the students were happy, that they didn't understand what I was doing. I can't understand it, I ran the whole day alone, and I thought it was perfect."

The Vietnamese cotrainer had his own view of their partnership.

"She wants to do things her way, and doesn't listen to my ideas. This is hard because her approach uses metaphors, which are common in Vietnamese, but difficult for participants (and me) to understand in English and in the way she means. It took me two weeks to understand what she was doing; maybe the managers do not follow what she says.

"One day I asked her to write on the board for me because the students used some words that I didn't know how to spell quickly in English. But she refused, and I lost face. I told a story one day about ladies, and she lost her temper. She told me that she would not talk in such ways in the United States because there are laws against it. That is true there, but here we do not have these laws. Maybe I was wrong to use the story, but she was wrong to be so angry. Then she said that the projector was outdated technology and that I should not use it—and she said this in front of the managers. Yesterday, I said there might be some problems with the course; she said, 'No, it was a perfect day.' I don't know how to work with her."

The critique stage of relationship development between foreign and local managers is characterized by detailed review of what works, and often yields to conflict and polarization in interpersonal interactions. The shock of confronting the reality of the situation can result in highly emotional responses from both parties. Participants start questioning their perceptions of the situation, and can become confused by the behavior that they observe in the other party. In some cases they erect defenses that stall relationship development.

The vignette about the two trainers in a state-owned university in Vietnam is characteristic of this stage of relationship development. Their differences in culture, age, perspectives, and knowledge about business and training contributed to how the conflict, which was inherent in the situation, became manifest. The relationship moved from one of cooperative accomplishment, to a frustrating critique of the interactions, and ultimately, to a serious misunderstanding and disharmony between two people. During the course of the disagreement, each person went to trusted outsiders to report perceptions and complaints, to look for support, and at least on the surface, to ask for advice about how to interact. Rather than resolving the discord themselves, they withdrew from their relationship and tried to teach the class of managers in parallel rather than together. Trust dissolved, and they no longer exchanged information in an open and honest way. Further, they heard and saw only the worst information about one another as their ability to perceive accurately deteriorated. Their expectations of each other soon turned from neutral or optimistic to negative and intransigent.

As the vignette suggests, at some point in relationships between local and foreign managers, the direction of the relationship can shift dramatically. The relationship may progress in a relatively positive manner for a long time. It can be several years, a matter of months, or within the time span of negotiations before something serious happens. However, as parties begin to review and critique the relationship and their interactions with counterparts, they often experience frustration and discouragement. Such experience can cause individuals to seek a new direction or new methods of interacting (e.g., Gersick 1989). Our interviews suggested that part of the disharmony between local and foreign managers is the normal course of culture shock and related events, where each side finds faults and cracks in the other and in their interactions.

One manager with experience in both developing and transition economies has seen a pattern between local and foreign managers who work together over time. Often, after two or three years of working closely together, the two groups of managers developed what he called apathy toward one another. Their daily work life became routine, as managers took each other, their work, and their motivation for granted. Sometimes they lost interest in trying to learn from each other or to find new and better ways to be efficient or effective. He noticed that local managers commented that foreign managers excluded them from discussions and decision making, acting without significant input from the local managers. This exclusion emerged even after months or years of the foreign managers seeking such input. Our interviewee observed that perhaps the local managers' dismay stemmed in part from their gaining more expertise and hence expecting to have more say and responsibility. As the foreign managers became more demanding and less willing to relinquish responsibility, friction arose.

Furthermore, the manager noticed that after a few years of working in a developing or transition economy country, foreign managers began to wear down, becoming weary of the working and living conditions. The manager commented that "sometimes these [developing and transition economy countries] get to them, they 'close down' and deal only with other expatriates or with the most senior local managers." This reaction also fits with the notion of the culture shock downward cycle as managers face the realities and frustration of living abroad. In transition economies, according to Feichtinger and Fink (1998), a similar process takes place for the country. It may take decades instead of months, but the pattern of curiosity and desire to succeed, followed by despair and slow recovery to a stable state, parallels the human experience.

This chapter examines the types of changes—in trust, sharing of information, and expectations—that can occur as local and foreign managers take stock of their relationship and interactions. Often, the interactions between transition economy managers and their foreign counterparts leads to friction, sometimes overt, sometimes more subtle. Equally often the critique stage leads to a change in the direction of relationship development.

TRUST

When managers began to confront the reality of the relationship, the shock was often expressed in lower trust. Often each group felt deceived in some way. They responded with three types of behavior. First, often the foreigners feared that local managers were trying to manipulate them (e.g., into a deal, into believing or doing things that the foreigner was uncomfortable pursuing). Second, the managers often felt betrayed when they perceived that their counterparts changed behavior unexpectedly or backed out of an agreement. Third, some local managers often saw their counterparts make mistakes that jeopardized the understanding and harmony between the two sides. Sometimes it was a cultural error, other times a lack of understanding of local business conditions. Unfortunately, the result of the breakdown in trust often led to defensive behavior in which each group blamed the other and refused to see the counterpart's viewpoint.

Fear of Manipulation

Foreign managers reported that they sometimes worried that local managers were trying to "put something over," or "make a deal behind my back." For example, a construction firm manager working in Mongolia feared that local partners would pass information along to competitors about his firm's pricing, wages, materials, and the like. As his unease grew, the foreign manager became more reluctant to share financial, costing, and personnel information. Still he was aware that his reluctance to share information affected the relationship, and he never felt completely at ease with his partners. This mistrust, he realized, created an ongoing low level of friction.

Negotiations, the first stage of many relationships, often started on a positive note but faced discord later, also due to fear of manipulation. A general manager of a housing firm wanted to set up a distributorship in China in the late 1990s. When he and his partner began negotiations, they worked with three Chinese (two men and a woman) whom they initially assumed were the buyers and decision makers for the deal. One of the Chinese men spoke English and called himself a facilitator. However, he conferred with the Chinese couple before giving information or presenting an offer to the Americans. The Americans quickly learned that as the middleman shuttled information and quotes between the foreign managers and the Chinese customers he added a percentage on each quote for himself. The Americans' Chinese-speaking secretary (who did not look Chinese and spoke no Chinese during meetings) reported on the discussions that the facilitator had with the non-English speaking Chinese couple. The foreigners, confronted by this reality, and feeling they had been manipulated, broke off discussions and walked away from the deal.

An environmental consultant who worked on projects in the Czech Republic (1993) and Georgia (1998) had similar experiences. He went into the projects expecting difficult conditions but also hoping to help each country move forward. In each project, his role was to assess the financial and environmental conditions (e.g., likely cleanup costs) and to give clients a recommendation about whether to pursue a deal. In the Czech Republic, the client was an American corporation considering the purchase of a plant; in Georgia, a U.S. governmental agency sought confirmation about the wisdom of building an oil processing facility, in part to help spur the Georgian economy. In both cases, the American felt his efforts were thwarted, if not sabotaged, by local counterparts at various steps in his assessment. When he went into meetings, he sensed that his counterpart had told participants what to say to try to convince him that the plants had no serious problems. That is, he felt meetings and discussions were orchestrated to present a positive image about the possible future business and relationships. He felt manipulated. As a result, he began to filter out disconfirming information. That is, he began to use selective avoidance by discounting information that did not fit the expectations he developed. Thus, his expectations of the level of trust became a self-fulfilling prophecy.

The same manager became even more frustrated when he realized that local managers had little knowledge about international standards and yet wanted to argue with him about what was acceptable or not. For example, the manager encountered a local Czech manager who was incensed when he thought that the American consultant was questioning his qualifications and understanding of geology. Likewise, a senior local manager in Georgia tried to convince the consultant that the oil firm would meet international standards for operations, production quality, and output even though the Georgian had never been outside his country, and the American believed, would have had little exposure to what international customers expected.

During his investigation on the feasibility of building the oil processing plant in Georgia, he became nervous about the government agency in which he worked. When the foreigner asked for oil samples, for instance, his local counterpart quickly identified and subcontracted the work to a local drilling firm. The American felt uncomfortable because to him it felt . . . "[too] slick and easy to get it arranged . . . [there were] no problems in the contracting or financial arrangement." The foreign manager learned later that his local counterpart, a senior politically appointed manager, "carried weight with a privatized association of geological survey people and maybe that's how [the local manager] worked it through the other side." Although unable to confirm his suspicions, the consultant continued to feel something was amiss and was not able to trust his counterpart. Eventually, he recommended that the U.S. agency not pursue the business opportunity.

Finally, some foreign managers seemed overwhelmed by the fear of manipulation or of not understanding the local conditions. In these cases positive outcomes were rare. Sometimes local managers ignored the foreigners; sometimes the foreign manager simply gave up and left or withdrew from the situation. One Russian manager spoke of the conditions he saw in 2002 that could generate misunderstandings and friction.

I really think that in such conditions a Russian is a very serious danger for foreigners here. The flexibility of Russians will be lost at this stage [if the relationship does not improve]. Before, we were such open and sincere hedgehogs [sic], ready to get pushed and squeezed; everything was interesting . . . everything was new. And now Russian traditions, Russian business, a notion of a good Russian manager are getting formed. Especially since we have [examples of some] very successful ones, and their stories are in everyone's mouth.

I think it will be very difficult for foreigners. I can see that my supervisor has been already experiencing some problems. I mean he wasn't able to fight with them. . . . He couldn't do it. He wasn't able to understand it. He was getting scared, and Russians were manipulating him, and he couldn't do anything about it.

Feelings of Betrayal and Shifts in Behavior

A second observation about relationships at this stage was that some foreign managers became frustrated when they felt the local managers reneged on a deal or agreement. These responses were laden with emotion. Managers raised questions about the motivation of their counterparts and felt betrayed by what they perceived to be shifts in behavior. The inability to accurately assess the cause of this behavior led to a reliance on stereotypes to guide future interactions. For example, a foreign manager working in China in the mid 1990s felt misled when the Chinese vendor changed the deal at the last minute.

Two years ago, we had a contract; the cost was U.S.$45 for a dozen. Two days before they go to ship, [the Chinese said] "No it can't be 45 dollars, too low. We want 10 dollars more per dozen." The goods were going to [be shipped the next day] so at first we said, "No, we wouldn't do it."

However, we [later] renegotiated the deal, and I said, "I'll pay an extra 50 percent of what you want." He agreed. But when it came time for him to pay the factory, he deducted [the amount of money he sent them]. [The Chinese] get you no matter which way you turn. They just squeeze you. . . . Contract on a piece of paper doesn't mean anything.

This manager's similar experience with the Chinese on at least two other occasions led her to conclude that she would never be able to trust the Chinese.

Not all issues relating to trust dealt with perceptions of the behavior of transition economy counterparts. For example, the key managers of an automotive lubricant product in the United States met several times with the CEO of a Russian distributor during the early 1990s. The CEO led the Americans to believe that his firm would place a major order with them. The order never materialized, and the Americans discovered later that the order went to the Russian firm's existing (Russian) vendor. The Americans were shocked since they thought they had the CEO's word on the deal. In fact, the Russian firm's purchasing manager had overridden the CEO's decision and instead had given the order to the existing vendor. In this case, the Russian CEO lost face with his potential American suppliers. He later demanded that his purchasing manager switch to the American firm for the following year's order. The two firms have since become strong partners, although the Americans have remained wary of the Russian purchasing manager.

Cultural Errors and Lack of Knowledge

A third way that trust broke down between transition economy and foreign managers was when one side made an error, often because of an inaccurate attribution, which led to a lack of trust. Often this happened when foreign managers were unaware of the implications of questioning local managers' judgment or abilities. For example, a foreign manager working on a project to build a hospital told us that he had worked for months to build trust among local managers and employees. He then invited a manager from another, well-regarded American firm to help increase awareness among employees about safety issues on construction sites. In a matter of moments, the foreign safety expert destroyed the trust and credibility that had taken so much time to build.

> The safety person came to town, and at a big meeting of all employees, he asked to say a few words. I asked him to tell the interpreter what he would say and told him "don't surprise the interpreter" and encouraged him to say very little and *not* go into lots of details. The guy stood up, hands on hips, and pointed to the man on the floor in front of him.
> "How would you like to lose a foot?" The man sitting in the audience, the translator—*no* one understood where this was going. Then the safety expert said "Sell me your hand. What's it cost?" The whole thing was a disaster. I tried to do damage control. . . . [It] took months for the safety guy to realize he'd blown it, no one listened to him in meetings, employees avoided him.

The local managers and employees were not just baffled, they were angry. The foreign safety expert's actions confirmed their stereotypes of the aggressive Americans they saw in movies and heard about from colleagues. In this case, a single event undercut the other foreign manager's efforts to build trust and credibility.

It is, however, not always easy to predict the effect of culturally inappropriate behavior. For example, in Vietnam an American known for being enthusiastic and emotional had periodic outbursts in meetings with his Vietnamese counterparts. While the Vietnamese despised similar behavior by other foreigners, they accepted this American's outbursts of anger. Their rationale was philosophical. They said they knew that when this American exploded, he was "upset for us and with us, not at us."

Thus, they accepted normally inappropriate behavior from someone whom they had come to trust.

In another example, a young Russian manager watched his expatriate boss fall apart during the year they worked together, as the expectations and trust that the Russian thought they had developed withered away. As the foreign manager's enthusiasm declined and he became less tolerant, the Russian manager's attitudes changed as well, as he described:

> The foreign manager was quite optimistic at the start of the project, but as we were discovering all the technical problems which required his attention and taxed his understanding of some things like transformation of Russian realities . . . he felt down, depressed very quickly, and the work went worse and worse. At our level we were doing a lot, but as it was getting up to some level, it didn't go further. The work was getting worse; our manager couldn't process in time the work we did for our top management, saying that "it's impossible to do anything in Russia, it's a wretched country, and nothing is understandable here, it's impossible to do business here," and so on.

For several months, the young Russian tried to ignore the weaknesses he saw in his expatriate boss. In the early 1990s, shortly after the breakup of the Soviet Union, foreigners were considered experts. The young Russian wanted to believe that his American boss could overcome his emotions and show the local managers and employees how to get the work done. That is, he selectively avoided information that disconfirmed his expectations. Ultimately, he eventually lost faith and trust in the foreign manager as he watched the foreigner's frustration grow.

Also the mindless, semiautomatic behavior of foreign managers sometimes created the conflict and resistance to building trust that is common at this stage of relationship development. For example, foreign managers or their headquarters' managers were often mistaken in their assessment of the local labor, were perceived to not take their local counterparts seriously, or treated them as second class citizens within the firm. This was especially hard for the locals to take when headquarters sent poorly prepared or less competent expatriates to run their offices. Local managers often felt they could have done a better job. The foreigners' scripted semireflexive behavior sent signals to the locals that they did not trust or respect them. A Russian manager described such a situation:

> [I]f a western company opens a representative office, the headquarters sends here not the best employees for the top positions. Meanwhile Russian managers will never get these positions . . . although they could be

much brighter. So there is a dilemma, even if a Russian manager is one thousand times better, and he knows more, he will never get that position. Even if he gets it, he will never get a chance to work in other branches of this international company as we are [perceived as] a third world country.

INFORMATION SHARING AND COMMUNICATION

The confusion and questioning about communication and information sharing is characteristic of this stage of relationship development. However, communication is fundamental to creating and keeping trust between foreign and transition economy managers. Some foreign managers seemed suspicious of their local counterparts. Others attributed the lack of information flow to cultural or historical causes, including remnants of socialism. For example, a regional marketing director for a major U.S. pharmaceutical firm operating in China speculated that, under communism, leaders hoarded information as a form of power. With no tradition of sharing information with employees, let alone with foreign partners, the system lacked transparency in many areas, such as business plans or management succession plans. This foreign manager acknowledged, however, that Chinese managers may simply not have had the information that foreigners needed or wanted.

A result of the decline in communication was often a move toward a them-versus-us attitude. Several of the foreigners admitted that when they thought that the local managers were holding back information, were not pulling their weight, or were unwilling to play a fair game, they withdrew from the interaction. Local managers saw unprepared or frustrated foreign managers who resisted working with them or made assumptions that their actions were manipulative when they had no such intentions.

Beyond intuitive feelings that managers had about how a relationship was changing, some managers monitored more mundane but informative changes, such as language use. For example, in Vietnamese, two phrases refer to *we*. There is *we (trung toi)* as in "we on our side" wish to do something and "you on your side" wish to do something. There is a second form of *we,* however, that refers to "we together, working as a group or team" *(trung ta)* that means the two sides are pulling together in the same direction. In this case, small indicators, along with more intangible feelings, helped foreign managers to recognize shifts in their interactions.

EXPECTATIONS ABOUT LOCALS

In the previous contact stage of relational development, transition economy and foreign managers often seemed willing to suspend judgment about the other. In the critique stage, as they encountered conflict, resistance, and uncertainty, each side seemed more sensitive and alert to the behavior that emerged. Their expectations of each other also shifted, sometimes subtly, as they worked to resolve interpersonal and task interactions.

While perceptions and expectations about local managers ranged widely, several triggers were common among the managers we interviewed. For example, foreigners often became frustrated that transition economy managers avoided risk taking, that they sometimes resisted taking on a customer orientation (as the foreigners saw it), or that they tried to tell the foreigners (who were sometimes the vendors) how to run their businesses. Furthermore, foreign managers took offense when local managers sometimes expected "payments" that fit local conditions or culture or acted in ways that foreigners felt showed they were not team players.

Avoiding Risk

One of the key characteristics of transition economy managers has been a general reluctance to take risks. While many foreign managers we interviewed admitted that they had expected this, some were unprepared for the extent to which this characteristic affected them. One manager from an infrastructure firm with experience in East Germany just after the Berlin Wall fell, as well as in Romania, Poland, Estonia, Russia, and Mongolia, found this pattern of behavior in each place. He remembered his initial reaction when he encountered this learned helplessness immediately after 1989 in East Germany and much later from Polish managers who continued to act as they had under socialism, even late into the 1990s.

> They called themselves "gray mice." They didn't want to be noticed, just wanted to make the quota that came from central government and not to be noticed beyond that. They didn't want to expose themselves—if they stood out in good or bad ways—to the hardships that would come or to the secret police. They weren't risk takers, wanted to keep the old system and job-for-life approach.

When these same managers were unable or unwilling to adjust to the practices regarding plant productivity (i.e., layoffs) and production improvements introduced by their partner firm, the American manager eventually fired them.

Customer Orientation

Some foreign managers reported that they became frustrated at the attitude of local managers toward customer service. The foreigners saw it as disdain toward doing business with them as customers. An accounting manager with a large American manufacturing firm in China felt frustrated and helpless with her Chinese supplier's reaction:

> In the West, we understand the customer is always right. The customer comes first. In China, it's not that way. It's opposite. Although we are the customers, we have to do what the vendors should be doing. For example, if I go to a vendor to buy something, he should be glad that I come. First of all, I shouldn't be going in, he should be looking for me. But in China, you have to look for him. He should be happy that he has a customer. No, he isn't. He says, "*No,* I don't really need you." If you know the person, you know he needs some money under the table. He might do a deal with you, only give you so much. He says "You have to prove to me how good you are." Even if he gives you so much, and you have the contract, he can break the contract any minute.

In another case, a manager bristled when he felt his Russian customer tried to tell him how to run his business. This began after the Russian manager uncovered a mistake on the American firm's shipping order. Even though the Americans corrected the order, his Russian customer continued to insist that the American firm should take action against the person who made the mistake.

> We sent a crate to the Russian company, and the Russian purchasing manager thought that we should have fit 20 more cases on the freight shipment. It was a mistake—once a packer miscounted on an order, put in less than what the company said was shipped, and the purchasing manager got *all* upset and asked "whose fault is it?" He wanted us to *fire* the packer. We said "it was a mistake," but the Russian wouldn't accept that behavior and kept going on about firing the guy. So next time, we put more onto the shipment.

Later, the foreign manager visited the Russian operation and saw how the local manager treated his own employees. After observing the hierarchical and authoritarian approach, the foreign manager understood the demand to "fire the packer." However, the friction between the two firms remained.

Expectations of Payments

Some foreign managers were frustrated at the constant expectation of payments—whether higher than what they felt was a reasonable market rate or beyond what a particular contract or job would demand. The expectation arose in several countries, ranging from Poland to China to Far East Russia. When local managers demanded payment or fees above the bid price on work, some of the foreigners refused to pay; others paid, but they were not happy about it. As a real estate developer in Shanghai described, this expectation is often accommodated:

Today I had a client who complained about what he sees as harassment in the security of the building. The security guards stand in front of the building and ask everyone who enters a lot of questions. . . . My client said, "Well, wait a minute. Shanghai is very safe; I don't want to be interrogated every time I go home, and I don't want my guests to be asked questions." . . . So I . . . [asked the building manager to tell the security guards] not to ask questions for people who come into this unit. They said "No! If we do that, and something happens in the building, we have no way to track it." In Chinese terms, this is security. But in western terms, it is invasion of privacy. So I brought cigarettes and chocolates to the office staff and asked them to ask the guards to say "hello" [to guests] and . . . do it with smile. I didn't want to do this myself, so I always asked my staff to do it. But if I bring them more gifts and goodies, then they will ask for more.

Adapting to the local behavior is common among managers trying to accomplish tasks in foreign environments. One manager commented that when she vacationed in the United States and told her friends about her work in China, she was horrified to realize that she had begun to take for granted the notion of paying extra to get things done.

The first thing that came to my mind, even when I needed to get something done in the United States, was the kind of goodies we should give them. I don't think I can survive in the real world outside of China because all I can think of is how to bribe.

Team Player Mentality

A key cultural dimension involved in interpersonal interactions is whether a society is collectivist or individualist. For example, are people more comfortable in groups or in striking out on their own; do they seek rewards that single out individuals or that promote and strengthen group efforts?

Many managers who worked in Asia—China and Vietnam or Far East Russia or Mongolia—expected to find that the group was important in how their counterpart managers behaved and viewed their jobs. Furthermore, many foreign managers initially assumed that collective societies with formerly socialist structures (or currently communist structures, like China and Vietnam) would hold that groups were key. They assumed that *groups* and *collectivism* were the analogous and that this would mean an easy transition to using the concept of teams. Foreign managers faced a surprise—and unexpected frustration—when they discovered this was not so (Vu and Napier 2000).

Part of the misunderstanding and frustration emerged from cultural views of an individual's position in society. In America, where individualism reigns, managers and employees think of themselves as individuals first, not as members of some group(s). When they form a team, they join with other individuals to achieve a common goal. The team members may or may not be people who know one another well, who have worked together before, or who care to know one another socially. Instead, their focus is on using the resources, skills, and knowledge of the team members to accomplish something bigger than themselves.

However, in much of Asia, including transition economies of China and Vietnam, people see themselves as group members first. People may belong to several groups—family, village, circle of school friends, or colleagues in a firm. One's identity then stems largely from being in or out of the group. For Vietnamese, for example, team is a concept outside that definition, hence outside the cultural norm. In fact, most Vietnamese would not accept the idea of being taken from one group to form another with people who may be unknown to them and of spending limited and intense time with those members as they tackle a task. Vietnamese sometimes say they feel "wrenched" from their group when they are forced into a new, unknown circle or team. Some call the entity a "group called team" since they have no clear word for it in Vietnamese.

The outcome in a business setting where foreigners expect results from teams may be difficult to predict. Vietnamese in "groups called teams" have no background or expectations about what to do. Whereas American teams will meet, form an identity, and act, Vietnamese "groups called teams" will have no such expectations. Instead, the individual local managers or employees will try to solve a problem separately, might discuss it together briefly, but often cannot decide, as a team, how to solve or address some issue.

Several of the managers we interviewed faced similar issues with "nonteams" in other transition economies. Managers found differences in getting people to understand the benefits of teams (versus groups). However, several managers also confirmed what Vu and Napier (2000) found in their discussions with Vietnamese and foreigners working in Vietnam: some younger managers—in Vietnam and elsewhere—seemed to be rebelling against the notion of the collective or group. As the market economy has become stronger and people see more opportunities, some of the younger managers have found ways to look out for themselves, rather than adhering to the strict rules of sacrificing for the common good. The implications for teams may be unclear at present, but until those same younger people look at each other as having skills and resources that can be pooled, the notion of teams, as foreigners perceive it, may continue to be a concept with different expectations for foreign and local managers.

EXPECTATIONS ABOUT FOREIGNERS

The lack of harmony in the local and foreign manager interactions at this stage often stemmed from inaccurate or unmet expectations about foreigners. Local managers told how their expectations about foreigners had changed or how they were surprised and irritated when these expectations were not confirmed in reality. Foreign managers mentioned the disappointment that they felt when they were unable to adjust to situations, even after months of working in a transition economy. In the following section, we discuss each of these perspectives.

Local Manager Expectations about Foreigners

Many transition economy managers continued to be wary of foreigners because of a history of national conflict. Suspicion also existed because of a sense that some foreign experts used transition economy countries as economic guinea pigs in the early 1990s. Because many transition economies had little experience with foreigners, they assumed their international expertise, knowledge, and advice would help their countries progress. Based on such a belief, the locals did not raise questions when several western economists approached the transition economies almost as experiments, suggesting a range of policies from shock treatment to gradual change.

It is now clear that many of those policies subsequently failed (Galbraith 2002). For example, in the first years of Russia's transition, well-known

Harvard professors frequently offered wide-ranging advice on economic and financial issues (Soulsby and Clark 1996; Wedel 1998). Unfortunately, much of the work over several years was disregarded when those same professors were found guilty of using inside information to generate large financial gain for themselves. Given such failures, some transition economy managers felt they were deceived by trusting the experts. As a result, they became more skeptical, even antagonistic toward outsiders (Galbraith 2002).

Furthermore, some local managers felt an arrogance or xenophobic attitude from foreigners, making communication difficult between the groups. One young Russian manager working for an international accounting firm found that dealing with all-knowing foreigners was hard. "It's difficult psychologically for Russians to talk to people who think that Russia is a backward country. It's difficult for me too."

Whereas earlier in the relationship, transition economy managers seemed more willing to accept misunderstandings or lack of respect, over time this behavior became less well-received. One Russian manager was furious when foreigners exhibited disregard for the locals, treating them almost like children:

> At first, I personally was very depressed by the systematic approach of everything. . . . I thought it was completely crazy to create policies for everything. Some of them were written and repeated many times. They seemed to be so obvious to me that I thought: "What a nonsense! How can you even talk about it?" Often they [the policies] were related to some organizational moments, like what time you come to work, what time you leave, how you should be dressed. And you think: "Do they take us for idiots?"
>
> It happened to be true, and my second supervisor confirmed it. When he started working here in 1997, as a representative of the most progressive country in the world, the United States of America, he was saying: "Guys, you are just Africans here! Just Africans!" I was saying to him: "Do you understand what you are saying?"

Another Russian manager found the different approaches to doing business and the lack of willingness to adapt to local conditions irritating:

> When you are interacting with foreign managers, there are always some differences in understandings, in approaches. They keep to the conditions of the environment they learned at their mothers' knees, or I don't know, in high schools and in business schools later on. . . . A main reason for difficulty was that we didn't agree about money . . . foreigners pay more

attention to property and other similar issues and less attention to money spent. They like to involve lawyers, pay them thousands of dollars. They find some clause that is not acceptable for foreigners, and try to do something about it, involve a "Big Five" company for an inspection . . . it's not how we do business.

Often, as foreign companies urged certain practices, such as human resource policies (Bjorkman and Lu 2001), onto their local counterparts, interactions became more strained. Sometimes local managers felt that the foreigners were too limited in the ways they viewed their jobs. In some cases, for example, local managers may have wanted more responsibility than they perceived the foreigners were willing to give. One manager's perception was that foreigners wanted local managers to remain in their initial (limited) jobs and roles and that they might be threatened if the locals became more responsible. As he said, "If we start to grow or improve, it's not acceptable to foreigners, because they got used to the idea that everything should go step-by-step."

Similarly, another felt limited by his perception of the ways that foreigners (versus Russians) designed and thought about their own jobs:

I heard . . . that in any western company every employee has a very narrow spectrum of what he is doing. For example, he can just copy numbers from one paper to another, and he will be doing this for years. And our Russian people want to respect themselves, and they aim to look in all directions, be experts in all issues, and to look at everything comprehensively. He will always know how to copy the numbers he should copy, the numbers his neighbor should do, and someone else too. So he wants to know everything.

Foreign Manager Expectations about Themselves

As the reality of the relationships between transition economy and foreign managers began to become exposed, both groups sometimes became more introspective. Foreign managers sometimes recognized that their mistakes or the assumptions, they made which later came to haunt them, led to conflict with local managers. Some foreign managers were willing and able to adjust their behaviors to meet expectations about how they should be interacting with their local counterparts. Others did not, however, either because they did not realize the need for change or because nothing in their background allowed them to make accurate perceptions. Sometimes, as in the following example, managers who made mistakes questioned their own abilities, which often led to the withdrawal mentioned earlier.

A human resource manager of an automobile manufacturer that set up a plant in Vietnam altered his normal hiring practices to fit what he saw as solving a problem. Whereas in the United States he hired people based on their technical skills (e.g., ability to weld, program a computer) and job-related qualifications, he used a different tactic, which ultimately proved faulty, in Vietnam. There he hired people based primarily on their ability to speak English, assuming that the American production managers could train the Vietnamese in the technical aspects of the job.

During the first six months of training and before production began, this practice seemed sufficient. A year later, however, the manager learned from the American managers of widespread performance problems and discontent with the production workers. The human resource manager realized that in solving a short-term problem by hiring Vietnamese who could speak English, he had created a much more difficult long-term problem. Since the Vietnamese personnel regulations made layoffs difficult, the American managers were forced to spend more time training the Vietnamese workers, and tensions grew. The manager's faulty assumption was based on an inaccurate expectation about the situation in a transition economy. While he later recognized his error, repairing the damage proved difficult.

Other managers seemed to choose methods of interaction based on previous success without realizing the possible consequences in a different context. One manager who had worked in Russia and then in Vietnam used what she called "the explosion" technique in both places. When something was not going well, she grew angry, yelled, and created a ruckus. "It worked in Russia," she said. "It's what everyone did to make a point." Unfortunately, she tried the same technique in Vietnam, where anger is rarely exhibited except under very unusual circumstances. In Vietnam, she lost credibility, had difficulty reestablishing good relations with counterparts, and never quite understood that the technique was part of the problem.

Interestingly, another manager chose a similar approach, but had considered whether and why to do it. In this case, a manager in a European chemical firm operating in Shanghai chose to cause conflict, even though she knew it was not culturally expected or accepted:

We have different values from the local staff's. Last year, I was screaming and yelling for six months. My local Chinese friend would ask me, "Have you ever thought how your Chinese [workers] do things? Why don't you think in their terms?"

But I said, "I can't because in this business I deal with foreigners, and I have the same values as the foreigners do, and that's why I have the edge. If I start thinking like the Chinese, then I don't have any edge." But that is the most difficult part for expatriates here—to manage local people—because we always think we are right, and we always think they are wrong.

A Chinese-American, who had a master's degree in international management, spoke Chinese, and had spent much time trying to understand Chinese culture, followed yet another pattern. He worked for a multinational food-processing firm, and felt he was a bridge between the Chinese and American managers, both those on site in China and those in the U.S. headquarters. However, he was surprised when he realized he had misunderstood the culture and work environment in China. A year into his assignment in China, he reviewed his situation and expectations:

My understanding of communicating and managing effectively was based primarily on trial and error. I learned the hard way, falling on my face. But each time I fell, I'd assess what the critical learnings of each incident were. I think that one must have an open mind when accepting an expatriate assignment. China, as you probably know, has one of the highest expatriate assignment failure rates in the world. I believe that the lack of ability to manage across cultures is at the top of the list as well. And the reason for this is because expatriates fail to understand the thought process and motivations of local employees.

Sometimes, foreign managers were tougher on themselves about expectations than were their local counterparts. In fact, one Russian manager became quite positive about foreigners as he got to know them. We asked whether he thought there were aspects about Russians and working in Russia that he thought foreigners would never be able to understand. He said:

I think there is nothing that foreign managers will never understand. To be honest, as I mix with foreign managers a lot, I think that as soon as a foreign manager has broken away from the idea that Russia is a godforsaken hole, that people are not well educated here, and that they don't know how to do business, then that person becomes totally adequate to me, the same as I am.

SUMMARY

This chapter discusses the stage of relationship that managers face when they confront the reality of their relationship and begin to review and critique their interactions with one another. At this stage, managers are often confused about the cause of the behavior they observe. Their responses to the confusion, conflict and polarization of the relationship, are often highly emotional. The frustration is often revealed through their comments about declining trust, about their worry that they will be manipulated, about their concern that the other party is changing its behavior on agreements, and about each side making mistakes but not recognizing them. The managers reported that information and communication became strained or dissolved completely.

In addition, both local and transition economy managers learned that their expectations of one another were not being met or were inaccurate. Foreign managers become frustrated when they sensed that the local managers consistently avoid risk, did not have a strong customer service orientation, or were unable or unwilling to create and work in teams to accomplish goals. Local managers found that the foreigners held unflattering views of them and were unknowledgeable about local conditions and ways of conducting business. Foreigners also found themselves making decisions to adapt to local conditions that they would not make in their home environments. This adaptation was not always successful, however. When the inherent conflict in the situation emerged, it precipitated a change in the relationship that affected its future course. The next chapter discusses how some of the managers we talked with were able to move successfully past the critique to a more productive understanding.

Chapter 8

CONVERGENCE: FINDING WAYS TO MAKE IT WORK

All that matters is that the miraculous become the norm.
—Henry Miller, playwright (1970)

A project manager in Vietnam in the mid-1990s experienced a jolting lesson in working with the Vietnamese. A report on the experience follows.

"The air in the conference room in Hanoi was stuffy. Four Vietnamese academic colleagues and I sat around a table, stiff from tension.

"The other project manager and I had made a decision, in the best interests of the project, not to renew the contract of another foreigner. While he had contributed much and showed great enthusiasm, we decided he had become increasingly disruptive and required more monitoring than we could reasonably do. His demands for much higher pay, bid for more authority than made sense for the work he was doing, as well as some infractions with his visa, made it hard to justify keeping him for another year. Many of the problems we had with him were not evident to the Vietnamese, however, since they had no involvement in salaries for foreigners and heard none of the complaints he gave us about his job.

"Still, before the decision, I'd asked my Vietnamese colleagues for input. Personnel issues of any sort were very sensitive in Vietnam, which still considered foreigners suspect and put them under close observation. The Vietnamese university managers rarely asked us for input about its people and bristled if we made comments or suggestions about who might be good in certain positions or who might need more training. Yet they had difficulty understanding that we too had sensitive personnel issues that sometimes were better settled without their involvement. Now some of them were upset with the decision and wanted to have a face-to-face discussion.

" 'You cannot do this. We do not want it,' said the vice director of the business school.

"I sat with my hands in my lap. Listening. This was not the time to be defensive.

"His voice got louder, his tone angrier as he started railing against me, the other project manager, and how we had an explanation different from that of the foreign professor about what had occurred. The implication was that he believed the other person and not us.

" 'There is something going on behind the curtain,' he said. His face became red, his mouth was pursed as he continued. I tried explaining our position, some of the reasons for the decision (while trying to save face for all of us). It did no good. We spent 45 minutes as he grew angrier and as I tried to stay calm and explain that the decision was not arbitrary.

"One of the others in the meeting was an older faculty member, a woman. She played the role of 'aunt' or 'older sister' for the Vietnamese, including the vice director, 10 years her junior. During the meeting, she tried to play mediator and to calm the vice director without making a big scene. The next day we had a long talk.

" 'I am amazed you stayed calm, and I am not happy that he got angry. Showing anger is not good in Vietnam. He showed his, and you did not show yours.'

"The explosion (and my staying calm) turned out to be a watershed for several reasons, some of which I did not understand at the time. Interestingly, after several of us reflected, others who had attended the meeting helped analyze what might have happened. First, I had gained some credibility because I'd been able to follow a cultural norm and not become angry when even the Vietnamese thought I had reason to blow up.

"Yet the fact that the manager had shown his anger so directly also turned out to be important. While Vietnamese rarely show anger to strangers, or even to most work colleagues, the manager had exploded at me in front of others in the school. While it was perhaps unconscious on his part, the manager's explosion may have indirectly signaled that I had become enough of a part of the group that he was comfortable showing that anger. Normally, the other in-the-group-person (me) would react in kind, the two people having a loud and vigorous discussion. So in a sense, we had each moved toward the other—in an odd sort of way. We were off-kilter and yet, in the end, things worked out; we moved toward one another and to a different level in our future interactions."

At some point, relationships between local and foreign managers reach a fork in the road in terms of the nature of their future interactions, and ultimately, whether or not the relationship continues. Continuing requires that new standards of behavior and more realistic expectations evolve. That is, individuals must reform the relationship and create a new path for themselves. Initially, this may mean that they adapt their expectations and behavior to be more like that of their counterpart. Often these behavioral concessions are made without any real understanding of their basis other than that they seemed to be effective.

This chapter discusses some of the approaches that foreign and transition economy managers have used to reform and change their interactions so that they could move forward together in their relationships. As in the previous chapters, the ways that the relationship develops with regard to trust, to information sharing and communication, and to managers' expectations of one another are reviewed.

TRUST

Building trust following the critique stage, where interactions have been strained by conflict and polarization, is difficult but feasible. Several interviewees suggested ways that they tried to build trust and improve relationships. They tried both formal and informal, direct and indirect methods. We categorized these methods as training, being patient and allowing time to pass, and adapting or adjusting behavior to be more like their counterpart. (Usually the foreigners claimed to adjust more to the transition economy managers than the reverse.)

Training

The managers we interviewed suggested that formal training was more often a tactic used by foreigners. Training, conducted by foreigners for locals, was often done within the country and informally. For example, two food-processing firm managers commented that they often sent American managers to China and Russia to work with and train farmers and plant operators on how to increase yields and how to package and distribute their products as part of building an initial relationship. The local managers trained their foreign counterparts only informally, and several of the Americans mentioned that the training they received was often unplanned. Sometimes the lessons were uncomfortably gained, such as the manager who discovered an unwanted facilitator in his Chinese negotiations who was tacking on additional fees for himself throughout the negotiation. The American manager left the deal and eventually found a way to hire and pay a flat fee to a facilitator—meeting both the Chinese expectations for additional money and his own desire for more control of the negotiation situation.

A construction firm with projects in several transition economy sites used a variety of methods to train managers at different levels. In this case, the need developed when the firm discovered that the local managers it hired were reluctant to change certain behaviors. For example, these local managers refused to carry out layoffs to increase plant productivity. This firm eventually changed its personnel strategies to compensate. It hired younger, untested employees and promoted them to assistant managers. There they worked along side senior foreign managers who acted as mentors for up to two years. In this way the young local managers learned the business firm's culture on site.

As these local managers became more involved in overall plant or project management and took over senior management positions, the firm initiated two more informal training methods. It created networks of transition economy (and some developing country) managers who met periodically to discuss common issues and problems. This was a self-training approach in some ways, since the transition economy managers and their countries were at different stages of development and could learn from each other. At each stage of the training, interactions improved as the managers understood each other better and engaged in more mutually beneficial behavior.

Following from the network, this firm added a peer evaluation process in which senior local managers (the ones trained by foreigners) from equivalent or similar operations were matched with transition economy managers. They then visited the others' sites to conduct progress reviews. This peer evaluation process reduced the foreign managers' involvement in direct evaluation. Transition economy peers could, therefore, work with and learn more effectively from each other.

This multi-staged and multi-focused training and evaluation system helped build trust among foreign and local managers at several levels. First, the transition economy managers, who faced similar problems in their various settings, were able to work with and learn from one another. Second, the local managers now responded to senior foreign managers with greater assurance, building trust and respect among the foreigners. Finally, as the peer evaluation-network approach developed, the firm brought foreign managers together with the local managers to compare notes, receive more formal training, and learn from each other and from the senior foreign managers. The direct involvement with each other on tasks of significant importance helped to break down stereotypic expectations and to improve trust.

Another firm used both formal and informal training approaches perhaps uniquely associated with its business. The general manager of a wood construction products firm brought representatives of the Chinese governmental agencies (i.e., Ministry of Construction and the State Administration for Building and Materials Industry) to his home state and had them construct a building with his product. Only after the Chinese experienced the efficiency and benefits of the American firm's product, did the relationship improve and move toward a successful business venture.

An agribusiness manager brought several groups of Russian and Chinese farmers to the United States for two or three weeks, hoping they would become potential vendors for the processing firm. During the short visits, the farmers learned about growing, storage, and distribution practices. This convinced some of the farmers of the importance of adding value to their own products and farms so that they could do business with the foreign firm. The firm also brought young managers and technical employees to the home site for stays of up to two years. During the sojourn, the transition economy managers shadowed foreign managers, built their own areas of expertise, and learned about U.S. style market economics.

One manager who brought several Russians to the home office in the United States found knowledge transfer to be easier than he expected. The Russians could relate to discipline (i.e., budgets and schedules) and liked the idea of the western management controls, once they understood them. Seeing the foreign managers use such techniques further cemented their understanding and trust. While the training took more time and effort initially, it usually had a better human resource payoff in the long run.

Another foreign manager commented that English language training helped improve communication in more ways than he expected. As local managers gained knowledge of the language, they also began to better understand the concepts behind some of the business practices they had learned. Additionally, the classroom interaction (interactive discussion versus lectures) helped the local managers become more comfortable with the behavior expected in the work place. The learning approach also helped reinforce some of the business concepts such as participation and giving feedback without negative repercussions. Training, therefore, required participants to make adjustments in attitudes and behavior. In so doing, local managers suspended distrust enough to accommodate activities that were in their own best interest. Foreign managers also adjusted their expectations, although this may have happened almost unconsciously. Therefore, both groups moved toward mutually beneficial behavior that over time resulted in trust.

Being Patient

Another tactic that interviewees said was influential in building trust was simply being patient and allowing time to have an effect. Both local and foreign managers commented that having more time with one another allowed them to realize the talents and strengths of the other managers. Time also allowed the foreign managers a chance to understand more about the conditions in the transition economy. Stereotypic expectations began to break down and interactions became smoother and trust grew. A manager whose firm worked over a six-year period to renovate run-down utility plants in Mongolia watched the reaction of Mongolians go from strident refusal to cooperation and gratitude.

> Once they realized we were keeping the plants going, that we were helping to keep the heat and lights on, people started stopping us on the streets to thank us. Instead of being the bad guy Americans, we were the good guys.

The safety expert, whose disastrous introduction at a plant site described in a previous chapter, found patience worked in his favor as well. After being ignored for his first month, he realized his aggressive American approach (i.e., "How much is your hand worth?") was not working. Because he was to remain on site for a year, he knew he had to change tactics and find ways to interact successfully. When local employees and managers realized that he was not leaving soon (he also had toned down his strong approach), they slowly began to open up. Over time he made it clear that he was interested in employee safety and in finding ways to protect employees, not in intimidating people. Employees and managers then became more willing to listen. He began to visit with employees one-on-one, took small groups to lunch, and met each unit separately in the plant. As he helped them understand that he would reward them for finding and solving safety problems, employees slowly began to accept him. Six months on, the relationship had developed a high level of trust, and it continued to be quite successful through the balance of the expert's stay. Time and patience had worked for both groups.

In another example, a Russian manager, watching interactions between Americans and Russians in a professional organization, noted a change in the mix of the organization's membership. He realized that as it changed, so too did the interaction and relationship between the groups. In the early 1990s, the composition of the American Chamber of Commerce of St. Petersburg International Business Association was 90 percent foreigners. Unaware of the meetings or feeling that they were unwelcome, only a few Russians attended. The Russian manager also felt that a subsurface tension existed in the organization.

By late 2001, the situation was reversed. People holding the same positions in their organizations attended the meetings, but the group was 90 percent Russian. "So there is Russian management everywhere," noted the manager, "It is a serious trend. Everything reverses to Russian." It had simply taken time for foreigners to believe they could turn over their businesses to Russians, and for the skills and knowledge of the Russians to develop. This contributed to increasing the level of trust between the two groups.

A final example of being patient comes from the senior manager of a food-processing firm operating in China for seven years. He observed that interactions among locals and foreigners improved markedly over time. In large part, he attributed this improvement to the changes in the local managers that had occurred over time. They had received training in the United States, and had developed a clearer understanding of the concepts of market economics, the firm's culture, which had increased their level of confidence in doing business. He watched the younger Chinese managers, in their 30s and 40s, who had been with his company for six to seven years, become increasingly comfortable with and successful at concepts like participative management. These young Chinese managers continued to follow long-standing patterns of behavior with their Chinese superiors (e.g., acting subservient), but could switch to alternative ways of communicating and behaving with their foreign bosses and counterparts. The patience of foreign managers in allowing their Chinese counterparts to develop adaptive behavior had paid off.

Adapting

A final tactic toward building the trust required for relationships to progress was a more conscious and active adapting behavior to become more like counterparts. Some foreign managers commented that, ultimately, they had had to reach out to their local counterparts. They did so by learning more about the other culture and by seeking out and getting to know their counterparts on a deeper level than in the earlier relationship stages. They then took actions that were more acceptable in the transition country environment, and many became well-liked and respected.

For example, an American manager disliked the Russian expectation of late night celebrations after finishing negotiations, a phase in a project, or signing a new business deal. However, he understood doing business in Russia involved "a lot of talk and vodka, since they needed to get to know us and to understand how we were trying to help them." In this case, it included helping farmers understand how to store, package, and market their crops instead of simply dumping a week's worth of product in the back of a truck and carting it to market. The manager said he longed for a simple way to close out a business event, but realized that the drinking and celebrating were part of the package.

A manager in China found that pricing his product as he did elsewhere meant constant niggling with the Chinese. Instead, he decided it was "easier to price things the way the Chinese did than to 'reeducate' them on pricing concepts." His normal approach was to offer a price for a finished house or building; but the Chinese preferred to set a price for a shell and then add components, pricing them separately. Despite the different approaches, the final price still turned out to be about the same.

Finally, some managers noted that at times the best way to "move toward one another" was to loosen some control. In Russia, one foreign manager became so frustrated at his inability to understand the process of doing business that he considered leaving or shutting down the project. Instead some of his colleagues within the firm encouraged him to relinquish some control to his Russian subordinates and managers, allowing them to take responsibility for completing the work that the foreigner was in charge of. In addition to completing the project, the local managers were able to use the situation to do some training of the foreigner. As one local manager explained:

> [T]he foreign manager just devolved his power onto lower level employees. And my colleague and I, both senior managers, we did the entire job he was supposed to do and reported to him. It was a very unusual situation. At the end we finished all the work and made a quite quality product. At that stage, [the foreign manager] changed his opinion . . . we explained to him how to interpret the information he thought was impossible to interpret. The project turned out to be successful, and [the foreign manager] even reaped laurels.

Improving the level of trust in relationships between foreign and local managers took a variety of courses at this stage of the relationship. The tactics included training, patience, changing interaction characteristics, and adapting behavior. Of course, the characteristics of both the situation and the individuals involved contributed to the effectiveness of building trust.

INFORMATION SHARING AND COMMUNICATION

The managers we interviewed blended their actions that led to increased trust with the ways that they changed the nature of communication. In particular, they commented that they altered the characteristics of their interactions, which often meant being more willing to share certain types of information or finding ways to give or receive information.

Some managers found they needed to alter the way they interacted with potential partners and counterparts, and doing that affected the way they exchanged information. A general manager, frustrated by a middleman in China, initially left the deal, but later recontacted and worked directly with the buyer. He then found another facilitator in China. The conditions the manager offered were that the facilitator would have to stay within the maximum price set by the firm, but that the firm would add another 10 percent on top for the middleman. The middleman was initially shocked, being accustomed to negotiating with each side, but he soon saw the benefits. He would get a guaranteed commission, would be paid immediately, and would no longer have to carry the risk of whether and how he would be paid. This new form of interacting reduced uncertainty, increased trust, and made subsequent deals easier.

In another case, foreign managers working in the Czech Republic and Russia became frustrated in their dealings with their older senior manager counterparts. They felt that they could not easily communicate with or understand these managers because the local managers were too concerned with status, used an authoritarian approach with employees, and were struggling to accept new ideas. The Americans found that they could more easily interact and communicate with the younger managers of their partner firm.

Slowly, the younger managers began to work around the older managers and became informal mediators between those managers and the foreign counterparts. The younger managers were respectful of their seniors and were careful not to offer suggestions outside their own areas of expertise. But they also encouraged the older managers to try to understand the motives of the foreign partners and to work toward mutually beneficial objectives.

The final example emerged almost accidentally in the interviews with managers. Both foreign and local managers, often without realizing it, admitted that they became chameleon-like in their interactions. Depending upon the setting, the group, or the individuals they interacted with, these managers adjusted their language, communication styles, and ultimately, modes of behavior. The comment related earlier from the senior manager of the firm in China that the younger Chinese managers were "comfortable with participative management—at least with the foreigners" reflects this circumstance. That is, not only could these younger Chinese managers act in ways that were acceptable to and comfortable for foreigners (e.g., being more aggressive, asking more questions, taking initiative rather than waiting to be told what to do), but they could also shift gears to interact successfully with their Chinese superiors and counterparts. Likewise, westerners who were capable of changing the characteristics of the interaction talked of being more restrained, remaining calm, using less direct forms of communication, observing protocol.

This notion of developing chameleon-like, or adaptive, skills has received more attention as the business world becomes more global. Rosen, Digh, Singer, and Phillips (2000) have referred to the *global literacies,* including the social and cultural skills that will allow for switching among different environments, that any individual will need in the future. Zachary (2000) has written about the *hybrids*—people born in one country, living in others, having mixed heritages and religious backgrounds—that increasingly populate the global world and has suggested they will be more comfortable working across business and other boundaries.

EXPECTATIONS ABOUT LOCAL MANAGERS

As they sought ways to build trust and to improve their relationships, both local and foreign managers reached new realizations about each other as their stereotypic expectations began to break down. Such insights came as they learned more about the conditions each faced and as they moved, often quite subtly, from the polarized attitudes of earlier stages. Over time, foreign managers gained knowledge about the less obvious aspects of working in a transition economy. They became more realistic in their expectations of local managers, which was reflected by two insights. Local managers often face pressures of which foreign managers are unaware. Local managers simply will not change some characteristics in the short term, so foreigners need to learn to accept them.

Pressures Faced by Local Managers

As they built relationships, foreign managers often recognized that their local counterparts sometimes felt pressures that the foreigners had not known about, had not understood, or that represented holdovers from state socialism. For example, under socialism, employees' jobs were rarely threatened. As a result of holding on to these beliefs, local managers often resisted layoffs that foreign managers considered necessary. A manager of an infrastructure engineering firm who had worked in East Germany, Albania, and Poland said that American managers had to carry out certain tasks such as initial layoffs because local managers were unfamiliar with and uncomfortable about doing it. He said he had to

> look for and identify the pressures that the local guys are under. We Americans assume that we're the ones with pressures—to complete a job, within budget and on time. We don't realize that the local guys have pressures that are really different but just as difficult.

Often the pressures on local managers were beyond the ability of either party to control. For example, in Vietnam, local managers sometimes had politically appointed subordinates, who were forced on their organizations. These appointees sometimes had little expertise or training related to the firm's function or were unable or unwilling to perform specific tasks. Often foreign managers were unaware of this. To a foreign manager, such people seemed likely candidates for dismissal. But, of course, the local manager was unable to do so. The recognition of this type of constraint on the behavior of local managers was often a milestone in relationship development.

Similarly, a manager working in China for many years commented that even though his firm had trained local managers in western business practices, the Chinese system dominated the behavior of local employees and managers. For some local managers this meant a traditional chain of command, with a "no questions asked" expectation. Because he had worked in eastern Europe, Latin and South America, and Asia for 20 years, he realized that it takes time for the pressures on local managers to diminish or for old behaviors to change. He tried to speed the process, however, by transferring managers among all the countries in which the firm operated. Thus, key managers, including local Chinese, experienced different company sites in Chile, Australia, Germany, the United States, and Brazil as well as in China. His rationale was that only as local transition economy managers take those assignments elsewhere will they absorb the company culture and find ways to incorporate and blend it with their traditional systems.

Acceptance that Some Characteristics May Not Change

Some foreign managers eventually realized that certain aspects of the values, attitudes, and beliefs of local managers would not change as the relationship progressed. A manager whose firm operated in Mongolia over a 10-year period found that despite surface changes, local managers shifted back to previous ways of thinking over time. He watched as local attitudes toward foreigners changed from stark abhorrence to gratitude and then to antipathy. In the early 1990s, the Mongolians were skeptical and resistant to having the foreigners on site to rebuild their decrepit utilities. However, after two or three years, they came up to the Americans on the street to thank them for "keeping the lights and heat on." After another few years, the attitude shifted again to one of resentment. As the American manager put it, the Mongolians felt the Americans were "too expensive." They just wanted the Americans to "give them the money and leave." Accepting that people would never be able to fully accept the American engineers working there, he realized that the best he could hope for was that the relationship remain professional until his firm completed its work. A recognition that the relationship had reached its potential, optimal or not, often marks the end of this stage of relationship development.

EXPECTATIONS ABOUT FOREIGN MANAGERS

As locals and foreigners got to know one another better, and the relationship developed through the convergence stage, two patterns of behavior were described by local managers. Some foreigners seemed to become more patient and accepting and, ultimately, adjusted. Others fought the situation, finished the job, but never really adjusted to the transition country environment. The interaction between locals and the first type of foreigners may have led to more satisfying relationships. However, sometimes managers achieved only short-term business outcomes.

Overall, the managers we interviewed reported a sense of determination, and they were committed to making the business and professional situation clear and attainable. But many were also trying to adjust to conditions they now knew well. They mentioned the importance of finding ways to structure the jobs and relationships to be clear about what outcomes the foreigners wanted from their local counterparts, but they were also aware that some of those structures would be hard to implement.

One manager said his firm tried to prepare and train its local employees by giving orientation about the company, by providing employees with English language and technical expertise, and then by reviewing the progress of the firm. He said the intent was that employees would understand the bigger picture and gain the expertise they needed to help the firm reach its objectives when they eventually took over operations.

Other foreign managers commented that they had learned to incorporate local approaches in the ways they dealt with local counterparts, although these sometimes went against their own beliefs about the way things should be run. One Chinese-American manager realized that his approach of asking for input and feedback made his Chinese managers uncomfortable because they saw the process of giving feedback as challenging the boss. Thus the foreign manager reoriented his approach to fit the Chinese expectations:

> I had a new style: Don't ask any questions. Tell the employee what he should have done. Tell him how I, and thus all of us, lost face in front of our superiors for our failure to perform. Do not criticize him directly or point out what he did wrong.

The foreign manager found it difficult to use this approach that, to him, seemed so high-handed, but discovered that it was more acceptable and effective with his Chinese employees. He told us that he expected to slowly adapt his participative style to fit the Chinese conditions and eventually hoped that the Chinese would appreciate his more western approach. Initially, however, he decided to restrain it.

Another senior manager's observation after 30 years working in a range of transition economies and developing countries, was that foreign managers will likely always "be educators" for local counterparts, both for partners and for clients. Still other managers, however, were less ethnocentric and arrogant when they talked of "being educators." These talked more about being mentors, but acknowledged they also had much to learn.

The wood products manager selling building products in China exemplifies the realization of needing to change his thinking and ways of interacting. At first, when the Chinese asked technical questions, he responded with technical information. He assumed that "engineer to engineer" talk would triumph, but finally realized that since the Chinese had no experience with the construction and engineering properties of wood, giving them technical information as a way to sell the product would not work. As a result, he altered his thinking:

> I shifted to selling the concept and design of western style housing—issues of comfort and energy efficiency. . . . That began to help the Chinese think differently but was still not enough. Ultimately, I invited about 20 representatives from the key ministries to our plant in the United States.

Finally, a form of "show and tell" emerged as a new way of thinking with several foreign managers. For example, when the manager showed the Chinese officials how to build a house using his product, it made the difference. When the officials saw for themselves the ease of construction and the benefits of this style of housing, they agreed to the approvals he needed.

SUMMARY

This chapter focuses on the stage of relationship development in which both local and foreign managers work through their conflicts and find ways to develop new standards of behavior and more realistic expectations. The processes they use to build trust following the conflict and polarization of previous stages include both formal and informal training, patience, changing the characteristics of the interaction, and adapting their behavior to be more like that of their counterpart.

The patterns of communication and information flow start to become two-way. That is, both foreign and local managers begin to understand the reality of the others' behavior, and stereotypic expectations begin to break down.

Furthermore, each group tries to see the interaction from the others' perspectives. Foreign managers finally recognize that there often are pressures on local managers that they will never fully know about or understand. As they begin to recognize these pressures, they adjust their tactics for working with the locals. Also, as is true in any relationship, both sides begin to realize that some values, attitudes, and beliefs are unlikely to change, at least in the near term. Finally, some foreign managers find they have to change their expectations about themselves. It is this kind of self-realization that often marks the transition to the final stage of the relationship, which is the topic of the next chapter.

Chapter 9

CONTINUE? POSSIBILITIES AND OUTCOMES

Lets face it . . . most relationships you have in life don't work out.
—Alex Bennett, radio broadcaster

That is what learning is. You suddenly understand something that you've understood all your life, but in a new way.
—Doris Lessing, writer (1919–)

Hanoi, Vietnam

"So how do the changes in Vietnam influence people's lives? I can see three groups of people with different dynamics. The first group includes more conservative people, who fear every change. These people are either incapable of coping with changes or afraid of losing their power. They know change is inevitable, yet try to slow it down.

"The second group is young, mostly 20s or 30s, dynamic people. They take any opportunity of the market system. What worries me is that these people only care about themselves, acting opportunistically. These people try to get funding from the government to study abroad, and then stay for better jobs. They form a company and sell fake products. The search for money threatens their sense of ethics. And that is even more serious in Vietnam since we don't have a strong legal system.

"What makes changes harder is that these two groups look at and use each other as a reason for their viewpoints. In between, the third group, people who foster changes, take advantage of changes, yet try to do good things for the country. These people have a sense of ethics, but they are rare. They would be the leaders of the changes. The challenge for me is not how to cope with changes. It is how to lead the changes."

In the final stage of the development of relationships between local and foreign managers in transition economies, many of the aspects of the relationship have been resolved. Each party has had enough time to experience and review the situation and has made decisions about the future. The conflict of previous stages has been replaced with more accurate expectations about the behavior of oneself and of others. However, the future is still uncertain, and both local and transition country managers still face many challenges.

The main focus of this book is on the ways that foreign managers learn to work with their local manager counterparts in transition economies. However, it is also important to remember the immense challenges that local managers in transition economies have experienced, in addition to dealing with foreign business counterparts. The vignette at the beginning of this chapter, written by a 35-year-old university faculty member, is a reminder that each person in a transition economy is making a decision—consciously or not—about how to deal with change and how to live the next stage of his or her life. Some, like the accounting student in the canteen (in a prior chapter vignette) and the Vietnamese faculty member, will seek to lead change in a way that contributes to the futures of their countries. Others will absorb market economic principles and thrive using them, reaching levels of economic achievement surprising even to their foreign counterparts. For example, Mr. Li Qinfu, one of China's wealthiest business people, started his work life as a red-kerchiefed Young Pioneer, before taking advantage of early economic reforms in 1983, at age 21 (Smith 2002). He paid the government U.S.$240 a year to take over a failing textile factory and its employees; after a year, he had made U.S.$7,000 in profit by supplying the fast growing Beijing and Shanghai markets. When the factory exceeded anyone's expectations and made U.S.$50,000 in one year, the government took back the factory, demoting Li to an employee. He left the factory, partnered with Japanese investors in 1990, continued to build and run factories in the textile industry, and began a high quality printing business as well. He has since bought out the government's share of his original factory and built a headquarters on its site that is a replica of the U.S. Capitol, complete with an 18-foot Statue of Freedom (but in his own likeness) atop the dome.

Younger managers, like the ambitious young Vietnamese entrepreneur who started the Internet investment advising firm and who also wants an advanced degree, will seek the advantages of market changes, but may continue to be influenced by the ideals of socialism. He will seek economic gain by taking advantage of the market economy but will also try to contribute to the country by, as he says, "becoming an employer of others, giving them a chance to earn money." Others will focus solely on finding ways to build their personal wealth, expertise, or own futures. They may leave their countries and decide not to return, thereby making significant and positive gains for themselves but giving little back to their countries or people.

The pressures on transition economy participants come from many sources. Their interactions with foreign managers are but one set of expectations on their behavior. However, these relationships have a significant and lasting impact on how these managers perceive their role both in business and as members of society. Our interviews suggested that managers face four options in the final phase of the relationship: managers press on in a positive way with the present relationship; they muddle through the relationship to complete the current task; they abandon the relationship; or they may find a completely new way to move forward. They will follow one of these paths in a future that is hard to know yet important to consider as managers debate whether and how to continue their relationships.

PREDICTING THE FUTURE

Because we do not know how transition economy business people will react to role pressures in the future, we are less clear about the relationship development in this fourth stage; hence, the chapter title is in question form (i.c., "Continue?"). After cautiously starting relationships with varying degrees of trust in each other and then encountering potential tension, some managers found ways to smooth and improve their interactions and build their relationships so that they could complete a project or phase of a project. However, when we interviewed managers, the next, longer-term outcome of the relationship was still developing and undecided for many.

As we have suggested, many people—foreign and local managers, scholars and journalists alike—have been astounded that some changes in transition economies did not occur faster. The early reports and literature, as well as memories of managers who worked in transition economies in the late 1980s and early 1990s, led to an expectation that by the early 2000s, the transition economies would have absorbed market economics concepts and principles and be flourishing.

While surface-level tangible changes were remarkable, attitudes and behaviors have changed more slowly. The manager who worked for a large infrastructure firm in Mongolia noted changes in acceptance of some western economic principles and practices during the decade he spent working there. He commented that his firm's on-site (foreign) managers

> had to repeat the ideas and concepts . . . had to repeatedly say that the local manager had to take responsibility. Four to five years later, some—not many—of the Mongolian managers rose to the top. The older people never did get it—some of the younger ones did.

However, as we conducted the research for this book, managers commented on the changes that, over time, had begun to occur. For instance, some local managers were simply more aware of what they did (and did not) know about market economics and business and what their weaknesses were. A foreign manager who worked in Hungary for many years saw a change in the Hungarian perceptions of their own economic role in the region. He said that, despite (or perhaps because of) Hungary's economic gains, its managers were now recognizing that its low wage competitive advantage during the 1990s may disintegrate in the coming decade. As neighboring transition economy countries (e.g., Romania, Albania, Bulgaria) become more stable and focus on doing business regionally and as Hungary moves toward European Union membership, Hungary's wage advantage will dissolve. The recognition that wages, as an advantage, will not exist forever was a new realization for local managers.

The duration of the relationships that our interviewees reported on tended to be less than three years. Most of the managers we talked with, both foreign and local, had several relationships over the years, or had more recent ones that were still developing. Some foreign managers with long-term transition economy experience had worked in several settings and, therefore, had several relationships on which they could report, but few lasted longer than three years. Of course, some relationships ended because a project concluded or because the relationship failed.

Exceptions existed, however. The senior manager whose firm built a food processing plant in China had worked with the same group of senior- and middle-level Chinese managers for almost six years. He commented on the changes he had seen over that time:

[T]hey had a very primitive understanding of market economics when I started going there in 1991. They understood production and costs since theirs had been a production-oriented economy, but they had little understanding or appreciation of quality or farming practices and the relationship of those costs. . . . Now, in 2001 . . . in our joint venture, which has gone on for several years, the Chinese have begun to ask questions in a more sophisticated way, challenging the foreigners about why the company should spend more money for certain things or asking, "What if we did something differently?"

This same manager described his firm's local managers as shifting from "knowing costs" to fully "understanding costs." In the early 1990s, he watched other companies, including a large British firm, lose money because they uncritically accepted information about costs, assumptions about prices, and availability of raw materials that the Chinese gave them. In his view, the problem was not one of intentional misleading. Rather he saw it as a lack of information, an inability on both sides to assess the problem well, or an unwillingness to believe that the information was a problem. By the early 2000s, he claimed, the Chinese in larger cities had improved on all counts, and foreigners who go to China now are more knowledgeable than they were a decade before. Finally, our own experience (over eight years in Vietnam for one of us) suggested that many of these relationships continue to be under construction and to have uncertain long-term futures.

Uncertainty about the future seemed to characterize the relationships between local and foreign managers in transition economies. The managers we interviewed frequently commented that they did not yet know the outcome of their stories. Given the generally short tenure of the relationships that we examined and uncertainty about the future, the managers were able to tell us less about this final stage than they could about the earlier stages of the interactions.

There is another reason for our hesitation to forecast longer-term outcomes for relationships between local and foreign managers working in transition economies. It is that the assumptions each side makes about the other and the conditions surrounding the relationship may simply not allow for accurate predictions. Holden (2002) questioned whether it was feasible to speculate confidently about the nature of future relationships between managers of different cultures. It may be unreasonable, difficult, and risky to try to fit possible outcomes into any model, no matter how carefully conceived, based upon western expectations.

One of the difficulties stems from an assumption, underlying a developmental model, that the knowledge or skills transition economy managers may have developed in a planned economy are not useful in a transition or market economy. Many of the comments of our interviewees suggested that (at least initially) they held this assumption. As suggested in earlier chapters, this assumption was not always accurate. Indeed, local managers often identified, and many foreign managers confirmed, that the transition economy managers had skills and knowledge that continued to be useful.

For instance, shortly after reunification in Germany, Siemens AG purchased an East German electronics plant (Litchfield 1992). It then cut the managerial workforce by half, doubled productivity, and started training programs for the remaining managers in business functions such as marketing, human resource management, and finance. During the training, the Siemens group found that East German managers excelled in two key areas. First, they were extremely resourceful at solving certain types of problems that required creative thinking. In addition, the East German managers were better able to master certain management game scenarios than were their West German counterparts. Wolfgang Hampl, long-time East German manager of the plant that Siemens purchased, was not surprised (Litchfield 1992). In the planned economy system, he explained, managers had to

> improvise in a system of chronic short supply, constant surveillance, and arbitrary leadership. What could be better training [for operating in transition economies?]

Under socialism, the East German managers had to become resourceful at finding ways to achieve, despite obstacles of chronic shortages, political restrictions, reluctant employees and supervisors, and lack of economic or emotional support. The foreign managers we interviewed noted that this resourcefulness and ability to manage in chaos remained with the local managers even as they sought to learn about market economies. In some ways, these managers were better equipped to adjust to changes in the environment than those trained in market economies. In other words, uncertainty and chaos sometimes perturbed transition economy managers less than it did their foreign counterparts simply because those conditions had often been part of their lives. Therefore, as the environment continues to change, it is difficult to predict if managers with experience under state socialism or in transition economies will be at an advantage or a disadvantage.

Another part of the difficulty of understanding and predicting future relationships stems from our inability to anticipate the unexpected (from western perspectives) outcomes or events that may occur as relationships, particularly cross-cultural ones, develop (Holden 2002). For example, persistence is one of the cornerstones of Vietnamese behavior in war, in interacting with business partners, and in dealing with foreigners. The Vietnamese resisted and persisted against their Chinese conquerors for a thousand years before they took back their own country. Many foreigners in Vietnam become accustomed to that persistence, expecting the Vietnamese to refuse to adjust to foreign practices or to accept demands by counterparts. Yet the Vietnamese are also practical and good at understanding a situation where persistence will not work, where they either adjust or do not do business with a partner. Learning to anticipate which type of situation will be one where the Vietnamese will resist and persist versus the one where the Vietnamese will accept (quickly) and move forward is part of the challenge that foreign managers face with their counterparts there.

Given the inability to predict accurately what might occur in longer term cross-cultural relationships, we chose in this book to discuss possible outcomes based on what managers told us as well as on the obvious choice—of continuing or not—that confronts these managers at this stage of relationship development. We had few long-term or "completed" stories of interactions and relationships that lasted for more than three years. More often, we had examples of works in progress, approaches that transition economy and foreign managers were still working through. Even so, the managers gave us insights into what they saw occurring. Three that emerged in our discussion are ones that are relatively obvious and common in western partnerships: persist and continue, accept and compromise, or abandon the relationship. The first, a desire to continue the relationship, appeared to be the most common. Once the managers worked through early friction or tension, many seemed more committed to a longer-term business relationship. The second and third approaches—to simply accept and get through the required business activities or to abandon them—were mentioned much less frequently by this stage of the relationship. A final pathway would be leaving open the possibilities, living with uncertainty and expecting "unexpected outcomes" (Holden 2002).

PERSIST AND CONTINUE

Even though few of the managers we interviewed had long-term relationships, they did offer a number of observations regarding the likely futures of managerial interactions. A common theme was that, by this stage of the relationship, managers decided to persist. Many transition economy and foreign managers reported that they tried to be tenacious, particularly in recent years, about making their interactions and relationships succeed. By the time they had worked through the contact, critique, and convergence stages, they were committed to working hard to make a relationship succeed for the longer term. While several foreign managers tried (and failed) in business relationships in the early 1990s (e.g., in Poland, Albania, Georgia, or Sakhalin Island), by the early 2000s many reported being very serious about finding ways to do business with transition economy counterparts. Their persistence may have stemmed from increased sophistication on both sides or from greater awareness and acceptance of the challenges of working together. They also appeared to develop increasing respect for the knowledge that the others held. One young Russian manager's response to our interest in "what foreigners will never understand about your country and its managers" is indicative.

> Our country has been moving ahead a little bit. Everything is getting more transparent. . . . We don't need to turn something on its head so that a foreigner could understand it. . . . So, as for what foreign managers will never understand in Russian managers? I suppose they can understand everything.

That is, by this stage of the relationship one outcome was a realization of possible success. This realization supplanted the conflict and confusion of earlier stages, and a willingness to try to make things work was evident.

Furthermore, once the partners decided to find ways to continue their relationships, their attitudes seemed to shift. They appeared to be more positive and to seek ways to adjust, rather than resist, each other. Indeed, transition economy managers steeped in planned-economy methods seemed increasingly willing to unlearn habits that hindered their performance in a new market economy (Holden, Cooper, and Carr 1998). Likewise, foreign managers too appeared to recognize the need to unlearn assumptions about transition managers and to be ready to adjust their own approaches. One manager who worked many years in the Czech Republic said that he had learned to have no expectations. He encouraged his counterparts to find their own ways rather than to take on foreign ways or to hold fast to former Czech approaches. In essence, the managers on both sides gave us the impression that if they had worked hard to get through earlier tensions and frustrations, they felt more committed to working together to achieve mutually beneficial outcomes.

Thus, as their interactions improved over time, their relationships became positive and stronger. As counterparts found ways to move the business relationship to a new level and adjusted to each other and to the conditions in which they worked, the real possibility of success became apparent. In addition, both local and foreign managers found that as counterparts adjusted to each other and to the environmental and business conditions, they understood and appreciated the pressures that the other faced. As transition economy managers took on and performed well in additional responsibilities, foreign managers relinquished tight control, began to delegate, and adjusted to follow some of the local practices. For example, the vice president of an international food-processing plant reported that, after several years in China, the company increasingly pulled expatriates out, since local managers were able to successfully manage both the processing plant and customer interactions.

Sometimes it was the local managers who adjusted and showed more willingness to accept foreign methods. The senior manager of a wood construction products firm found, over two years, that the Chinese he dealt with adjusted to the idea of his firm paying a flat fee to a middleman rather than using the traditional Chinese approach of a middleman who negotiates a cut for himself from buyer and seller. Additionally, the government officials that he worked so hard to convince of the value of wood finally saw the value of the building approach and product. Having recognized the benefits of wooden buildings (energy efficiency, ease of construction, and cost) and the drawbacks of concrete (inconsistency with the environment and aesthetics), the officials were seeking new applications for wood construction.

Likewise, a Chinese-American manager who was surprised at the early tension between him and his local employees found that, after several years, many of his local employees admitted that his style had, in fact, benefited them:

> If you ask most employees to pick out my faults, they will probably say that I can be difficult, fussy, overly detail oriented. Yet, four out of five employees who leave . . . on their own will come back with comments such as "I can see exactly why you were the way you were," because they ended up with the same expectations of their colleagues.

His interpretation of the adaptation he observed was reflected in his comment, "I believe that the 'western' practice I bring of motivation, empowerment, thinking outside of the box is being accepted by my Chinese employees."

Our respondents indicated that adjustment to ensure the continuation of the relationship was a two-way street. Just as the local managers adjusted to western business practices, modes of operating, and perspectives, their foreign counterparts also adjusted. A long-term consultant and instructor at a Vietnamese university commented that

> no matter how much we foreigners try to instill "international business practices," the Vietnamese will find their own ways of using those practices. They will find a new approach and thrive in their own way. Not like we would; not like we think they should. But they'll find their own way.

Rather than trying to force western practices, she concluded that she could offer help and guidance, but that, ultimately, the country's, the university's, and individuals' decisions were theirs, not hers.

Another foreign manager wrestled with whether to step in and help local managers in Central Europe and Asia with a new performance system that his infrastructure firm was implementing worldwide or to wait and let them adapt it to their own situations. Based on his years working with managers in transition economies (from central and eastern Europe to Mongolia and Russia), he felt it important to introduce a companywide performance system as the time came for turn over of projects to the local management. The system required company managers to identify eight to ten performance criteria that were then communicated throughout the firm to all managers and employees. In theory, the local firm managers were to implement and use the system for their employees. Since the local managers would receive a bonus for unit performance, the foreigner thought there was an incentive for them to implement the new system. However, the foreign manager found that the local managers were initially unclear about how to interpret the performance criteria and to use them for their employees. Many of the local managers did not introduce or carry out the performance system as quickly as the foreigner expected. As he assessed the situation later, he speculated that the local managers' reluctance to use the system stemmed from differences between the market and socialist systems, from the managers' misunderstandings, and also from their concern about making mistakes using the system. He became frustrated as transition economy managers brushed off the system and conducted business in their traditional ways. Later, the foreign manager was convinced that the locals knew that bonuses depended upon firm performance but that they hadn't made the connection initially.

Although the local managers were responsible for carrying out the system, he worried that employees and other managers did not fully grasp the criteria, the purpose of the system, the expectations for performance, or the relationship to pay. Furthermore, he resisted asking the local managers to conduct information sessions because he was waiting for those managers to assume the responsibility for the system. Since he had built a good relationship and strong interaction, he wanted to find a way to maintain those without direct involvement or interference in the local managers' jobs. His normal approach was to nudge and urge, but he realized this was not effective in these cultures. So, he continued to stress the link between performance and pay with all units. Eventually, over the course of a year, the local managers (and employees) understood that the system was to benefit (and not punish) them and made the connection between performance and compensation. They then learned to manage the system on their own. While the adjustment in this manager's style may seem subtle, it was just this sort of quiet persistence that was an effective tactic.

ACCEPT AND COMPROMISE

A second approach that emerged from discussions with the managers we interviewed was one of acceptance, or making the best of a (bad) situation, even though neither side felt completely satisfied. In this case counterparts worked through a project and moved on or found ways to turn the work over to the local (or another foreign) managers and eased themselves out. Often the decision to accept a suboptimal situation was mutual. At other times business objectives had been met, even though interpersonal interactions were discordant.

Sometimes this approach came from a festering disharmony that resulted from much earlier actions. For example, an infrastructure firm that agreed to help restructure and increase productivity of firms (East Germany in the early 1990s and Mongolia in the late 1990s) saw in both cases that a reduction of the labor force was critical to improve plant productivity. In both sites, local managers disagreed with the conclusion to reduce employees and refused (or did not know how) to carry out the decision. Because of their socialist backgrounds they held a continuing strong belief in employment as a right for workers. They argued with the foreign managers' decisions, but eventually accepted the situation. However, in each case, eight years apart and in quite different countries, the foreign managers, rather than the local managers, implemented the reduction. In both cases, plant output, efficiency, and long-run stability all increased. The remaining local managers, although surprised, eventually agreed that the result, though painful and almost unimaginable for them, was positive.

The same manager watched the relationship he had with local managers in Mongolia go through a dramatic transformation over the course of the decade of the 1990s. While it was never fully positive, neither was it poor enough to abandon. And there was an underlying sense of acceptance throughout his time there. In the early part of the decade, the relationship between him, his American colleagues, and their Mongolian counterparts moved from a state of distrust, especially on the part of the local managers, to one of acceptance. For example, the American managers felt that local employees, managers, and even citizens realized that the firm, by working to renovate a local utility firm, was helping them. Somewhat later his impression was that the Mongolians had simply been accepting the situation. There was, after 1997, a shift in political affiliations within the parliament—from almost completely communist to less so, then back to more communist in its representatives. The shift suggested a less positive view of market economics. Apparently people failed to see the benefits of free markets and hoped that a return to the communist party would improve things. By that point, the American firm had completed the project and left. As the manager commented, they finished the project, accepted the relationship as it had developed, and moved on. They saw no reason to continue the relationship beyond the life of the initial business project.

ABANDON

A few managers reported that they could or did not want to continue in their relationship. In such cases, the relationship ended or began to unravel at the critique stage. The reaction on each side was often quite negative because interpersonal conflicts had not been resolved. In some cases, of course, the local managers sought to pursue their own paths or returned to more traditional ways of operating. Foreign managers often felt that changes would be so long or so difficult to achieve that the relationship would cost more to sustain than the expected benefits.

In a typical example, a manager who became frustrated working in the Czech Republic, felt that the senior local managers tried to manipulate his activities and the course of a project. He abandoned the relationship, but returned several years later. His reaction was that, on some levels, little had changed—the old guard was still running the public sector oil company, still using authoritarian approaches, and still seeking to work the system in ways that were not always transparent. On the other hand, he found the younger, lower level employees increasingly knowledgeable about western practices and technology; they just were unable to break out from the dominant managers above them.

In other cases, relationships die or are abandoned because of neglect. In several cases in the Vietnamese university where one of us worked, the university established and pursued relationships with foreign academic and business partners in an effort to offer academic degrees or executive training. It seemed, in many cases, that the university was desperate to accept most offers from foreign institutions for fear of not having another opportunity in the future. As a result, they often had what amounted to more relationships than any of the managers inside the university could handle. From the foreign managers' perspective, the relationships often died because the Vietnamese had not nurtured and taken personal care of the relationship, as the foreigners had expected.

LEAVE OPEN THE POSSIBILITIES

The difficulty of determining future directions for relationships suggests that we consider at least one more option. Managers may discover opportunities or pathways that are unlike any they have encountered and seek to explore them and adapt them for their own situations. Several scholars have suggested that new routes open up in interactions among individuals from different cultural backgrounds (e.g., Holden 2002; Thomas and Ravlin 1995). We might expect new possible outcomes to emerge among managers in their interactions in the transition economies as their environments, organizations, and individual knowledge and motivations change. Thus, rather than forcing a fit in what may occur, we leave open the possibilities for new and unseen modes of operating. As Holden (2002) suggested, spontaneous, unpredictable, and unexpected outcomes may emerge in cross-cultural management relationships.

In another Vietnam example, one of us spent years working with counterparts on all aspects of building their business school (e.g., creating academic programs, support systems for human resources, finance and accounting practices, technology and library resources). Even after those five years of building trust and working together, the Vietnamese counterparts did not tell the foreign partners about a critical and potentially devastating internal disagreement until it was almost too late to help. The university's internal politics and conflict nearly ended one of the school's crucial programs as well as the funding support from an external donor. Thus, an unexpected—and to the foreigners, bizarre— behavior on the part of the Vietnamese influenced subsequent trust and pursuit of the relationship. The Vietnamese saw their reluctance to report on the situation as one of handling their own internal problems; the foreigners saw it as a lack of trust that they could help solve the problem.

SUMMARY

This chapter suggests that the nature of future relationships between transition economy and foreign managers are difficult to predict. Most of the relationships we observed, if they survived the first three stages, were ones that managers were motivated to continue for some reason. They found ways to adapt in order to maintain the relationship. Notable was a quiet persistence and a belief that making change was worth the effort. Another set of outcomes involved an acceptance of less than optimal interpersonal relationships in order to complete the task or project at hand. And, of course, a certain percentage of relationships were abandoned for a variety of reasons. Western managers, in particular, described this abandonment in terms of the costs of maintaining the relationship in comparison to future benefits. Finally, some relationships may evolve in unpredictable and unexpected ways. Our ability to predict the future in intercultural relationships is very limited.

Chapter 10

MANAGING RELATIONSHIPS IN TRANSITION ECONOMIES

> For every complex human problem there is a simple solution, and it's
> always wrong.
> —H. L. Mencken, American journalist (1880–1956)

Managing the relationship with transition economy managers is indeed
a complex endeavor. Foreign managers face significant challenges when
their firms seek entry into these economies as they join the broader global
marketplace. This chapter draws on what we have learned in our investigation to suggest ways to overcome some of the challenges discussed
in earlier chapters. As the Mencken quote suggests, we have no neat and
tidy prescription. We do, however, have an approach that, while recognizing the complexity of the situation, offers managers a practical avenue
for achieving more successful interpersonal interactions in transition
economies.

First, the chapter reviews the elements of the broad model we used in
our investigation and then summarizes the effects of the model of relationship development outlined in Chapter 5. Then a three-phase iterative
approach to improving interpersonal interactions between foreign and
transition economy managers is introduced. This approach involves helping foreign managers gain knowledge about transition economy managers, developing a mindful approach to interactions, and finally, learning
and practicing adaptive skills. Each of these elements is reviewed in
detail below.

Figure 1.1 in Chapter 1 illustrates the elements that make up the context of interpersonal interactions in these transition economies. The interaction of foreign and local managers in transition economies is complicated because the managers approach these interactions with different backgrounds, knowledge, experience bases, and motivations—in short, different grounding. These grounding differences are exacerbated by the contextual differences brought about by the different firm types that have emerged in transition economies and by the variation in the type of transition toward more market-based economic structures that exists in different countries.

First, the legacy of state socialism indelibly etched attitudes about what is normal or expected behavior in the minds of transition economy managers. These attitudes include norms of centralization and bureaucratic control, quantity of production over quality, paternalistic behavior by superiors, soft budget constraints, weak response to prices, and a general disregard for the external environment. To the extent that these norms for behavior are inconsistent in a more market-oriented environment, managers must suppress or unlearn them. The willingness and ability of transition economy managers to make such change is influenced by many factors, including learned helplessness about making change and a healthy paranoia of out-groups. These managers may have become so conditioned by their previous experience that they function in an almost automatic or mindless manner that feels correct to them. While they may actively acknowledge the need to change behavior to be effective in the new environment they face, there are strong subconscious forces at work that make such changes extremely difficult.

Second, the behavior of transition economy managers is influenced by the ability of organizations in which they work to absorb extreme change. The types of firms facing the most upheaval and having the least ability to absorb change are state-owned enterprises and newly privatized firms. While entrepreneurial start-ups and foreign firms may respond better, they must still absorb a significant amount of change in an already turbulent environment.

Three suboptimal responses to extreme change are apparent (Newman 2000): clinging to comfortable yet obsolete routines; a complete lack of direction or concept for the future; and uncritical mimicry of perceived successful examples. In this way, organizational responses to extreme change place demands and constraints on managers' behavior, which limit their ability to choose more appropriate alternative behavior. For example, recently privatized SOEs in Bulgaria often retained the same top management group that guided the state-owned enterprise (Manev and Gyoshev 2001). Managers in Chinese enterprises have been found to have little power to change their officially defined role because jobs have traditionally been characterized by tight rules and technical regulations (Boisot and Xing 1992).

Our research suggests that the relationships between local and foreign managers in transition economies progresses through identifiable stages that we labeled Contact, Critique, Convergence, and Continue?. At each stage, fundamental psychological principles help to explain and predict the characteristics of the interpersonal interaction. In our study, these characteristics were most clearly manifested in the perceptions of trust that existed between the parties, in the accuracy of the expectations of the behavior and attitudes of participants, and in the nature and flow of information. However, passing through the stages of the development model did not guarantee a successful interaction. The characteristics of the final stage of the development model appears to differ across individuals and situations. Since we have little evidence of what happens in the long term in these relationships, the story is as yet unfinished. However, we have documented general trends and possible outcomes that may emerge over the longer run. Some managers want to withdraw from future interaction, some successfully complete their current projects and then pursue no others, and yet others hit a sort of plateau in which they ultimately adjust their goals and expectations in order to move forward. Still others create different paths forward, developing unique new ways to operate.

Given the differences among individuals, some idiosyncratic, unexpected, and sometimes hard-to-imagine experiences emerged within the context of their relationships. Transition economy managers come from different cultures; they have different knowledge and experiences under socialism than their foreign counterparts had in their countries. As a result some issues, experiences, or images may arise that are unfamiliar and unexplainable in a rational way for foreign managers (Holden 2002). Rather than assuming foreign managers will be able to understand and categorize all of their interactions or outcomes with transition economy managers, the following sections offer ideas to help these managers become more aware of and to improve their interactions with transition economy managers.

As suggested previously, individual managers might define a successful interaction in transition economies in a variety of ways. Our interviewees typically focused on task accomplishment—getting the job done—but in some cases, they mentioned having positive feelings about the situation. This book suggests a somewhat broader definition of what it means to be successful in transition economy relationships. Following Brislin (1993), a successful interaction is defined as consisting of four parts. First, individuals must feel that they are having a successful relationship. That is, they report that they are working cooperatively and look forward to interacting with the other party. Second, they must be accomplishing their work goals or tasks. Third, they are able to develop and maintain good interpersonal relationships with their counterparts. Finally, they are conducting their business or accomplishing their tasks with no greater stress than they would be experiencing working with people in their own countries. Only when all four of these criteria are met can managers say that they truly have a successful interaction. Success defined in this way encompasses the shorter-term, getting-the-job done criteria, but adds a longer-term developmental component that is equally important.

It is important to consider all four criteria of success because it may be possible to achieve success in one dimension while neglecting another. For example, the short-term success of task accomplishment may actually occur at great cost with regard to the stress it places on the individual manager. Focusing so intensely on the specific task may also cause the manager to neglect the development of good relationships with counterparts that is critical for success in future interactions. Many of the stories we heard from managers in transition countries about foreign managers suggested that the well had been poisoned for future foreign managers by the actions of their predecessors. Therefore, successful interactions are important for one's self and for one's successors. The following section discusses an approach to managing interactions between foreign and transition economy managers that addresses all four of these outcome criteria.

MANAGING INTERACTIONS

The complexity of the situation in which foreign managers must interact with transition economy managers prohibits a simple prescription for success. That is, every variant of individual, organizational, and environmental factors that a manager might face cannot be documented and then combined with the developmental stage of the interaction to list drills and routines that fit each specific case. Such a focus on country specific knowledge ignores the fact that certain aspects of cross-national and cross-cultural interactions are applicable across settings. Also, the sheer magnitude of acquiring and cataloging the breadth of detailed knowledge required in even a single country makes the task virtually impossible.

However, simply leaving the task of managing an interaction to the transition economy manager or expecting him/her to adjust completely to foreign (typically western) approaches is also ineffective. First, as noted above, transition economy managers may be constrained in their ability to adjust their behavior and attitudes. That is, there may be individual, institutional, and cultural factors that make adjusting to normal western style market behavior difficult or impossible. Additionally, as our interviewees found, transition economy managers may possess knowledge and skills, often not immediately apparent to the foreign manager, that make blanket adjustment to western approaches inadvisable and ultimately less effective in a particular context. This tacit knowledge, or in-the-bones expertise, is learned through socialization in a particular environmental context (Nonaka and Takeuchi 1995). Therefore, foreign managers are unlikely to recognize such knowledge because local mangers have difficulty making it explicit. When local managers say "that won't work here," and are then unable to explain why, they may actually be saying; "I have tacit knowledge about whether the approach you propose will be effective." These factors suggest the need for an approach that does not rely solely on either factual knowledge or experience.

Thus, a three-stage iterative approach for foreign managers to use in improving the ability to manage relationships with transition economy managers is suggested. The first stage involves recognizing the need for and acquiring several kinds of knowledge—both specific knowledge about managers in these economies and the way that their behavior might be similar to and different from that of foreign managers and also general knowledge about concepts and experiences that apply to any cross-national or cross-cultural interaction. The second stage involves developing a mindful approach to interactions by paying attention, in a reflective and creative way, to cues that indicate how the context of culture, history, the organizational setting, and the stage of relationship development are at work in a given situation. Finally, based on knowledge from understanding and mindfulness, foreign managers can develop adaptive skills to manage effectively their interactions with transition economy managers in a variety of contexts. Table 10.1 presents an overview of the interactive process.

With each iteration of the approach depicted in Table 10.1, new interactions help the foreign manager develop competency in managing relationships and interaction with transition economy counterparts. That is, a basis in knowledge allows for a mindful approach that helps turn this knowledge into skills. Each specific piece of knowledge builds a more general base on which to build interaction skills. The major

Table 10.1
Effects of Stage of Relationship Development

Stage	Trust	Expectations	Information Flow
Contact	Neutral, healthy skepticism, or optimism	Stereotypic expectations	Based on initial perceptions and expectations
Critique	Disorientation, conflict, and lack of trust	Disconfirmed expectations, confusion	Communication barriers have emerged
Convergence	Stereotypes begin to break down, trust develops	Realistic expectations emerge, new standards of behavior	Flow of communication begins to be two-way; non-conflicting goals emerge
Continue?	Evaluation of the level of trust; consideration of future relationship	More accurate attributions of behavior; active thought about own behavior	Active two-way communication; new meanings are negotiated

advantage of this approach is that each specific competence gained simultaneously results in a general competence that makes each new interaction easier to manage. The elements of this iterative model are discussed in the following.

Knowledge

Although it is impossible for foreign managers to know everything about their counterparts from transition economies, knowledge is a key component of managing these relationships. Three types of knowledge are important. First, self-knowledge helps foreign managers recognize the factors that influence their own values, attitudes, and behavior and how these elements may bias perceptions and judgment. Along with self-knowledge, foreign managers need knowledge of their counterparts helps managers recognize areas of potential agreement or conflict. This knowledge can be only a first best guess because of the significant amount of individual variation that exists even among individuals in a single country or organization. A second type of knowledge involves understanding the process by which contextual elements influences the values, attitudes, and behavior of individuals. This type of knowledge can help foreign managers predict the responses of transition economy managers both to external factors and the actions of foreign managers. A final knowledge type involves the recognition of the stage of development of the relationship as outlined in Chapter 5. This type of knowledge allows foreign managers to anticipate outcomes of interactions based on more accurate expectations. That is, the behavior they observe both in local managers and in themselves may be the result of the normal stage of development in the relationship.

Self-Knowledge and Knowledge of Others

Two critical types of knowledge for foreign managers are of the self and others. While self-awareness is very much an individual matter, foreign managers share some common self-perceptions. That is, their values, attitudes, and behaviors have been conditioned by the expectation of others about what it is managers do and how managers should behave. As discussed previously, because of the inherently western conceptualization of management and the similarity of management education around the world, western managers will share a great deal of explicit information as well as a significant amount of tacit knowledge about what it means to be a manager.

Foreign managers also need to develop understanding and knowledge of how they view others: the values, attitudes, and behavioral assumptions that they have about transition managers, given the historical, cultural, organizational, and institutional background of each group of managers. Previous chapters of this book have discussed the content of this knowledge in some detail. Here the discussion focuses on the limitations of these general expectations about managers in another cultural or organizational environment.

When the characteristics of a group or category of people are generalized to the individual, a stereotype is being used. Stereotypes are not necessarily bad or noxious. They result from the natural process of applying a limited amount of information about a group to all members of that group. The process is natural because it is impossible to have detailed knowledge about every individual a person might encounter, so that person generalizes.

These generalized expectations can cause problems in managing relationships in several ways. First, of course, not every individual will match the simple expectations that even a great deal of knowledge permits. There is typically a huge amount of variation within a group. Each individual is more or less representative of a cultural norm, and no individual matches the stereotype exactly. Also, individual behavior is the product of the situation and personality as well as of a culture. Second, stereotypes often elicit strong feelings, particularly about groups with which people may have had a long history of interaction or conflict. The deep feelings that people have for members of other cultural or ethnic groups cannot be ignored. The effects of the cold war between East and West, the cultural revolution in China, and the American conflict in Vietnam may now be part of history, but their effects on the attitudes of individuals toward groups of people from those regions remain. Third, national stereotypes often ascribe to a generally accepted hierarchy because of economic dominance or other presumed desirable characteristics of nations (Sidanius 1993). For example, some individuals from developing countries rank the United States as a desirable culture because of its economic strength.

Finally, as Chapter 5 mentions, after individuals develop an expectation of people from a particular category (Russian managers, Vietnamese engineers, etc.), they tend to hold to those expectations even in the face of new and disconfirming information. That is, when they meet a person who does not fit their expectation, they discount that person as being atypical and hold to their stereotype of the group.

Despite these limitations, even knowledge that produces only broad stereotypic expectations of transition economy managers can be useful if these stereotypes are:

- consciously held, that is, managers recognize they are dealing with limited information;
- limited to describing members of the particular category or group and are not evaluative;
- an accurate description of the broad behavioral norm for that group;
- used as a first best guess about behavior of that group; and
- modified based on additional information gained through observation or experience (Adler 1997).

Knowledge of Context

A second type of knowledge has to do with the process through which different contextual elements influence managerial values, attitudes, and behavior. That is, understanding how context (broadly defined as organizational, institutional, historical, and cultural influences) affects what managers do can aid in understanding management behavior in transition economies. A useful tool for examining the factors that influence managerial behavior in organizations is to think of what managers do as role behaviors (Katz and Kahn 1966). Role behaviors are the recurring activities of individuals that are associated with a particular position in the organization (Sarbin and Allen 1968). The exact composition of the role of any individual manager depends on the expectations and influences both from within the organization and from the external environment.

Four concepts are important to understanding the idea of roles that managers play. First is *role expectations* that are the standards of behavior that others associate with a given position in an organization. Second is the idea of a *sent role,* which are the messages about what his/her role should be that influence the individual manager. Third is the *received role,* which is the manager's perception of the sent role and any role expectations that the individual sends to him/herself. Finally, *role behavior* is the response of individuals to the information and influence. All roles have multiple senders. A manager's role behavior may be a response to simultaneously sent roles from the organization, from elements of the external environment, and to his or her own reflective internal role expectations. To the extent that sent roles are contradictory or are mutually exclusive, the manager experiences *role conflict.* To the extent that these sent roles are incomplete, the manager will experience *role ambiguity* (Kahn, Wolfe, Quinn, Snoek, and Rosenthal 1964). The role stress created by these situations has been shown to have a very negative effect on job-related attitudes (Fisher and Gitelson 1983).

A complimentary approach to understanding managerial behavior, useful in making comparisons among managerial jobs, is Stewart's (1982) demands, constraints, and choices model. *Demands* are what anyone in the managerial job must do. These are such things as meeting minimum performance criteria and doing certain kinds of work (e.g., attending required meetings or filing a particular report). *Constraints* are the factors both internal and external to the organization that limit what managers can do. These include limitations with regard to resources, technology, geography, legal and trade unions, and any organizational restrictions placed on the manager. *Choices* are the activities that the manager can, but does not have to, do. These involve choosing what work is done and how it is done. Combining the ideas of role behaviors with demands, constraints, and choices in what transition economy managers do provides a framework that can be used to understand the effects of organizational, institutional, and cultural factors on managerial behavior. Our interviews suggest the following.

- Managers in transition economies are likely to have very different role perceptions from their foreign counterparts. For example, both western and transition economy managers may recognize the need to scan the environment for new business opportunities. However, while western managers may be thinking about the potential demands for new products or services, transition economy managers may be thinking about how to exploit political connections.

- Managers in transition economies are more likely to receive conflicting role expectations from their environment, and these role expectations are changing rapidly. For example, as state-owned enterprises shift from a production target motive to a profit motive, local managers will be expected to control costs, which is a new role for them and may conflict with their own perceptions of what their role should be and, perhaps, with employee expectations of their managers.

- Transition economy managers experience more role conflict, role ambiguity, and role stress than their foreign counterparts. For example, because laws regarding business transactions were unnecessary in socialist economies, the absence of such a system of laws posttransition creates an ambiguous message about what is appropriate business behavior. Also, when laws are introduced, they may conflict with role behavior that local managers adopted to function without a formal legal structure. The short-term opportunistic behavior that some transition economy managers exhibit reflects those ambiguous role messages.

- The demands, constraints, and choices in managerial jobs in transition economies are undergoing extreme change. For example, activities such as marketing and finance, did not exist pretransition. These new functions place new demands on managers. While the constraints of central planning have been removed, new constraints, such as the need for quality control imposed by the market, are introduced. And, as noted previously, the amount of discretion in managerial roles has increased, in part, because of incomplete role messages.

Thinking of the managerial behavior in terms of roles encourages a search for the sources of role messages, for how roles may be different in the particular context, and also for how roles may change overtime. As their role expectations are recognized, the behavior of transition economy managers appears less idiosyncratic.

Knowledge of Relationship Stage

The final type of knowledge required to effectively manage the relationship with transition economy managers is knowledge about the developmental process of the relationship. Our research indicated that these relationships typically progress through identifiable contact, critique, convergence, and continue? stages. Although this general developmental model does not fit each individual case perfectly, it can be a useful tool in anticipating the stage of relationship development on such indicators as the level of trust, accuracy of expectation, and information flow between the participants. Table 10.1 summarizes the effects of stage of relationship development.

This section suggests that three types of knowledge form the basis for managing relationships with transition economy managers. They are knowledge about one's own grounding as well as that of one's counterpart, knowledge of the process through which differences in grounding affect behavior, and knowledge of the stage of development through which these relationships typically progress. Knowledge by itself is not sufficient to effectively manage a relationship. Because these managerial relationships are so complex, managers must also learn from experience. The experiential learning needs to be more than trial and error, however. A key concept, *mindfulness,* is needed to turn experience into the repertoire of skills necessary to manage the complex interactions with transition economy managers.

Mindfulness

Mindfulness is a Buddhist concept that has been adopted and applied in the fields of psychology (Langer 1989) and communications (Ting-Toomey 1999). Mindfulness means attending to our internal assumptions, cognitions, and emotions, while simultaneously attuning to another's assumptions, cognitions, and emotions. It also involves learning to see behavior or information presented in a situation as novel or fresh, viewing a situation from several vantage points or perspectives, attending to the context and the person in which we are perceiving the behavior, and creating new categories through which we can understand this new behavior (Langer 1989; Thich 1991). The antithesis of mindfulness, *mindlessness,* is exemplified in the following example:

> The route one man drives from work is designed to avoid a certain run-down section of the city and to minimize traffic. He takes this route every workday. On occasion his spouse calls him at the office and asks him to pick up something for supper. Doing so requires a very slightly different route. However, he often arrives home without making the supermarket detour, and doesn't realize it until his wife asks where the groceries are.

The act of operating an automobile on city streets is a complex activity, yet most people do it in this seemingly mindless, semireflexive manner. Typically, as in the example above, they learn and repeat their routes so often that even a slight adjustment is difficult. In this case, a familiar, repetitive activity leads to a kind of mental laziness.

As discussed in earlier chapters, much of human behavior occurs in this scripted, seemingly mindless manner, which is a semireflexive response to the situation. However, mindlessness can occur even when people have not learned an activity through constant repetition (Langer 1989). This happens when people uncritically accept pieces of information when they are first presented and then hold on to these impressions in subsequent encounters. For example, television may present images that suggest particular traits about people of a certain ethnicity (e.g., Scots are thrifty, Americans are brash, the British are reserved). Because the information may have been irrelevant when it was first presented, people accepted it mindlessly. Subsequently, when they meet a person of this ethnicity, they may uncritically (and unconsciously) draw on this piece of now relevant information. In this way, the uncritical use of cultural stereotypes can be seen as a form of mindlessness.

The adverse results of mindless behavior in interacting with individuals from other countries and cultures are wide ranging. For example, managers with different grounding can easily misunderstand this semireflexive behavior. Likewise, mindlessness prevents managers from understanding the true meaning of behaviors of their counterparts. The outcomes of mindlessness fall into three categories: narrow thinking, unintended outcomes, and loss of control.

Narrow Thinking

A classic case of narrow business thinking induced by mindlessness is "marketing myopia" (Langer 1989). Levitt (1975) said that the decline of the railroads in the United States occurred because the industry managers assumed that they were in the railroad business rather than in the transportation business. Likewise, foreign managers who assume that their role is to enlighten transition economy managers on correct behavior in a market economy suffer from the narrow thinking that limits alternatives.

This type of thinking was revealed in several of our interviews. For example, the environmental consultant who insisted that the only way to conduct studies was the way he had done it in the United States showed an admirable desire to follow international standards, but a reluctance to be creative in finding new or alternative ways to solve problems. Had he been able to consider alternate ways to work with his counterparts, he might have been able to gain the information he needed.

Unintended Outcomes

The unintended consequences of mindlessness occur because of creeping commitment. That is, when a manager accepts an inconsequential event uncritically or performs a behavior mindlessly, those actions form the basis for a small next step, then another, and still another, until the outcome is not at all inconsequential. The incremental nature of their actions prevents managers from realizing that they have behaved in ways that they may not have chosen.

For example, this type of mindlessness appeared in the two trainers in Vietnam who worked together for several weeks before their blow up about "writing on the blackboard." They refrained from facing issues as they arose in their interactions, they made more commitments to each other and to the course participants, and then when the difficulties became too obvious to ignore, they had already committed to completing a training course, and neither wanted to compromise on making changes.

Loss of Control

Finally, mindlessness reduces the ability of managers to control their own behavior. For example, managers who experience success naturally want to persist in the behavior they believe created that success. Many do so, even in the face of changed circumstances. Thus, foreign managers who try to uncritically transfer the techniques that served them well in their home settings to transition economies are guilty of a type of mindlessness. In our interviews, an extreme example of this behavior was the American manager in Russia who lost control and ranted that the country was an impossible place to get things accomplished, hurting his credibility and sacrificing his subordinates' respect for him.

Mindlessness is present when people experience the learned helplessness condition discussed in Chapter 5. That is, after repeated failure, managers abandon activities that have failed even though the circumstances may now allow those same activities to be successful. For example, one of our interviewees saw evidence of this type of mindlessness in the apathy of foreign managers after two or three years on a project in a transition economy: "They just settle in and do the job without the enthusiasm or creativity that it needs." The managers began to carry out tasks without thinking critically and carefully about them, and eventually felt unwilling and powerless to make changes.

Since all three types of mindlessness were present in the interactions between foreign and transition economy managers we interviewed, we see its antithesis, mindfulness, as a key mediating step in linking knowledge with skillful practice. Mindfulness has been conceptualized as a cognitive ability, a personality trait, and as a cognitive style. Mindfulness puts managers in a stage of readiness to effectively interact with people who are different from themselves and is within the ability of individuals to control. Consistent with research on cross-cultural communication and training we suggest that to fashion effective interaction with transition economy managers requires mindful observation and listening. (Ting-Toomey 1999).

Mindful Observation

Mindful observation involves observing, describing, interpreting, and suspending evaluation of new and unfamiliar behaviors. It is founded on the self-awareness described previously. Managers need to monitor their reactions to the different behaviors and interactions before deciding how to respond. When western managers observe behavior that is inconsistent with their own expectations, they need to think through the answers to several questions, before reacting: Why might someone act this way (e.g., what possible sources of the role expectations underlie the behavior)? How can I interpret this behavior in light of what I know about these expectations? What is my intuitive reaction to this behavior? Why would I react this way? What is the likely outcome of my behavior? In other words, what managers need to do is reflect on their experiences and remain nonjudgmental. Some of the managers we interviewed mentioned their conscious attempts to remain nonjudgmental in the early stages of their relationships. That is, they took a wait-and-see approach to building trust by suspending their evaluation of the situation. Learning to stop and reflect in a nonevaluative way is a critical first step in developing mindfulness.

Mindful Listening

Mindful listening means hearing more than just the words that are spoken. It also means checking for accurate perception and paraphrasing the speaker's message into one's own words. Checking for mutual understanding and shared meanings is critical in overcoming the possible barriers to effective interaction. Managers often find that it is much easier to hear what they expect to hear than it is to accurately decode and understand a message from a counterpart with very different cultural and institutional grounding. When transition economy managers responded to requests from foreign managers with phrases like "whatever you say, you know best," some foreigner managers saw this as a signal to check for understanding, but many did not.

Finally, mindful listening means paying attention—to the spoken words and also to nonverbal aspects of communication, such as tone of voice, gestures, body position, pauses, and even silence. Other contextual elements such as the physical location and the relative status of the speaker also come into play. This type of listening—beyond the words— is especially difficult for North American managers who rely heavily on words to communicate meaning. For mindfulness to influence and enhance interactions between foreign and transition economy managers, it must be translated into skills and behaviors that managers can use. Those skills and behaviors are discussed next.

Skills

This final stage of the iterative process of learning to manage interactions with transition economy managers involves foreign managers building on basic knowledge and mindfulness of their own and their counterparts' behavior. By developing *knowledge* and *mindfulness,* managers can more accurately understand the behavior of themselves and others. Thus, the final step for managers is to use this information to guide their skill development and choose appropriately from a repertoire of behaviors to improve the interactions they have with transition economy managers. Two general skill sets are especially helpful—identity confirmation and collaborative dialogue (Ting-Toomey 1999).

Identity Confirmation

Identity confirmation refers to a set of actions that managers (and others) use to indicate that they are sensitive to and respectful of the perceptions that others have of themselves. Such actions include addressing people by their preferred titles, labels, and identities and using inclusive, rather than exclusive, language. For example, one of the initial mistakes that some of the foreign managers made was not realizing the superiority of the education that their transition economy managers had. As a result, some made mistakes in the way they addressed and interacted with those counterparts. While transition economy managers may have lacked the language and skills associated with market-based business practices, they based their self-images on other experiences. For example, many of these managers identified strongly with their ethnicity, their professional qualifications, their social class, or their educational level. By being sensitive to people's self-identity and according them respect, managers recognize their worth. To effectively interact with transition economy managers, foreign managers need to pay close attention to the local managers' preferences for identity affiliation.

Collaborative Dialogue

Collaborative dialogue involves suspending one's assumptions about people who are different and refraining from imposing one's views on them. Engaging in collaborative dialogue means that western managers avoid pushing their own points of view or goals onto their transition economy counterparts and consciously seek alternative perspectives. It can be thought of as the exact opposite of ethnocentric behavior, which rests on assumptions of the superiority on one's own beliefs or behavior.

Translation of Skills to Behavior

The way in which the mindful experience of western managers can be transferred into a repertoire of behaviors is founded in social learning theory (Bandura 1977). Social learning theory suggests a process of learning that involves attention, retention, reproduction, and finally, reinforcement. In the transition economy context, this means that foreign managers need to pay attention to and appreciate critical differences in the culture and background between themselves and others; they must also pay attention to the context in which the interaction is taking place. Such learning also implies an attitude that sees the different behavior of others as legitimate and important. Retention requires mindfulness to retain and learn from experiences and to apply the learning to future interactions. To retain information provided by experience, managers must actively think about the interaction situation and what it means for them in future interactions. Reproduction means practicing the skills learned in future relationships. Finally, reinforcement implies that the more frequently and attentively managers reinforce successful behaviors, the more quickly they can improve their interactions.

Additionally, managers must recognize that alternative perspectives and ideas may not always be presented directly; they may be presented indirectly in stories, metaphors, or analogies. Managers must be attentive to the identity and the relationships that underlie the content of messages. Western managers who are interested in their counterparts' situations and show a willingness to learn are likely to improve their interactions. In summary, foreign managers can enhance their relationships with transition economy managers by:

- *being aware* of their own culture and background, its biases and idiosyncrasies, and the way these are unconsciously reflected in their own perceptions and behavior;

- deliberately *avoiding mindlessness* by expecting differences in others, seeing this different behavior as novel, and suspending evaluation of that behavior;
- *being mindful* of behavioral cues and their interpretation and to the likely effect of their behavior on others;
- *adapting their behavior* in ways that are appropriate for the situation;
- *experimenting* with methods of adapting intuitively to new situations and using these experiments to build competence and smooth interpersonal performance;
- *transferring behaviors* learned in one situation experimentally to new situations;
- *practicing new behaviors* that work until these behaviors become automatic; acquiring repertoires of new, skilled behavior.

Using an iterative approach to learning means that each new encounter provides an opportunity for additional knowledge that may be incorporated into an individual's skill set and applied in other situations. Skills learned in this way can be applied to a variety of different countries, cultures, and situations.

SUMMARY

This chapter suggests an approach to managing relationships with others who have different backgrounds, as is the case for western managers trying to function in transition economies. This approach builds on a model that first identifies both the internal and external factors that influence the behavior of transition economy managers. Then, the interactions are reviewed based on the relationship development model set forth in earlier chapters. Finally, an approach for building on this knowledge and on the experience gained in interacting with local managers is prescribed to transform these bases into a repertoire of skills that can be applied to future interactions. This transformation process relies on adopting a mindful approach to interacting with different others—breaking out of semireflexive, mindless modes of observing and behaving to create new categories of understanding. The iterative process is not a quick fix or simple solution; it is a way of being that can be transferred across countries, individuals, and situations.

BIBLIOGRAPHY

Abelson, R. P. 1981. "Psychological Status of the Script Concept." *American Psychologist* 36: 715–29.

Adler, N. J. 1997. *International Dimensions of Organizational Behavior.* 3rd ed. Cincinnati: South-Western.

Adler, N., and F. Ghadar. 1989. "Globalization and Human Resource Management." In *Research in Global Strategic Management: A Canadian Perspective,* vol. 1, edited by A. Rugman, 179–205. Greenwich, CT: JAI Press.

Aharoni, Y. 1986. *The Evolution and Management of State Owned Enterprises.* Cambridge, MA: Ballinger Publishers.

———. 1994. "How Small Firms Can Achieve Competitive Advantage in an Interdependent World." In *Small Firms in Global Competition,* edited by T. Agmon and R. Drobnick, 9–18. New York: Oxford University Press.

Albrow, M. 1997. *The Global Age.* Palo Alto: Stanford University Press.

Allmendinger, J., and J. Richard Hackman. 1996. "Organization in Changing Environments: The Case of East German Symphony Orchestras." *Administrative Science Quarterly* 41: 337–69.

Allred, B. B., C. C. Snow, and R. E. Miles. 1996. "Characteristics of Managerial Careers of the 21st Century." *The Academy of Management Executive* 10 (4): 17–27.

Antal, A. B., M. Dierkes, and M. Lutz. 1999. "Organizational Learning in China, Germany and Israel." *Journal of General Management* 25 (1): 17–42.

Argyris, C. 1960. *Understanding Organizational Behavior.* Homewood, IL: The Dorsey Press.

————. 1977. "Double-Loop Learning in Organizations." *Harvard Business Review* 55 (5): 115–25.

Asch, S. 1963. Effects of Group Pressure on the Modification and Distortion of Judgements. In *Groups, Leadership and Men,* edited by H. Guetzkow, 177–90. New York: Russell & Russell, Inc.

Au, K., and L. Sun. 1998. "Hope Group: The Future of Private Enterprises in China." *Asian Case Research Journal* 2 (2): 133–48.

Bandura, A. 1977. *Social Learning Theory.* Englewood Cliffs, NJ: Prentice-Hall.

Ben-Ner, A. 1988. "The Life Cycle of Worker-Owned Firms in Market Economies: A Theoretical Analysis." *Journal of Economic Behavior and Organization* 10 (3): 287–313.

Bjorkman, I., and M. Ehrnrooth. 1999. "HRM in Western Subsidiaries in Russia and Poland." *Journal of East-West Business* 5 (3): 63–79.

Bjorkman, I., and Y. Lu. 2001. "Institutionalization and Bargaining Power Explanations of HRM Practices in International Joint Ventures—The Case of Chinese-Western Joint Ventures." *Organization Studies* 22 (3): 491–512.

Black, J. 1999. "Market Realities Hit Poland." *BBC News,* 13 October, 16.09 GMT.

Boisot, M., and J. Child. 1996. "From Fiefs to Clans and Network Capitalism: Explaining China's Emerging Economic Order." *Administrative Science Quarterly* 41 (4): 600–628.

————. 1999. "Organizations as Adaptive Systems in Complex Environments: The Case of China." *Organization Science* 10 (3): 237–52.

Boisot, M., and G. L. Xing. 1992. "The nature of managerial work in the Chinese enterprise reforms: A study of six directors," "The Nature of Managerial Work in the Chinese Enterprise Reforms: A Study of Six Directors." *Organization Studies* 13 (2): 161–84.

Boyacigiller, N. A., and N. J. Adler. 1991. "The Parochial Dinosaur: Organizational Science in a Global Context." *Academy of Management Review* 16 (2): 262–90.

Breu, K. 2001. "The Role and Relevance of Management Cultures in the Organizational Transformation Process." *International Studies of Management and Organization* 31 (2): 28–47.

Brislin, R. W. 1993. *Understanding Culture's Influence on Behavior.* Fort Worth, TX: Harcourt Brace College Publishers.

Brzezinski, Z. 1989. *The Grand Failure: The Birth and Death of Communism in the Twentieth Century.* New York: Charles Scribner's Sons.

Burbach, R., O. Núñez, and B. Kagarlitsky. 1997. *Globalization and Its Discontents: The Rise of Postmodern Socialism.* London and Chicago: Pluto Press.

Campbell, R. W. 1991. *The Socialist Economies in Transition: A Primer on Semi-reformed Systems.* Bloomington: Indiana University Press.

Child, J., and L. Markóczy. "Host-Country Managerial Behavior and Learning in Chinese and Hungarian Joint Ventures." *Journal of Management Studies* 30 (4): 611–31.

Child, J., and D. K. Tse. 2001. "China's Transition and Its Implications for International Business." *Journal of International Business Studies* 32 (1): 5–21.

Clark, A. 2000. *Why Angels Fall: A Journey through Orthodox Europe from Byzantium to Kosovo.* New York: St. Martins Press.

Clark, E., R. Lang, and K. Balaton. 2001. "Making the Transition: Managers and Management in Transforming and Reforming Economies." *International Studies of Management and Organization* 31 (2): 3–8.

Clark, E., and A. Soulsby. 1999. *Organizational Change in Post-Communist Europe: Management and Transformation in the Czech Republic.* London and New York: Routledge.

Clarke, S. 1996a. "The Enterprise in the Era of Transition." In *The Russian Enterprise in Transition,* edited by S. Clarke, 1–61. London: Edward Elgar Publishers.

———, ed. 1995. *Conflict and Change in the Russian Industrial Enterprise.* Cheltenham, UK, and Brookfield, VT: Edward Elgar.

———. 1996b. *The Russian Enterprise in Transition.* London: Edward Elgar Publishers.

Collier, I. L. 1986. "Effective Purchasing Power in a Quantity Constrained Economy: An Estimate for the German Democratic Republic." *Review of Economics and Statistics* 68 (1): 24–32.

Cohen, M. 2000. "American Dream." *Far Eastern Economic Review,* 27 July, 22–23.

———. 2001. "From Cadre to Manager." *Far East Economic Review,* 27 September, 125–26.

Cohen, W. M., and D. A. Levinthal. 1990. "Absorptive Capacity: A New Perspective on Learning and Innovation." *Administrative Science Quarterly* 35 (1): 128–53.

Dallago, B. 1990. *The Irregular Economy: The "Underground" Economy and the "Black" Labour Market.* Aldershot, Eng., and Brookfield, VT: Gower Publishers Company.

Daniels, J. D., and L. H. Radebaugh. 1998. *International Business: Environments and Operations.* 8th ed. Reading, MA: Addison-Wesley.

Denison, D., ed. 2001. *Managing Organizational Change in Transition Economies.* Mahwah, NJ: Lawrence Erlbaum Associates.

de Tocqueville, A. 1835. *Democracy in America.* New York: Alfred Knopf.

Dewey, J. 1978. *Human Nature and Conduct, 1922.* Reprint, New York: Random House.

Dowling, P. J., D. E. Welch, and R. A. Schuler. 1999. *International Human Resource Management: Managing People in a Multinational Context.* Cincinnati, OH: South-Western College Publishers.

Drakulevski, L. 1999. "Managerial Style in Transition Economies—The

Example of the Republic of Macedonia." *Eastern European Economics* 37 (6): 26–34.

Dubow, C. 1997. "Great Doing Business with You, Grigori: And Thank You for Not Killing Me!" *Forbes,* 22 September, 140–48.

Dunbar, E. 1983. "Sociocultural and Contextual Challenges to Organizational Life in Eastern Europe: Implications for Cross-Cultural Training and Development." In *Handbook of Intercultural Training,* vol. 1, edited by D. Landis and R. W. Brislin, 349–65. Elmsford, NY: Pergamon.

Earley, P. C., and C. B. Gibson. 1998. "Taking Stock in Our Progress on Individualism-Collectivism: 100 Years of Solidarity and Community." *Journal of Management* 24: 265–304.

Edwards, V., and P. Lawrence. 2000. *Management in Eastern Europe.* New York: Palgrave, St. Martin's Press.

Erez, M., and P. C. Earley. 1993. *Culture, Self-Identity, and Work.* New York: Oxford University Press.

Ericson, R. E. 1991. "The Classical Soviet-Type Economy: Nature of the System and Implications for Reform." *Journal of Economic Perspectives* 5 (4): 1–18.

"Face Value: Behind the Throne." 1998. *The Economist,* 12 September, 76.

Feichtinger, C., and G. Fink. 1998. "The Collective Culture Shock in Transition Countries—Theoretical and Empirical Implications." *Leadership and Organization Development Journal* 19 (6): 302.

Fey, C. F., and P. W. Beamish. 2001. "Organizational Climate Similarity and Performance: International Joint Ventures in Russia." *Organization Studies* 22 (5): 853–82.

Fink, G., and N. Holden. 2000. "Collective Culture Shock: Contrastive Reactions to Radical Systemic Change." *CD-R Proceedings of the Annual Meeting of the Southern Management Association,* 7–12 November, Orlando, FL.

———. 2002. "Collective Culture Shock: Contrastive Reactions to Radical Systemic Change." IEF working paper no. 45, University of Economics and Business Administration, Vienna, Austria.

Finkelstein, S. 1992. "Power in Top Management Teams: Dimensions, Measurement, and Validation." *Academy of Management Journal* 35 (3): 505–39.

Fisher, C. D., and R. Gitelson. 1983. "A Meta-Analysis of the Correlates of Role Conflict and Ambiguity." *Journal of Applied Psychology* 68: 320–33.

Fisher, I. 2002. "As Poland Endures Hard Times, Capitalism Comes under Attack." *The New York Times,* 12 June, A1, 8.

Fiske, A. P. 1991. *Structures of Social Life: The Four Elementary Forms of Human Relations.* New York: Free Press.

Fox-Wolfgramm, S. J., K. B. Boal, and J. G. Hunt. 1998. "Organizational Adaptation to Institutional Change: A Comparative Study of First-Order Change in Prospector and Defender Banks." *Administrative Science Quarterly* 43: 87–126.

Friedman, M. 1991. *Monetarist Economics.* Oxford, UK, and Cambridge, MA: Blackwell.

Galbraith, J. K. 2002. "Shock without Therapy." *The American Prospect* 13 (15): 36–39.

Garber, J., and M. E. P. Seligman, eds. 1980. *Human Helplessness Theory and Applications.* New York: Academic Press.

Gersick, C. J. G. 1989. "Marking Time: Predictable Transitions in Task Groups." *Academy of Management Journal* 32: 274–309.

Ghauri, P. N., and S. B. Prasad. 1995. "A Network Approach to Probing Asia's Interfirm Linkages." *Advances in International Comparative Management* 10: 63–77.

Gioa, D. A., and P. P. Poole. 1984. "Scripts in Organizational Behaviour." *Academy of Management Review* 9: 449–59.

Gobeli, D. H., K. Przybylowski, and W. Rudelius. 1998. "Customizing Management Training in Central and Eastern Europe: Mini Shock Therapy." *Business Horizons* 41 (3): 61–72.

Goldman, M. C. 2000. "A Decade Later, the Czech Republic Has Morphed into a Vibrant Economy." *Cable News Network,* 24 September, 14.56 P.M. ET.

Greenwood, R., and C. R. Hinings. 1988. *The Dynamics of Strategic Change.* New York: Blackwell.

———. 1993. "Understanding Strategic Change: The Contribution of Archetypes." *Academy of Management Journal* 36 (5): 1052–83.

———. 1996. "Understanding Radical Organizational Change: Bringing Together the Old and the New Institutionalism." *Academy of Management Review* 21 (4): 1022–54.

Greider, W. 1997. *One World, Ready or Not: The Manic Logic of Global Capitalism.* New York: Simon and Schuster.

Greiner, L. E. 1972. "Evolution and Revolution as Organizations Grow." *Harvard Business Review* 50 (1): 37–46.

Hamilton, D. L. 1979. "A Cognitive-Attributional Analysis of Stereotyping." In *Advances in Experimental Social Psychology,* vol. 12, edited by L. Berkowitz, 53–84. New York: Academic Press.

Han, V. X., and R. Baumgarte. 2000. "Economic Reform, Private Sector Development and the Business Environment in Vietnam." *Comparative Economic Studies* 42 (2): 1–30.

Haroh, T. M. 1991. *Peace is Every Step.* New York: Bantam Books.

Harper, T. 1999. *Moscow Madness: Crime, Corruption, and One Man's Pursuit of Profit in the New Russia.* New York: McGraw-Hill.

Hewstone, M. 1990. "The 'Ultimate Attribution Error'? A Review of the Literature on Intergroup Casual Attribution." *European Journal of Social Psychology* 20: 311–35.

Hill, C. W. L. 2001. *International Business: Competing in the Global Market Place, Postscript 2001.* New York: Irwin-McGraw Hill.

Hofstede, G. 1980. *Culture's Consequences.* Beverly Hills, CA: Sage Publications.

Holden, N. 2002. *Cross-Cultural Management: A Knowledge Management Per-spective.* Harlow, Eng.: Pearson Education.

Holden, N., C. Cooper, and J. Carr. 1998. *Dealing with the New Russia: Management Cultures in Collision.* Chichester, NY: John Wiley.

Hraba, J., R. Mullick, F. O. Lorenz, and J. Vecernik. 2001. "Age and Czechs' Attitudes toward the Postcommunist Economic Reforms." *The Sociological Quarterly* 42 (3): 421–38.

Illes, K., and B. Rees. 2001. "Developing Competent Managers: The 'Shadow' of Hungarian History." *Journal of East European Management Studies.* 6 (4): 421–43.

Jarillo, J. 1988. "On Strategic Networks." *Strategic Management Journal* 9: 31–41.

Jones, D. 1995. "Employee Participation During the Early Stages of Transition: Evidence from Bulgaria." *Economic and Industrial Democracy* 16 (1): 235–45.

Kahn, J. 2002. "Some Chinese See the Future, and It's Capitalist." *The New York Times,* 4 May, Arts 1, 11.

Kahn, R., D. Wolfe, R. Quinn, J. Snoek, and R. Rosenthal. 1964. *Organizational Stress: Studies in Role Conflict and Ambiguity.* New York: Wiley.

Katz, D., and K. W. Braly. 1933. "Verbal Stereotypes and Racial Prejudice." *Journal of Abnormal and Social Psychology* 28: 280–90.

Katz, D., and R. L. Kahn. 1966. *The Social Psychology of Organizations.* New York: Wiley & Sons.

Kavanaugh, K. H. 1991. "Invisibility and Selective Avoidance: Gender and Ethnicity in Psychiatry and Psychiatric Nursing Staff Interaction." *Culture, Medicine and Psychiatry* 15 (2): 245–74.

Kelley, H. H. 1972. "Attribution in Social Interaction." In *Attribution: Perceiving the Causes of Behavior,* edited by E. E. Jones, D. E. Kanous, H. H. Kelley, R. E. Nisbett, S. Valins, and B. Weiner, 1–26. Morristown, NJ: General Learning Press.

Kets de Vries, M. F. R. 2000. "A Journey into the Wild East: Leadership Style and Organizational Practices in Russia." *Organizational Dynamics* 28 (4): 67–81.

Klebnikov, P. 1996. "The Seven Sisters Have a Baby Brother." *Forbes* 157 (2): 70–76.

———. 2000. *Godfather of the Kremlin: The Decline of Russia in the Age of Gangster Capitalism.* San Diego: Harcourt.

Kluckhohn, C., and K. Strodtbeck. 1961. *Variations in Value Orientations.* Westport, CT: Greenwood Press.

Knoke, W. 1996. *Bold New World.* New York: Kodansha International.

Kogut, B. 1989. "A Note on Global Strategy." *Strategic Management Journal* 10: 383–89.

Kolodko, G. W. 2002. *Globalization and Catching-Up in Transition Economies.* Rochester, NY: University of Rochester Press.

Konrad, E. 2000. "Changes in Work Motivation During Transition: A Case from Slovenia." *Applied Psychology: An International Review* 49 (4): 619–35.

Kornai, J. 1980. *Economics of Shortage.* New York: North-Holland.

———. 1992. *The Socialist System: The Political Economy of Communism.* Princeton, NJ: Princeton University Press.

Kornai, J., and Á. Matits. 1990. "The Bureaucratic Redistribution of Firms' Profit." In *Vision and Reality, Market and State: Contradictions and Dilemmas Revisited,* edited by J. Kornai, 54–98. New York: Routledge.

Kozlova, T., and S. Puffer. 1994. "Public and Private Business Schools in Russia: Problems and Prospects." *European Management Journal,* December: 462–68.

LaFraniere, S. 2001. "Cleaning Up Russia's Culture of Corruption; Putin Targeting All Who 'Feed Off' Small Business." *The Washington Post,* 29 December, A.

Lane, P. J., and M. Lubatkin. 1998. "Relative Absorptive Capacity and Interorganizational Learning." *Strategic Management Journal* 19: 461–77.

Lane, P. J., J. E. Salk, and M. A. Lyles. 2001. "Absorptive Capacity, Learning, and Performance in International Joint Ventures." *Strategic Management Journal* 22: 1139–61.

Langer, E. 1989. *Mindfulness.* Reading, MA: Addison-Wesley.

Lee, P. N. 1987. *Industrial Management and Economic Reform in China 1949–1984.* New York: Oxford University Press.

Leipziger, D. M. 1992. *Awakening the Market: Vietnam's Economic Transition.* World Bank discussion paper no. 157. Washington, DC: The World Bank.

Levitt, B., and J. G. March. 1988. "Organizational Learning." *Annual Review of Sociology* 14: 319–40.

Levitt, T. 1975. "Marketing Myopia." *Harvard Business Review,* September–October, 1–14.

Linville, P. W., O. W. Fischer, and P. Salovey. 1989. "Perceived Distributions of the Characteristics of In-Group and Out-Group Members: Empirical Evidence and a Computer Simulation." *Journal of Personality and Social Psychology* 57: 165–88.

Litchfield, R. 1992. "A Day in the Life of Wolfgang Hampl." *Canadian Business* 65 (10); 15–16.

Litvack, J. I., and D. A. Rondinelli. 1999. *Market Reform in Vietnam.* Westport, CT: Quorum Books.

Long, W. F., and D. J. Ravenscraft. 1993. "LBOs, Debt and R and D Intensity." *Strategic Management Journal* 14: 119–36.

Lorange, P., and J. Roos. 1992. *Strategic Alliances.* Cambridge, MA: Blackwell.

Luo, Y. 1999. "Environment-Strategy-Performance Relations in Small Businesses in China: A Case of Township and Village Enterprises in Southern China." *Journal of Small Business Management* 371 (1): 37–52.

———. 2001. *Strategy, Structure and Performance of MNCs in China.* Westport, CT: Quorum.

Luthans, F., K. Luthans, R. Hodgetts, and Brett Luthans. 2000. "Can High Performance Work Practices Help in the Former Soviet Union?" *Business Horizons* 43 (5): 53–60.

Lysgaard, S. 1955. "Adjustment in a Foreign Society: Norwegian Fulbright Grantees Visiting the United States." *International Social Science Bulletin* 7: 45–51.

"Managers Talk about the Pros and Cons as East Meets West." 1994. *HR Focus* 71 (2): 12.

Manev, I., and B. Gyoshev. 2001. *Privatisation of Small and Medium Sized Enterprises: Five Case Studies from Bulgaria.* Paper presented to Academy of Management Annual Meeting. Washington, DC.

Maniero, L. A., and C. L. Tromley, eds. 1994. *Developing Skills in Organizational Behavior.* Upper Saddle River, NJ: Prentice Hall.

Markus, H. R., and S. Kitayama. 1991. "Culture and the Self: Implications for Cognition, Emotion, and Motivation." *Psychological Review* 98 (2): 224–53.

Martin, J. H., B. A. Martin, and B. Grbac. 1998. "Employee Involvement and Market Orientation in a Transition Economy: Importance, Problems and a Solution." *Journal of Managerial Issues* 10 (4): 485–502.

Mathur, L. K., K. Gleason, and I. Mathur. 1999. "Managing Expansion to Transition Economies: The Evidence from Eastern Europe." *Journal of East-West Business* 5 (3): 41–62.

McCarthy, D. J., S. M. Puffer, and A. Naumov. 1997. "Case Study—Olga Kirova: A Russian Entrepreneur's Quality Leadership." *International Journal of Organizational Analysis* 5 (3): 267–90.

McCarthy, D. J., S. M. Puffer, and S. V. Shekshnia. 2001. "The Resurgence of an Entrepreneurial Class." *Journal of Management Inquiry* 2 (2): 125–37.

McLean-Parks, J., and D. A. Schmedemann. 1994. "When Promises Become Contracts: Implied Contract and Handbook Provisions on Job Security." *Human Resource Management* 33: 403–23.

McLuhan, M., and Q. Fiore. 1967. *The Medium is the Message.* New York: Random House.

McNulty, N. G. 1992. "Management Education in Eastern Europe: 'Fore and After." *The Executive* 6 (4): 78–87.

Meyer, A. D., J. B. Goes, and G. R. Brooks. 1993. "Organizations Reacting to Hyperturbulence." In *Organizational Change and Redesign,* edited by G. P. Huber and W. H. Glick, 66–111. New York: Oxford University Press.

Meyer, K. E. 2001. "International Business Research on Transition Economies." In *The Oxford Handbook of International Business,* edited by A. M. Rugman and T. L. Brewer, 716–59. Oxford and New York: Oxford University Press.

Michailova, S., and K. Liuhto. 2000. "Organisation and Management Research in Transition Economies: Towards Improved Research Methodologies." *Journal of East-West Business* 6 (3): 7–46.

Milliman, J., M. A. Von Glinow, and M. Nathan. 1991. "Organizational Life Cycles and Strategic International Human Resource Management in Multinational Companies: Implications for Congruence Theory." *Academy of Management Review* 16 (2): 318–29.

Minniti, M. 1995. "Membership Has Its Privileges: Old and New Mafia Organizations." *Comparative Economic Studies* 37 (4): 31–48.

Mintzberg, Henry. 1973. *The Nature of Managerial Work.* New York: Harper & Row.

———. 1993. *Structure in Fives: Designing Effective Organizations.* Englewood Cliffs, NJ: Prentice Hall.

Murrell, P. 1996. "How Far Has the Transition Progressed?" *Journal of Economic Perspectives* 10 (2): 25–44.

Naisbitt, J. 1994. *Global Paradox.* New York: W.R. Morrow.

Napier, N. K., S. Hosley, and T. V. Nguyen. Forthcoming. "Conducting Qualitative Research in Vietnam: Observations about Ethnography, Grounded Theory and Case Study Research Approaches." In *A Handbook of Qualitative Research Methods for International Business,* edited by R. Marschan-Piekkari and C. Welch. Cheltenham, UK, and Northampton, MA: Edward Elgar.

Napier, N. K., M. H. Ngo, M. T. T. Nguyen, T. V. Nguyen, and T. V. Vu. 2002. "Bi-cultural Team Teaching: Experiences from an Emerging Business School." *Journal of Management Education* 26 (4): 429–48.

Napier, N. K., and D. C. Thomas. 2001. "Some Things You May Not Have Learned in Graduate School: A Rough Guide to Collecting Primary Data Overseas." In *International Business Scholarship,* edited by B. Toyne, Z. L. Martinez, and R. A. Menger, 180–97. Westport, CT: Quorum Books.

Neilson, R. P. 2000. "Entrepreneurship as a Peaceful and Ethical Transition Strategy toward Privatization." *Journal of Business Ethics* 25: 157–67.

Newman, K. L. 2000. "Organizational Transformation During Institutional Upheaval." *Academy of Management Review* 25 (3): 602–19.

Newman, K. L., and S. D. Nollen. 1998. *Managing Radical Organizational Change.* Thousand Oaks, CA: Sage.

Nguyen, Thang V., C. T. H. Giang, and N. K. Napier. 2001. "Entrepreneurial Strategic Orientation and Environmental Uncertainty: Vietnam's Small and Medium Sized Enterprises Face the Future." *Journal of Asian Business* 17 (3): 71–87.

Nonaka, I., and H. Takeuchi. 1995. *The Knowledge-Creating Company.* New York: Oxford University Press.

Oberg, K. 1960. "Cultural Shock: Adjustment to New Cultural Environments." *Practical Anthropology* 7: 177–82.

Offe, C. 1995. "Designing Institutions for East European Transitions." In *Strategic*

Choice and Path Dependency in Post-Socialism: Institutional Dynamics in the Transformation Process, edited by J. Hausner, B. Jessop, and K. Nielsen, 47–66. Cheltenham, UK: Edward Elgar.

Parker, B. 1998. *Globalization and Business Practices: Managing across Boundaries.* London: Sage Publications.

Parker, S., G. Tritt, and W. T. Woo. 1997. "Lessons for Economic Transition in Asia and Eastern Europe." In *Economies in Transition: Comparing Asia and Eastern Europe,* edited by Wing Thye Woo, Stephen Parker, and Jefferey D. Sachs, 3–18. Cambridge, MA: MIT Press.

Pearce, J., and I. Branyiczki. 1993. "Revolutionizing Bureaucracies: Managing Change in Hungarian State-Owned Enterprises." *Journal of Change Management* 6 (2): 53–65.

Peng, M. W. 1994. "Organizational Changes in Planned Economies in Transition: An Eclectic Model." In *Advances in International Comparative Management,* edited by Joe Cheng, 9, 223–51. Greenwich, CT: JAI Press.

———. 2000. *Business Strategies in Transition Economies.* Thousand Oaks, CA.: Sage Publications.

———. 2001. "How Entrepreneurs Create Wealth in Transition Economies." *The Academy of Management Executive* 15 (1): 95–110.

Peng, M. W., and Y. Luo, Y. 2000. "Managerial Ties and Firm Performance in a Transition Economy: The Nature of a Micro-Macro Link." *Academy of Management Journal* 43 (3): 486–501.

Peng, M. W., and J. J. Tan. 1998. "Toward Alliance Postsocialism: Business Strategies in a Transitional Economy." *Journal of Applied Management Studies* 7 (1): 145–48.

Powell, B. 2001. "China's Great Step Forward." *Fortune,* 17 September, 128–42.

Puffer, S. M. 1994. "A Portrait of Russian Business Leaders." *Academy of Management Executive* 8 (1): 41–54.

———. 1996a. "The Booming Business of Management Education." In *Business and Management in Russia,* edited by S. M. Puffer and Associates, 96–106. Cheltenham, UK, and Brookfield, VT: Edward Elgar.

———, ed. 1996b. *Business and Management in Russia.* Cheltenham, UK, and Brookfield, VT: Edward Elgar.

———. 1996c. "A Portrait of Russian Business Leaders." In *Business and Management in Russia,* edited by S. M. Puffer and Associates, 17–33. Cheltenham, UK, and Brookfield, VT: Edward Elgar.

Puffer, S. M., D. J. McCarthy, and A. Zhuplev. 1996. "Meeting of the Mindsets in a Changing Russia." *Business Horizons* 39 (6): 52–60.

Ralston, D. A., C. P. Egri, S. Stewart, R. H. Terpstra, and K. Yu. 1999. "Doing Business in the 21st Century with the New Generation of Chinese Managers: A Study of Generational Shifts in Work Values in China." *Journal of International Business Studies* 30: 415–27.

Ralston, D. A., T. V. Nguyen, and N. K. Napier. 1999. "A Comparative Study of the Work Values of North and South Vietnamese Managers." *Journal of International Business Studies* 30 (4): 655–72.

Ridley, C. R. 1984. "Clinical Treatment of the Nondisclosing Black Client." *American Psychologist* 39: 1234–44.

Robinson, I. 2000. "Organizational Change in Post-Communist Europe: Management and Transformation in the Czech Republic." *Journal of Management Studies* 37 (7): 1050–53.

Robinson, I., and B. Tomczak-Stepien. 2000. "The Socialist Legacy and Worker Perceptions of Transformation: An Analysis of Post-Socialist Polish Enterprises." *Journal of East-West Business* 6 (2): 7–31.

Robinson, R. D. 1984. *The Internationalization of Business: An Introduction*. Chicago: The Dryden Press.

Rock, C. P., and V. Solodkov. 2001. "Monetary Policies, Banking, and Trust in Changing Institutions: Russia's Transition in the 1990s." *Journal of Economic Issue* 35 (2): 451–58.

Rokeach, M. 1973. *The Nature of Human Values*. New York: Free Press.

Rona-Tas, A. 1994. "The First Shall Be Last? Entrepreneurship and Communist Cadres in the Transition from Socialism." *American Journal of Sociology* 100: 40–69.

Rosen, R., P. Digh, M. Singer, and C. Phillips. 2000. *Global Literacies*. New York: Simon and Schuster.

Rousseau, D. M. 1989. "Psychological and Implied Contracts in Organizations." *Employee Responsibilities and Rights Journal* 2: 121–39.

———. 1995. *Psychological Contracts in Organizations*. Thousand Oaks, CA: Sage.

Rupp, K. 1983. *Entrepreneurs in Red: Structure and Organizational Innovation in the Centrally Planned Economy*. Albany, NY: State University of New York Press.

Sarbin, T., and R. Allen. 1968. "Role Theory." In *The Handbook of Social Psychology*, edited by G. Lindzey and E. Aronson, 489–567. Reading, MA: Addison Wesley.

Schein, E. H. 1965. *Organizational Psychology*. Englewood Cliffs, NJ: Prentice-Hall.

Schneider, F., and D. H. Ernste. 2000. "Shadow Economies: Size, Causes, and Consequences." *Journal of Economic Literature* 38 (1): 77–114.

Schrage, C. R., and A. Jedlicka. 1999. "Training in Transition Economies." *Training and Development* 53 (6): 38–40.

Schumpeter, J. 1911. *The Theory of Development: An Inquiry into Profits, Capital, Credit, Interest, and the Business Cycle*. Translated 1934 by R. Opie. Cambridge, MA: Harvard University Press.

Senge, P. 1990. *The Fifth Discipline: The Art and Practice of The Learning Organization*. New York: Doubleday Currency.

Shekshnia, S. V. 2001. "Deputy Prime Minister Aleksei Kudrin on Creating a Positive Business Climate in Russia." *Academy of Management Executive* 15 (4): 10–15.

Sidanius, J. 1993. "The Psychology of Group Conflict and the Dynamics of Oppression: A Social Dominance Perspective." In *Explorations in Political Psychology,* edited by S. Iyenger and W. McGuire, 183–219. Durham, NC: Duke University Press.

Smith, C. S. 2002. "For China's Wealthy, All but Fruited Plain." *New York Times,* 15 May, A, 12.

Smith, P. B., and M. H. Bond. 1999. *Social Psychology across Cultures.* Boston: Allyn and Bacon.

Snell, R., and C. S. Tseng. 2002. "Moral Atmosphere and Moral Influence under China's Network Capitalism." *Organization Studies* 23 (3): 449–78.

Snyder, M. 1981. "On the Self-Perpetuating Nature of Social Stereotypes." In *Cognitive Processes in Stereotyping and Intergroup Behavior,* edited by D. L. Hamilton, 183–212. Mahwah, New Jersey: Lawrence Erlbaum Associates.

Soulsby, A. 2001. "The Construction of Czech Managers' Careers." *International Studies of Management and Organization* 31 (2): 48–64.

Soulsby, A., and E. Clark. 1996. "The Emergence of Post-Communist Management in the Czech Republic." *Organization Studies* 17 (2): 227–47.

Spar, D. L. 2001. "National Policies and Domestic Politics." In *The Oxford Handbook of International Business,* edited by A. M. Rugman and T. L. Brewer, 206–31. Oxford and New York: Oxford University Press.

Stahl-Rolf, S. R. 2000. "Transition on the Spot, Social Structure and Institutional Change." *Atlantic Economic Journal* 28 (1): 25–36.

Stanojevic, M. 2001. "Industrial Relations in 'Post-Communism': Workplace Co-operation in Hungary and Slovenia." *Journal of East European Management Studies* 6 (4): 400–420.

Starobin, P. 2001a. "The Oilman is a Teacher." *Business Week Online,* 25 June, http://www.businessweek.com:/print/magazine/content/.

———. 2001b. "Putin's Russia." *Business Week,* 12 November, 66.

Stewart, R. 1982. *Choices for the Manager.* Englewood Cliffs, NJ: Prentice-Hall.

Stewart, R., J. L. Barsoux, A. Kieser, H. D. Ganter, and P. Walgenbach. 1994. *Managing in Britain and Germany.* New York: St. Martin's Press.

Stiglitz, J. E. 2002. *Globalization and Its Discontents.* New York: W.W. Norton & Company.

———. 1999. "For Economists, No Time to Party." *Newsweek,* 29 November, 58.

Sundaram, A. K., and J. S. Black. 1995. *The International Business Environment.* Englewood Cliffs, NJ: Prentice-Hall.

Svejnar, J. 2000. "Economics Ph.D. Education in Central and Eastern Europe." *Comparative Economic Studies* 42 (2): 37–51.

Tajfel, H. 1981. *Human Groups and Social Categories.* Cambridge: Cambridge University Press.

Tan, J. J. 1998. "Management in China and Eastern Europe: The Blurry Picture." *Journal of Applied Management Studies* 7 (1): 131–33.

———. 1999. "The Growth of Entrepreneurial Firms in a Transition Economy: The Case of a Chinese Entrepreneur." *Journal of Management Inquiry* 8 (1): 83–89.

Thomas, David C. 1998. "The expatriate experience: A critical review and synthesis." *Advances in International Comparative Management,* 12, 237–273.

———. 2002. *Essentials of International Management: A Cross-Cultural Perspective.* Thousand Oaks, CA: Sage.

Thomas, David C., and Elizabeth C. Ravlin. 1995. "Responses of Workers to Cultural Adaptation by a Foreign Manager." *Journal of Applied Psychology* 80 (1): 133–46.

Thompson, G. R., and C. Valsan. 1999. "Early Privatization in Romania—The period of Management and Employee Buyouts, 1991 to 1995." *Eastern European Economics* 37 (6): 35–53.

Ting-Toomey, S. 1999. *Communicating Across Cultures.* New York: Guilford Press.

Tongren, H. N., L. Hecht, and K. Kovach. 1995. "Recognizing Cultural Differences: Key to Successful U.S.-Russian Enterprises." *Public Personnel Management* 24 (1): 1–17.

Triandis, H. C. 1995. *Individualism and Collectivism.* Boulder, CO: Westview.

Tuckman, B. W. 1965. "Developmental Sequence in Small Groups." *Psychological Bulletin* 63 (6): 384–99.

UNCTAD [United Nations Conference on Trade and Development]. 1999. *World Investment Report 1999.* New York and Geneva: United Nations.

Valencia, M. 2001. "Limping Towards Normality." *The Economist,* 27 October, 3–5.

Vamosi, T. S. 2001. "Management between Continuity and Change—A Case Study from Hungary." *Journal of East European Management Studies* 6 (2): 121–51.

Vernon, R. 1966. "International Investment and International Trade in the Product Life Cycle." *Quarterly Journal of Economics* 80: 190–207.

Vu, T. V., and N. J. Napier. 2000. "Paradoxes in Vietnam and the United States: Lessons Earned: Part II." *Human Resource Planning Journal* 23 (1): 9–10.

Warner, M., ed. 2002. *Studies on the Chinese Economy.* New York: St. Martin's Press.

Wedel, J. R. 1998. *Collision and Collusion.* New York: St. Martin's Press.

Weiss, S. E. 1994. "Negotiating with the Romans—Part I." *Sloan Management Review* 35 (2): 51–61.

Williams, C. J. 1994. "Bulgaria's War of the Roses—Perfume Oil is a State

Monopoly That Stubbornly Resists Capitalist Inroads in the Eastern European Nation." *The Los Angeles Times,* 8 February, H6.

"The Withering Away of the Party." 2002. *The Economist,* 1 June, 40.

World Bank. 2000. *World Development Indicators.* Washington, DC: World Bank.

WTO. 1999. *WTO Annual Report.* Geneva: World Trade Organization.

Zachary, P. 2000. *The Global Me.* New York: PublicAffairs.

Zhao, D., and J. A. Hall. 1994. "State Power and Patterns of Late Development: Resolving the Crisis of the Sociology of Development." *Sociology* 28 (1): 211–30.

Zwass, A. 2002. *Globalization of Unequal National Economies: Players and Controversies.* Armonk, NY: M.E. Sharpe.

INDEX

Abandonment, 170–71
Acceptance: and compromise, 169–70; of unchangeable characteristics, 156
Adaptation: to build trust, 151–53; to change, 54–58; of expectations of behavior, 147; to local conditions, 140; persistence in, 166; resources for, 55
Adaptive behavior, 151, 154
Adaptive change, 43
Adaptive learning, 52
Adaptive skills, development of, 177
Adjustment: models of, 87; resistance to, 96
Adjustment phase, 87
Adler, N., 87
Agreement, reneging on, 131
Agricultural and land reforms, 27
Agricultural reforms, 30
Alekperov, Vagit, 49
Alliances, types of, 50–51
Americans, stereotypes of, 132, 180
Anatomy of socialism, 17–18
Anger, exhibition of, 142, 146
Apathy, 127, 185

APEC (Asia-Pacific Economic Cooperation), 32
Arrogance and national identity, 91–92
Asia, 138. *See also specific Asian country*
Attention, 188
Attitudes: adjustments in, from training, 149; towards employees, 79–80; towards outsiders, 80
Attribution: defined, 91; differences in, 91–92; effects of inaccuracy in, 132; of in-groups and outgroups, 92
Authoritarian approach of local managers, 136

Banana (slur), 123
Behavior: adaptive, 151, 154, 189; adjustments in, from training, 149; causal attribution of, 93; changes to, after conflict, 135; culturally inappropriate, 132; expectations of, 94; new standards of, 147; nonjudgmental, 74, 186; as scripted semireflexive, 133; shifts

About the Authors

NANCY K. NAPIER is Executive Director of the Global Business Consortium and Professor of International Business and Management at Boise State University in Idaho, U.S.A.

DAVID C. THOMAS is Professor of International Management and Area Coordinator of International Business at Simon Fraser University in Canada.